FACULTY RETIREMENT

FACULTY RETIREMENT

Best Practices for Navigating the Transition

EDITED BY

Claire A. Van Ummersen,

Jean M. McLaughlin, and

Lauren J. Duranleau

Foreword by Lotte Bailyn

Published in association with

American
Council on
Education™

Leadership and Advocacy

STERLING, VIRGINIA

Published by Stylus Publishing, LLC
22883 Quicksilver Drive
Sterling, Virginia 20166-2102

Library of Congress Cataloging-in-Publication Data
Faculty retirement : best practices for navigating the transition /
edited by Claire Van Ummersen, Jean McLaughlin, and Lauren
Duranleau.
    pages cm
Includes bibliographical references and index.
ISBN 978-1-62036-191-7 (cloth : alk. paper)
ISBN 978-1-62036-192-4 (pbk. : alk. paper)
ISBN 978-1-62036-193-1 (library networkable e-edition) (print)
ISBN 978-1-62036-194-8 (consumer e-edition)
1. College teachers—Retirement—United States. 2. Universities
and colleges—Faculty—Retirement—United States.
I. Van Ummersen, Claire
LB2334.F34 2014
378.1'2—dc23
                                              2013040902
13-digit ISBN: 978-1-62036-191-7 (cloth)
13-digit ISBN: 978-1-62036-192-4 (paperback)
13-digit ISBN: 978-1-62036-193-1 (library networkable e-edition)
13-digit ISBN: 978-1-62036-194-8 (consumer e-edition)

Printed in the United States of America.

All first editions printed on acid-free paper
that meets the American National Standards Institute
Z39-48 Standard.

Bulk Purchases

Quantity discounts are available for use in workshops and for
staff development.
Call 1-800-232-0223

First Edition, 2014

10   9   8   7   6   5   4   3

This book is dedicated to Dr. Claire Van Ummersen, whose vision for this work has been the driving force for over a decade.

CONTENTS

PART SIX: CHALLENGES OF AND OPPORTUNITIES FOR IMPLEMENTATION

PART SEVEN: CONCLUSION

The academic career has many wonderful characteristics. It's a career in which what a person is most interested in, what he or she has worked hard to master, provides a living wage—and when professors make it, they have a job for life. The academic career also permits a fair amount of control over time, over where and when work is done. At the same time it makes many demands. There is the initial hurdle of getting to tenure, which coincides with the years of family formation. And after that there are the multiple demands of teaching and mentoring students, researching and publishing, serving the university, mentoring junior colleagues, and serving the profession. And through it all is the pressure to establish and maintain a professional reputation. All aspects of the academic career require the full engagement of practitioners.

And that makes retirement a complicated topic indeed. Faculty simply aren't eagerly awaiting retirement. The full engagement their occupation demands makes it likely that not many avocational or nonprofessional pursuits will be readily available to retirees—they have hardly had the time or energy to establish them. And now the timing of retirement has officially been made voluntary, a freedom that may or may not be a blessing.

For institutions of higher education, voluntary retirement is a problem. On the one hand, these institutions need to replenish themselves, and that means their older employees need to retire. But many faculty hang on well into their seventies, even their eighties, and create for themselves and their institutions complicated dilemmas. On the other hand, there is a phasing problem: mass retirements can decimate a department and create the need for mass hirings, which guarantee another crisis some 40 years hence. Occasional lucrative incentive plans deal with the first issue but may create the problems of the second. Also, different kinds of institutions and different disciplines may be particularly subject to one problem or the other.

So, what to do to ease these dilemmas? The examples in this book provide many useful suggestions for the period leading to retirement, the transition period, and retirement itself. One might say that the retirement dilemma could be eased from the beginning of the academic career, by decreasing pressure and demands at all stages from hiring to tenure and beyond and perhaps even by actively encouraging outside interests. Indeed, research has shown that time-outs and alternative activities boost creativity, which may actually be hampered by overwork. Some of the institutions represented here do start discussions about retirement early; they talk with faculty not only about financial planning but also about making nonwork interests part of their ongoing activities. All institutions should seriously consider implementing such discussions.

Phasing into retirement by reducing duties before official retirement is frequently mentioned throughout this book. Approaching retirement in phases allows faculty burdened by the multiple demands of the academic career to reduce or finish their scholarly endeavors. But for many professors, their discipline is their identity, and they have spent their careers developing this identity. For them, retirement may create a real crisis.

The institutions discussed in this book have various ways of addressing potential identity crises. Some allow faculty to continue with their work, permitting them to stay at the university and use its resources; they even provide small grants to make continuous scholarly work possible. Others see their retired faculty as a resource, asking them to fill in occasional teaching needs, participate in short-term projects, and act as mentors. And data show that most faculty want to continue to stay involved with their institutions—it is important to them. Of course, retired faculty members are different demographically from new assistant professors, and hence using them as mentors may not address an institution's needs for diversity. Also, the relative values placed on teaching and research have changed, particularly in what were previously "teaching" institutions. Regardless, if institutions see their retired faculty as a resource and continue to include them in relevant activities, both sides may benefit.

Let me end with a personal note: I taught my last class in spring 2013, a PhD seminar that I have taught for decades and that was a particular pleasure because it centered on student research and hence kept me up to date in ways I could not have been otherwise. I felt sad when it was over, but also relieved. The class ended a period of postretirement employment that had provided me with a salary and relieved me from having to use my pension funds just as they dramatically declined in the financial crisis. What I noticed this last time I taught the class is that I felt much lighter, under less pressure—even though I had not previously been aware that I felt pressure at all. I discovered a joy in retirement I had not anticipated, and I wonder how one could convey that to people who are just beginning to contemplate this decision. Of course, this feeling of relief does not happen for everyone. Some want to continue with their scholarship and research until they die. The examples in this book cater to this individuality by combining transparency with options. They do not necessarily provide blueprints to be copied, but they raise problems and suggest solutions that can be useful to all institutions of higher education.

Lotte Bailyn
T. Wilson (1953) Professor of Management, Emerita
MIT Sloan School of Management

Kathleen Christensen, *Working Longer Program,*
Alfred P. Sloan Foundation

For over a decade the Alfred P. Sloan Foundation has been privileged to work with the American Council on Education (ACE) in identifying and advancing the structural and cultural changes needed to increase flexibility in faculty careers. Our shared belief has been that these changes will assist institutions of higher education in recruiting and retaining highly talented and diverse faculty members.

As a Sloan program director, I approached ACE in the early 2000s with the idea that ACE and Sloan should partner to increase the awareness within higher education of the issues facing young faculty members as they tried to pursue meaningful careers and start and raise families. By then I was already nearly a decade into a research program that I had started at Sloan in 1994 to understand the issues facing working parents at a time when the majority of children in the United States were raised in households in which all adults worked. Sloan-supported studies consistently revealed that parents were experiencing a time famine—feeling that they did not have enough time to be good parents *and* good workers. These working parents expressed the desire to have more control over when, where, and how work was done.

The majority of Sloan-supported research focused on parents working in the private sector. But we also sought to understand the work-family challenges faced by the professoriate. While many young faculty members often had more control over day-to-day scheduling, they faced challenges in simultaneously jump-starting their careers and families and sustaining both, specifically during their tenure-track years. For young faculty, particularly women, the final years of childbearing collided sharply with the demands of obtaining their first faculty positions and securing tenure. Research by Mary Ann Mason and Marc Goulden revealed that compared with their male colleagues, women with children were much less likely to take tenure-track jobs; women without children who accepted tenure-track positions were much less likely to marry or have children; and if married, they were more likely to end up divorced and as single mothers. This was not a future to which many young women aspired.

At the time I initially approached ACE, I had just launched the Sloan-supported National Workplace Flexibility Initiative, coming off our research that showed the time famine faced by working parents. This initiative sought to make workplace flexibility a compelling national issue and the standard of the American workplace. While most of our efforts in this campaign focused on private-sector workplaces, I knew from our research and from personal experience, having risen to be a full professor as a mother of two young children, that there was a need to have a comparable flexibility initiative within higher education. The rigid, lockstep demands of the academic career path were unforgiving to those who wanted to have an academic career and a family; they had to be rethought. I reframed the flexibility initiative for higher education to focus on faculty career flexibility.

I was pleased that ACE welcomed the opportunity to partner with the Sloan Foundation on a program focused on faculty career flexibility. Through the masterful leadership of Claire Van Ummersen, Jean McLaughlin, and Lauren Duranleau, ACE has made the need for faculty career flexibility understood in all corners of academia and has further educated institutions of higher education as to best practices and policies. They have successfully achieved this awareness and education through multiple ways.

In February 2005 ACE published *An Agenda for Excellence: Creating Flexibility in Tenure-Track Faculty Careers.* In this report ACE and a national panel of 10 highly respected university presidents and chancellors outlined an ambitious agenda to reform and enhance the academic career path for tenured and tenure-track faculty. They made specific recommendations for augmenting the number of pathways to a successful academic career. Building on the success of this effort, ACE and the foundation designed and developed the Alfred P. Sloan Awards for Faculty Career Flexibility.

The purpose of this awards program was to accelerate institutional efforts toward broader implementation and evaluation of structural and cultural changes needed at institutions of higher education to create more flexible career paths and to make academic careers compatible with family caregiving responsibilities. First administered in 2006, this highly successful awards program recently completed its fourth and final cycle. Twenty-three institutions from three Carnegie classifications (doctoral/research universities, master's large universities, and baccalaureate) and medical schools have been awarded up to $250,000 each to accelerate their efforts. This awards program succeeded in large part because all applicant and winning institutions received benchmarking reports revealing their progress relative to peer institutions'.

ACE's team has effectively worked with these 23 winning institutions to meet the goals outlined in their individual accelerator awards statements. The winners have been networked so that they learn from one another, thereby creating a vibrant community committed to faculty career flexibility. Equally important, ACE has used the platform of the awards program to amplify lessons learned throughout higher education. Claire and her team have effectively done this through the development of a web portal, linking to winning campuses' web materials. They have provided technical assistance to campuses and systems to understand better how satisfied faculty were with current status and how they compare with their peers. And they produced the widely used *Toolkit of Best Practices and Key Resources for Faculty Career Flexibility for Administrators, Faculty, and Students.*

ACE's efforts did not end on the campuses. Claire, Jean, and Lauren presented results at national meetings hosted by numerous education associations, including the Association of Public and Land-grant Universities (APLU), the National Association of Independent and College Universities (NAICU), the College and University Work Family Association (CUWFA), the National Conference on Race and Ethnicity in American Higher Education (NCORE), the Association of American Medical Colleges (AAMC), AAMC's Group on Faculty Affairs (GFA), and the Southern Association of Colleges and Schools (SACS). ACE convened groups of federal agency heads and presidents to discuss the issues and solve the problems related to the agency-university disconnect. They published what they learned that would be valuable to colleges and universities. These lessons have been incorporated into ACE's Leadership Programs. They have created partnerships with systems, such as the Annapolis Group, Jesuit institutions, and state systems in California and Maryland.

Recently, ACE and Sloan have launched the National Challenge for Higher Education: Retaining a 21st Century Workforce, a campaign that asks college and university presidents to promote faculty career flexibility on their campuses. The National Challenge initiative will broadly disseminate information on and presidential acknowledgment of the need to develop more flexible faculty career paths and an accepting culture that supports faculty use of policies without bias. This new campaign comes at a critical time when many institutions are starting to see four generations of faculty in the workplace, with each group looking for different ways to balance their work and professional lives.

One of these four generations is at its culminating career stage, poised to transition into retirement. Retirement represents a critical career stage for any academic, but one that has been woefully ignored. It is a stage that involves major transitions in identity, community, and economic security.

At a time without mandatory retirement, institutions of higher education must find strategies through which they can meet their own needs while meeting faculty needs. Some of these strategies include helping faculty define their legacy and find meaningful roles within the community on campus and beyond once they transition into retirement. Select institutions of higher education are leading the way in developing innovative and effective ways to help faculty transition into retirement. Fifteen institutions from three Carnegie classifications (doctoral/research universities, master's large universities, and baccalaureate) were recognized in 2012 with Sloan Awards for Retirement Transitions for their effective policies and programs supporting faculty members in their transitions to retirement.

Just as ACE shone a powerful light on the institutional need to address faculty work-life challenges at early career stages, so now is ACE focusing on the culminating career stage. This book tells that story by letting the 15 winning colleges and universities discuss what has worked for their institutions and their senior faculty at the culminating stages of their careers.

References

American Council on Education. (2005). *An Agenda for excellence: Creating flexibility in tenure-track faculty careers.* Retrieved from http://www.acenet.edu/news-room/Documents/Agenda-for-Excellence.pdf

American Council on Education. (n.d.). *Toolkit of best practices and key resources for faculty career flexibility for administrators, faculty, and students.* Retrieved from http://www.acenet.edu/leadership/programs/Pages/Toolkit-Faculty-Career-Flexibility.aspx

ACKNOWLEDGMENTS

The editors would like to acknowledge the funding and support of the Alfred P. Sloan Foundation, especially the support of Kathleen Christensen, without whom these projects would not be viable. The editors would also like to acknowledge past staff and interns who have worked on the Alfred P. Sloan Projects at ACE: Gloria D. Thomas, Kate Quinn, Lauren Duranleau, Camisha Abels-James, Gailda Davis, Peck-Gee (Peggy) Chua, Won Choe, Jennifer Eliason, Yasir Kuoti, and Kadeem Thorpe.

PART ONE

SETTING THE CONTEXT

REDEFINING FACULTY RETIREMENT

Lauren J. Duranleau, *American Dental Education Association*, and
Jean M. McLaughlin, *American Council on Education*

M andatory retirement was eliminated nearly 20 years ago, and it has taken the higher education sector almost as long to realize the implications of voluntary retirement for the academic workforce. Today faculty are both living longer and choosing to work longer, and institutions must adapt. Since U.S. higher education employs a disproportionately higher percentage of employees age 55 and over, this sector is at the forefront of workplace challenges presented by a workforce aging at a faster rate than the U.S. workforce as a whole (Kaskie, Leicht, & Hitlin, 2012). Indeed, compared with its international counterparts, which are only beginning to uncap their mandatory retirement laws, the American higher education system is at the forefront of an opportunity to address these challenges worldwide. This means that U.S. higher education has the chance to serve as a model for both the U.S. business sector and international higher education institutions in redefining the senior stages of faculty careers and transitions through faculty retirement.

To understand why institutions need to adapt to fit today's longer lifespans, it is important to examine what the elimination of mandatory retirement has done to higher education, given its tenure structure and faculty employment dynamics. This chapter provides a brief history of the elimination of mandatory retirement, describes the landscape of faculty retirement today, and discusses how voluntary retirement affects both faculty and the institution. The chapter concludes by providing a win-win viewpoint for both parties.

The Problem

The history of mandatory retirement in U.S. higher education follows the different cultural and socioeconomic trends of the 20th century. In 1905 William Osler, an outgoing chief physician of the Johns Hopkins Medical School, proposed during a public address that U.S. higher education institutions adopt a policy of mandatory retirement for professors at the age of 60. He claimed that faculty over the age of 40 were unproductive and that faculty over the age of 60 were a nuisance (Ashenfelter & Card, 2001). Osler's proposal did not lead to immediate action, but he was among the first to publicly voice a stereotype of older workers that persists to this day. The pressing need for a mandatory retirement age in the early 20th century also stemmed from the availability of public pension plans, a system that many state institutions of higher education implemented in the 1920s and 1930s. The pension system prompted other sectors of the workforce to adopt mandatory retirement policies (Ashenfelter & Card, 2001). During the early half of the 20th century, many institutions of higher education put mandatory retirement rules in place (Hammond & Morgan, 1991).

By the 1960s the civil rights movement was in full swing and with it came a shift in public thought as to which labor rights should be protected by the federal government. This shift brought the perspective that retirement must be an employee's voluntary decision, made without coercion from the employer (Franke, 2011). Thus, in 1967 Congress passed the federal Age Discrimination in Employment Act (ADEA) to prohibit employers from discrimination based on age and to protect employees between the ages of 40 and 65. Since the act prohibited mandatory retirement before the age of 65, it had little impact on higher education, as most institutions already used 65 as the cutoff (Franke, 2011).

At this time about 40% of employees in the American labor force were forced into mandatory retirement (Fields & Mitchell, 1984). With the increased longevity of society came the need for a change to ADEA so that those who were living longer could be given the opportunity to work longer. In 1978 an amendment to ADEA outlawing mandatory retirement for employees before the age of 70 was passed (Fields & Mitchell, 1984). The amendment presented a challenge to higher education, and extensive lobbying by higher education representatives managed to delay the implementation of the law by 4 years; it went into effect in 1982 (Ashenfelter & Card, 2001). Although mandatory retirement at the age of 65 in higher education seemed nearly universal before the 1982 deadline, several states had by that time either raised the mandatory retirement age or abolished it altogether (Hammond & Morgan, 1991).

By the 1980s medical breakthroughs and improvement in quality of life had led to long life expectancy for Americans (Shrestha, 2006). As Table 1.1

TABLE 1.1
Average Life Expectancy for Americans at Birth, by Sex, Categorized by Howe and Strauss's (1991) Generation Theory

Years	Total (years)	Males (years)	Females (years)
1901–1924 (Greatest Generation)	52.0	50.4	53.8
1925–1942 (Silent Generation)	61.0	61.1	62.9
1943–1960 (Baby Boomers)	68.0	65.4	70.9
1961–1981 (Generation X)	71.5	67.9	75.3
1982–2004 (Generation Y)	75.8	72.6	79.0

Note: Data from *CRS Report for Congress: Life Expectancy in the United States*, by L. B. Shrestha, 2006. Retrieved from https://opencrs.com/document/RL32792/2006-08-16/

shows, the life expectancy rate jumped by almost 10 years between the greatest generation and the silent generation as well as between the silent generation and the baby boomer generation. The average life expectancy rate went from 52.0 years in 1901–1924 to 75.8 years in 1982–2004. This means that the effects of the increased longevity are just being felt now, as the silent generation has moved through retirement, and the large baby boomer cohort reaches the "traditional" retirement age.

Since the new retirement age of 70 was not based on an actual evaluation of an individual worker and could be considered an arbitrary mandate, Congress once again revisited ADEA. In 1986 an amendment was passed to outlaw compulsory retirement for workers in most sectors. The amendment allowed for an 8-year exemption for postsecondary faculty and called for the National Academy of Sciences to review the impact of the elimination of mandatory retirement in higher education (Ashenfelter & Card, 2001). A central argument for the exemption of postsecondary faculty was that higher education had long established a fixed endpoint that faculty and the administration could plan for (Franke, 2011). The National Academy of Sciences analyzed faculty retirement patterns and available studies on private and public institutions that had already eliminated mandatory retirement following the 1967 ADEA legislation. The key conclusions that it presented to Congress were that "at most colleges and universities, few tenured faculty would continue working past age 70 if mandatory retirement is eliminated" and that "at some research universities, a high proportion of faculty would choose to work past age 70 if mandatory retirement is eliminated" (Hammond & Morgan, 1991, p. 103). Congress concluded that continuing to delay the uncapping of the mandatory retirement age in higher education was unnecessary and thus allowed it to expire on schedule on December 31, 1993 (Ashenfelter & Card, 2001).

Although the National Academy of Sciences' study was comprehensive, it did not take into account that retirement patterns could change once the social construct of mandatory retirement was removed and choosing one's own retirement date became the norm. A quote from a Harvard faculty member in 2004 captures this change: "When I was approaching 70, people told me that I should retire. But that feeling that one had a responsibility to retire seems to have faded. There has been a general shift of views about age in this country. People live longer, they stay healthier longer" (O'Brien, 2004). The study also did not take into account that changes in the economy, coupled with the fact that the cohort of aging faculty waiting in the pipeline had different values, traditions, and beliefs from those of previous generations, might lead to a population of faculty who would both want and need to work longer (Ashenfelter & Card, 2001).

Retirement Landscape Today

The retirement landscape of today can be better understood by looking at the generations that are currently in the workforce. Table 1.2 shows these five generations, with the last column showing the age range for the generations in 2014. The middle column shows what the average age for each generation was as of the last *National Study of Postsecondary Faculty* (U.S. Department of Education, 2004), and in the 10 years since the study, the average ages will only have increased. Two of these generations are past the "traditional" retirement age, and one is rapidly approaching it. The academic workforce is aging, and each generation has its unique workforce philosophy.

Many faculty in the greatest generation left the academy under mandatory retirement, although a few remained in place owing to differing state laws or reemployment in later years. Improvements in medicine have given the silent generation the ability to work longer, and without mandatory retirement, many have decided to stay on. Institutions were not prepared for major changes in retirement transitions for members of the silent generation, as the average life expectancy when they were born was only 61 years.

The baby boomer generation is just beginning to approach traditional retirement age. Members of this cohort have distinct attitudes, expectations, and motivations, along with preferences for communication and

TABLE 1.2

Generations of American Workers Categorized by Howe and Strauss's (1991) Generation Theory

Name of generation and birth year span	Average age of U.S. faculty in generational cohort in 2004[a] (years)	Age range of generation in 2014 (years)
Greatest Generation 1901–1924	83	90–113
Silent Generation 1925–1942	67	72–89
Baby Boomer Generation 1943–1960	53	54–71
Generation X 1961–1981	36	33–53
Generation Y 1982–2004	N/A	10–32

[a]Data from *NSOPF: 2004 National Study of Postsecondary Faculty*, by U.S. Department of Education, Institute of Education Sciences, National Center for Education Statistics, 2004, http://nces.ed.gov/surveys/nsopf/.

collaboration that are different from those of the silent generation. These differences make it tricky for institutions to navigate retirement transitions for baby boomer faculty. A 2011 survey conducted by TIAA-CREF showed that only 25% of faculty were planning to retire at 66 years of age (Yakoboski, 2011); this means that beginning with the baby boomers, a larger group of faculty than ever before intend to work longer than ever before. Considering that the baby boomer generation is the largest cohort in academe (U.S. Department of Education, 2004), institutions will need to be prepared to work with this generation and to have supports in place to allow for them to work longer.

The financial crisis of 2007–2009 led many faculty to delay their retirement, with the baby boomer generation being hit the hardest. Many baby boomers' children fall into generation Y, a generation that has been unable to enter the workforce en masse owing to economic conditions. Members of generation Y have responded to these uncertainties by living at home with the support of their parents. Thus, many baby boomers are still supporting their children, while providing elder care for their parents—that is, caring for two generations. This caregiving adds to the financial burden that will force them to work past traditional retirement age. In addition, the composition of families is changing. Many baby boomers had children late in life or divorced, remarried, and have multiple families to support. For some, this means delaying retirement in order to pay for college for their children.

Although smaller in number than the baby boomers and members of generation Y, members of generation X believe that Social Security will not be available for their future and that they will likely have to dip into their retirement savings in order to survive (PwC, 2013). Researchers have claimed that members of generation X have opted out of careers in higher education, and others have suggested that traditional faculty roles and positions may not be available for members of generations X and Y in ways that would support a long-term career in academe. These last two generations may approach retirement in ways we cannot yet begin to imagine.

Given the expected longevity of the generations that currently compose American society and the financial issues plaguing each generation, faculty likely will continue to work longer. Thus, it is crucial that institutions adapt to the realities of their employees' living longer, working longer, and continuing to contribute well past the traditional retirement age.

Faculty View of the End of Mandatory Retirement

Positives

Ending mandatory retirement meant that faculty no longer had a prescribed exit from higher education. Retirement once marked "a rite of passage out of productive endeavor into decline, decrepitude, and impending death" (Albert, 1986, p. 24). Today, however, faculty are still competent, healthy, and motivated past the age of 70, and as a result, allowing them to retire when it is best for them personally makes sense in the 21st-century workplace. Senior faculty can still participate in teaching, research, and service (such as shared governance) without fear of dismissal, and they can continue to contribute to the public good. They can remain involved with and connected to their institution, which is important to faculty who have spent most of their careers and lives there (Van Ummersen, Duranleau, & McLaughlin, 2013). Continued involvement can also benefit the health of older faculty members, since challenging and self-directed work can delay the slowing of physical and mental functioning (Riley, 1986).

It is important that faculty are able to continue to save for retirement past the age of 70 if they need to. As new trends in the composition of families show, many adults at the traditional retirement age are still financially supporting their children. Eliminating mandatory retirement allows faculty to continue to earn a paycheck if they are not financially ready to retire. In addition, some professors may want to remain teaching so that their children can reap the tuition benefits. For those who were affected by the economic downturn, are still supporting their families, or do not have enough saved for retirement, being able to continue working until they are financially ready to retire lifts a massive burden off their shoulders.

Negatives

Faculty realize that by not retiring at 65, they are contributing to a bottleneck in the composition of the professoriate, and they feel guilty about this (Ruse, 2010). At the same time they are also worried that their tenure line will disappear once they retire and that their salary line will not go toward another full-time faculty member. Faculty who teach disciplines that are beginning to disappear, such as traditional foreign languages, do not want to see their classes or even departments slide into oblivion after they have retired. They feel a sense of duty to remain at the institution, passing their knowledge of the disappearing discipline on to new generations of students. Importantly, senior faculty also hold institutional knowledge and traditions and often think that they need to stay so that this information is not lost. Some faculty may be hesitant to announce that they are planning to retire because they may be treated differently by their colleagues. They may be left out of conversations and department meetings because their colleagues already consider them gone.

Not having a mandated retirement age means that today's faculty may not be as ready to retire as were faculty prior to 1994. The current economy works against retiring early, and some may not have made the necessary financial plans. Some faculty may also feel safer staying rather than going. Psychological and social factors can make retiring seem daunting. Faculty retirement is not a fixed event but rather a process that consists of pivotal decisions made during the latter stages of a faculty career (Riley, 1986). It is a socially constructed phase of life, involving questions about the length, meaning, and content of retirement—what do faculty retire to (Riley, 1986)? Ending mandatory retirement allows faculty to make these decisions for themselves. However, it can be difficult to know when the right time to retire is. The decision to retire is complex and depends on several individual factors, such as personal finances, health, family, and continuing career interests (Hammond & Morgan, 1991).

The decision to retire will affect each faculty member in a unique way. Retirement, lacking clearly defined content and rewards, has been called a "roleless role" (Riley, 1986). People adapt to this freedom in different ways: some relish the opportunity to participate in nonacademic activities; others experience culture shock after retirement and no longer feel like a part of academe. For the second group of individuals, retirement can be accompanied by lowered social esteem and lack of stimulation and can even lead to depression (Riley, 1986). The end of mandatory retirement means that faculty need to determine for themselves when to retire and what to retire to.

Institution View of the End of Mandatory Retirement

Positives

In an era of limited resources, the end of mandatory retirement means that institutions can retain senior faculty. Senior faculty are valuable resources, as they have shaped both institutions and higher education generally and can continue to do so. Senior faculty have decades of experience and bring in large research grants that benefit institutions economically and improve their reputations. Additionally, senior faculty are invaluable in orienting new faculty to their profession and to individual institutions (Bland & Berquist, 1997). Senior faculty also enhance the culture of the institution, as they "tend to take a long-term, historical perspective and are concerned with the overall welfare of the institution" (Bland & Berquist, 1997, p. 51). Culture is not self-sustaining; it requires attention to sustain its core values (Bland & Berquist, 1997).

Senior faculty play a crucial role in maintaining an institution's identity. Institutions cannot afford the time, energy, and resources necessary to relearn lessons from the past, and without the wisdom of senior faculty, institutions are likely to make mistakes (Bland & Berquist, 1997). As institutions make major shifts in their missions and organizational structures, having available the institutional memory of senior faculty will help to reduce operational vulnerability. Also, for any institution undergoing change, stability in faculty can serve as a vital anchor (Bland & Berquist, 1997).

Negatives

With the end of mandatory retirement, institutions could no longer plan for faculty retirement. Now administrators do not know in advance when faculty members will be retiring, and this can make long-term planning difficult. Some institutions are facing faculty shortages because a large number of faculty are retiring. Other institutions are struggling to persuade their aging population to retire. The decision to retire depends on factors that are different for each faculty member; it is challenging for administrators to create policy incentives for retirement because one standard policy will not appeal to all faculty. Institutions lacking financial resources may not be able to offer individual buyouts, in which faculty receive a lump-sum payment to retire by a certain date, and implementing expensive programs and activities may also not be an option.

Administrators grapple with how to entice faculty to retire because they are trying to manage faculty composition in terms of age, diversity, and popular majors. It is a tricky balancing act since administrators want to open slots for new faculty but at the same time avoid a mass exodus (American Council on Education, 2011). They want curriculum renewal and the fresh ideas and innovations that junior faculty can bring. Plus, with the student population growing more diverse, it is important to ensure that the faculty is also diversifying, a hard task to accomplish when the majority of professors are White males over the age of 50 (Berberet, Bland, Brown, & Risbey, 2005).

Institutions also worry about how to persuade senior faculty who are viewed as being past their most productive years and as having lost their passion and ability to connect with students. They have often not kept up with changes and advances in their field of study. It is difficult for institutions to get these faculty to retire because forced retirement is difficult and costly in legal, financial, and human terms (American Council on Education, 2011). Most institutions do not wish to engage in documenting the performance failures of a once well-respected scholar.

To make matters more difficult, administrators avoid discussing retirement with faculty for fear of being sued for age discrimination. Table 1.3 shows the trends in case resolutions and monetary benefits from ADEA from 1992 to 2012. Both resolutions and monetary benefits have risen, with the number of case resolutions going from 19,975 in fiscal year (FY) 1992 to 27,335 in FY 2012; correspondingly, monetary benefits rose from $57.3 million in FY 1992 to $91.6 million in FY 2012. As the workforce continues to age, these numbers will only increase. Thus, institutions want to avoid incurring these costly ADEA charges from faculty, which in turn makes initiating the conversation of retirement with older faculty complicated.

Win-Win View of the End of Mandatory Retirement

Although it may appear that the negatives of ending mandatory retirement outweigh the positives for both faculty and institutions, in fact the 21st-century workplace is still catching up with changing policies and practices that reflect increased longevity among the American population. Because retirement has been couched in structural terms (i.e., who can retire, when they can retire, what retirement policies are in place), institutions have been slower to address the cultural factors that also accompany this career stage. The abolition of mandatory retirement, combined with discrimination laws, puts institutions in a structural bind. From the faculty's point of view, "it is

TABLE 1.3

Total Number of Resolutions and Monetary Benefits From the Age Discrimination in Employment Act, Shown Biennially (FY 1992–FY 2012)

	FY 1992	FY 1994	FY 1996	FY 1998	FY 2000	FY 2002	FY 2004	FY 2006	FY 2008	FY 2010	FY 2012
Resolutions	19,975	19,618	15,719	15,995	14,672	18,673	15,792	14,146	21,415	24,800	27,335
Monetary benefits (millions of dollars)[a]	57.3	42.3	31.5	34.7	45.2	55.7	69.0	51.5	82.8	93.6	91.6

Note: Data from *Age Discrimination in Employment Act: FY 2007–FY 2012*, by U.S. Equal Employment Opportunity Commission, 2012. Retrieved from www.eeoc.gov/eeoc/statistics/enforcement/adea.cfm.

[a] Does not include monetary benefits obtained through litigation.

a monstrous wrong to send into job oblivion men and women whose only crime is a willingness to work and too many candles on their birthday cake" (Friedman, 1990). Institutions need to create a culture that supports successful and satisfying careers wherein retirement is part of the natural progression of an academic's life. The institutions discussed in the following chapters have found ways to work with senior faculty to promote both cultural and structural changes that satisfy each side, shifting their collegial conversation from concerns over an aging professoriate and faculty turnover to development of mutually beneficial environments, consisting of policies and practices that effectively facilitate the retirement transition for the institution and supportive programs for faculty.

Allocating resources to retirement transition policies, programs, and practices is cost-effective for institutions. An institution should want to promote a relaxed and smooth retirement transition so that retirees will leave on a positive note and want to continue their relationship with the institution. Senior faculty and retirees are wealthy in accrued capital—that is, their knowledge, expertise, and contacts. Institutions can tap into this capital in numerous ways, such as having retired faculty continue to teach, lecture, mentor, conduct research projects, and bring in grant funding. In addition, these valuable members of the collegial community can bring in donations, sponsor scholarships, promote the institution via word of mouth, enhance branding, facilitate community building, and serve as conductors for collegial interaction (American Council on Education, 2011). Such ambassadors are important for institutions because they are more genuine in their characterizations of the campus than are sterile marketing brochures.

Contributing to the institution in this capacity also benefits retired faculty members, since they can continue to remain involved in the academic community. Fostering an engaged, cohesive retiree community leads to an institutional culture that can help to recruit and retain faculty at all stages of the career life cycle by making the institution a desirable workplace for academics.

To facilitate this win-win scenario, institutions should promote faculty vitality at all career stages, ensuring that senior faculty receive professional development. Institutions should find a way to both manage faculty who want to retire and embrace those faculty who want to work longer. To do this, institutions should have policies and programs in place that foster an environment in which senior faculty are valued, while providing incentives and supports for faculty wanting to transition into retirement. According to Bland and Berquist (1997), faculty are most engaged in their careers at the latter stage. Institutions need to focus on this culminating stage and provide the necessary resources so that senior faculty can transition successfully into retirement and continue to offer their talent and services in a new postretirement role.

References

Albert, S. P. (1986). Retirement: From rite to rights. *Academe, 72*(4), 24–26.

American Council on Education. (2011). *Advancing an agenda for excellence: Supporting faculty retirement transitions.* Retrieved from http://www.acenet.edu/news-room/Documents/ACE-Faculty-Retirement-Transitions-exec-summary.pdf

Ashenfelter, O., & Card, D. (2001). *Did the elimination of mandatory retirement affect faculty retirement flows?* (IZA Discussion Paper No. 402). Bonn, Germany: Institute for the Study of Labor.

Berberet, J., Bland, C. J., Brown, B. E., & Risbey, K. R. (2005). *Late career faculty perceptions: Implications for retirement planning and policymaking.* New York: TIAA-CREF Institute.

Bland, C. J., & Berquist, W. H. (1997). The vitality of senior faculty members: Snow on the roof—fire in the furnace. *ASHE-ERIC Higher Education Report, 25*(7), 51–109.

Fields, G. S., & Mitchell, O. S. (1984). *Retirement, pensions, and social security.* Cambridge, MA: MIT Press.

Franke, A. H. (2011). *Supporting the culminating stages of faculty careers: Legal issues.* Retrieved from http://www.acenet.edu/news-room/Pages/White-Paper-on-Supporting-the-Culminating-Stages-of-Faculty-Careers-Legal-Issues.aspx

Friedman, L. (1990, November 7). Mandatory retirement is age discrimination. *New York Times.* Retrieved from http://www.nytimes.com/1990/11/07/opinion/l-mandatory-retirement-is-age-discrimination-854090.html

Hammond, P. B., & Morgan, H. P. (Eds.). (1991). *Ending mandatory retirement for tenured faculty: The consequences for higher education.* Washington, DC: National Academy Press.

Howe, N., & Strauss, W. (1991). *Generations: The history of America's future, 1584 to 2069.* New York: William Morrow.

Kaskie, B., Leicht, K., & Hitlin, S. (2012). *Promoting workplace longevity and desirable retirement pathways within academic institutions.* New York: TIAA-CREF Institute.

O'Brien, R. D. (2004). Older faculty stay on at Harvard. *Harvard Crimson.* Retrieved from http://www.thecrimson.com/article/2004/2/12/older-faculty-stay-on-at-harvard/

PwC. (2013). *Employee financial wellness survey: 2013 results.* Retrieved from http://www.pwc.com/en_US/us/private-company-services/publications/assets/pwc-financial-wellness-survey.pdf

Riley, M. W. (1986). On future demands for older professors. *Academe, 72*(4), 14–16.

Ruse, M. (2010). A prof at 70: Having fun, feeling guilty. *The Chronicle of Higher Education.* Retrieved from http://chronicle.com/blogs/brainstorm/a-prof-at-70-having-fun-feeling-guilty/22460

Shrestha, L. B. (2006). *CRS report for Congress: Life expectancy in the United States.* Retrieved from the Congressional Research Service website: https://opencrs.com/document/RL32792/2006-08-16/

U.S. Department of Education, Institute of Education Sciences, National Center for Education Statistics. (2004). *NSOPF: 2004 National Study of Postsecondary Faculty.* Retrieved from http://nces.ed.gov/surveys/nsopf/

U.S. Equal Employment Opportunity Commission. (2012). *Age discrimination in employment act: FY 2007–FY 2012.* Retrieved from http://www.eeoc.gov/eeoc/statistics/enforcement/adea.cfm

Van Ummersen, C., Duranleau, L., & McLaughlin, J. (2013). Faculty retirement transitions revitalized. *Change, 14*(26), 1–9.

Yakoboski, P. J. (2011). *Should I stay or should I go? The faculty retirement decision.* New York: TIAA-CREF Institute.

2

SUPPORTING THE CULMINATING STAGES OF FACULTY CAREERS

Lauren J. Duranleau, *American Dental Education Association*, and
Jean M. McLaughlin, *American Council on Education*

The American Council on Education (ACE) has partnered with the Alfred P. Sloan Foundation since 2003 to raise awareness of the importance of workplace flexibility in faculty careers. With generous support from the foundation, ACE has conducted five awards competitions to identify best practices for faculty career flexibility within various types of institutions. The earlier awards programs mainly focused on new and early-career faculty. Through more recent work, ACE realized that while flexibility is required throughout a faculty member's career, it is just as important during the latter stages. The faculty career is composed of many key transitions, such as recruitment as an assistant professor, the granting of tenure and promotion to associate rank, and the move to full professorship. These transitions are generally guided by the institution with good communication regarding how to prepare and what will be expected (Van Ummersen, Duranleau, & McLaughlin, 2013). The last stage of the faculty career—retirement—often occurs with far less communication and support. In 2011 ACE undertook a project focused on this last transition, with the goal of increasing understanding of the final stages of faculty careers. This chapter outlines the project activities and summarizes key findings. It then provides an analysis of survey results and concludes by highlighting the award-winning institutions from the project's awards competition.

ACE was guided by an advisory committee of subject experts that provided insight and vision. Project activities included completing an extensive literature review on faculty retirement transitions and conducting site visits to nine institutions. The site visits included focus groups and interviews with administrators and with faculty who were retired, retiring, or eligible to retire. ACE also held an invitational conference, during which input was solicited from the higher education community on best practices for transitioning into retirement. A legal issues white paper was published in 2011 by ACE. This document highlighted the different types of laws that campuses must contend with, and focused on how campuses can structure their retirement policies in order to avoid problems with the laws. The advantages and disadvantages for both institutions and faculty regarding different retirement plans that are commonly offered were also discussed. The culmination of this work, which gathered perspectives from both faculty and administrators on retirement transitions and analyzed what common supports could be improved, provided a conceptual framework to create survey instruments for an awards program.

Following these activities, ACE mounted an awards competition to identify best practices at 4-year colleges and universities. Institutions that applied for the award completed an institutional survey focused on the policies and supports they provide. The institutions also had their faculty complete a survey on their satisfaction with institutional policies, support, and culture. Fifteen institutions from three Carnegie classifications (baccalaureate colleges, master's large institutions, and doctoral/research universities) were selected by a panel of judges, comprising retired college and university presidents, to receive a 2012 Alfred P. Sloan Award for Best Practices in Faculty Retirement Transitions. The $100,000 awards are being used to further promote best practices and to implement new supports to smoothly guide faculty into the latter stages of their careers.

Project Findings

During this nearly 4-year project, ACE used a three-phase framework to explore faculty retirement transitions: (a) pre-retirement, the "preparation and planning stage," which is typically the 5 years before retirement, but could start earlier; (b) retirement, the "action stage," from within 6 months of retirement to 6 months after retirement; and (c) postretirement, the "maintenance stage" (LaBauve & Robinson, 1999, pp. 8–10). Using this guiding framework, along with a series of research questions, ACE identified common themes and issues for faculty retirement transitions across different institutional types. The research questions that shaped the project activities included the following: (a) What flexible retirement options do faculty know exist for them at their home institutions, and what options are still needed? (b) What structural and cultural obstacles exist to prevent both faculty and administrators from using their options? (c) What solutions to overcoming these obstacles have emerged in institutions? and (d) How do administrators and faculty work together to implement solutions? The next sections outline common themes and issues and analyze institutional and faculty survey results.

Lack of Transparency

ACE found that there is a lack of transparency in supports available for faculty and that most faculty are unaware of existing supports. Some faculty are in denial that the time has come for them to explore retirement, whereas others are waiting for the administration to walk them through the process, answer questions, and provide a tutoring session on the various options available. Faculty have trouble determining where to find information on retirement; some are looking in the wrong places, and others are getting misinformation from fellow colleagues. Institutions need to find legal ways to provide faculty with the information they need to make decisions. It is important that institutions tell retirees about all options and supports and have policies written in clear, understandable language readily available online. Faculty in public institutions found information about retirement more easily, whereas faculty in private institutions thought that the process was "secretive," especially because it involved individualized negotiation of options. Administrators should make sure that the retirement process is clear, transparent, and equal for all faculty.

Lack of Communication

Faculty are accustomed to having clear timelines and guidelines for their career transitions. Their institutions remind them that change is approaching and provide them with the necessary information. Faculty expect to receive the same straightforward support for retirement, and when they do not, they feel as though they are no longer valued or respected. Thus, institutions must better communicate all retirement transition support options to faculty. Institutions need to find ways to discuss the process with senior faculty without violating federal and state age discrimination laws. While a common frustration expressed by administrators during the site visits was that faculty deleted e-mails about supports such as financial seminars, they should still promote these supports by actively engaging in communication campaigns and ensuring that department chairs notify all faculty about supports, no matter what stage of their careers they are in. Institutions should proactively reach out to faculty using multiple communication vehicles. Having retired faculty assist with the process and share their experiences can help guide senior faculty through the retirement stages.

Generational Differences

Some senior faculty indicated that generational differences within their department were so sharply defined that they felt uncomfortable. One person expressed it thusly: "There is no tolerance for us old duffers." Another said, "We are no longer welcome." Yet another offered, "There is a rupture between young talented faculty and us." Administrators also noted that different expectations across faculty from different generations created friction among them. These tensions can decrease the efficiency of a department and create a culture unsupportive of senior faculty that permeates through the campus. Institutions should promote the view that senior and retired faculty are vital. This can be done by ensuring that department chair training, faculty mentoring, and seminars for all generations of faculty on these issues are regularly held.

Lack of Coordination and Communication Between Human Resources and Academic Administrators

Faculty are used to communicating with the provost or academic affairs department when going through career transitions. They are familiar with academic affairs and usually know the office leadership personally. However, for the transition into retirement, most policies and supports are located within the human resources office, an office that most faculty are not familiar with. Human resources can give the impression of being focused only on the hiring and termination of employees. Regardless, to ensure that integrated and comprehensive programming to facilitate retirement transitions is being provided, there must be coordination and communication between human resources and academic administrators (McLaughlin, 2013). Human resources employees should integrate themselves into the community of the provost or academic affairs office so that faculty can get to know them and feel comfortable going through the transition of retirement with them.

Pre-Retirement Supports

The preparation and planning stage of retirement is crucial, and while faculty may not know where to find retirement-planning information, ACE found that institutions were better at providing support for this stage of the retirement transition than they were at providing information for the latter two stages. The institutions' strong suit was financial planning. Most institutions had their campus retirement company (e.g., TIAA-CREF, Fidelity, Vanguard) state's pension plan, hold periodic workshops on campus, and in some cases faculty members could meet individually with company representatives to discuss their financial plans. Many campuses also held financial workshops facilitated by the human resources department. ACE found that faculty also wanted to be able to meet with an outside expert to confirm what they were told by the plan provider. Campuses should provide funds to allow each retiring faculty member one visit with a financial adviser.

Health insurance planning and preparation is less straightforward. Most faculty want the health insurance transition to be explained and are worried that their health-care costs will be higher following retirement. Others have specific needs, such as arranging bridge insurance for a younger spouse or dependent child. Institutions have started holding workshops on how to fill out Social Security and Medicare forms and how to determine what additional insurance faculty may need in retirement. These workshops are quite popular because they help faculty figure out whether their institution offers bridge insurance for faculty and dependents not qualified for Medicare, as well as whether their institution will pay a portion of the extra cost of insurance as faculty lose institutional coverage. For some, the answers to these questions determine whether they will put off retirement in order to retain the institutional health-care plan. Institutions should be proactive in making sure that faculty have all the information regarding health insurance planning and preparation ahead of time.

Another critical pre-retirement support is counseling. Many faculty experience an identity crisis as they approach retirement, as they face the huge challenge of understanding themselves outside of the identity forged by their academic role. In retirement, they are losing who they are, without knowing who they will be (Van Ummersen et al., 2013). Many institutions have employee-assistance programs that house counselors who are trained to work with individuals undergoing unusual stress. The programs usually provide five or six counseling visits, and faculty are often allowed to bring a spouse or the whole family to some of the sessions. These counseling programs are popular among faculty, and institutions should consider developing more extensive programs to help faculty deal with the psychosocial aspects of preparing to retire.

Retirement Supports

ACE found that the most widespread retirement support for the action stage of the transition was a phased retirement plan. These plans involve the gradual winding down of faculty responsibilities in a 3- to 5-year period. They usually allow faculty to negotiate percentages of effort for each year of phasing, which enables them to individualize the plan to meet their specific needs. Institutions should make sure that these plans are formalized and equitably applied to faculty in all departments. The retirement program that seemed to be the least advantageous for both the institution and faculty was individual buyouts. Individual buyouts were accompanied by the perception that faculty were being subjected to unequal treatment, coercion to retire, and age discrimination. Faculty didn't know what the rules around individual buyouts were or what others had received. Phased retirement plans, in contrast, provided transparency, which helps to create a smooth transition into retirement for faculty.

Faculty emphasized the importance of feeling respected and valued for their accomplishments and the service they had provided to their institution. The manner in which an institution handles the retirement process will have a lasting impact on a faculty member's view of the institution after retirement. Acknowledging the contributions of retiring faculty who are going is critical. Some institutions have celebrations for faculty as they retire, and some invite faculty members to showcase their research before they enter retirement. Many institutions support the completion of faculty legacy projects—which include everything from digitizing art history slides to completing laboratory experiments or major administrative assignments—by providing grants to fund the projects or offering sabbatical time to allow faculty to focus on them. Legacy projects are a means of recognizing the value of faculty work to the institution at the conclusion of a successful career. Additionally, ACE found that some institutions are gathering oral histories and documenting the importance to the campus of each retiring faculty member's career.

Postretirement Supports

ACE found that retired faculty had the least amount of support during the postretirement stage. Although most faculty thought maintaining a relationship with their campus was important, some found that it was difficult to do so owing to a lack of information and support from the institution. Retired faculty would like to remain active academically, via teaching, research, or volunteer service. They would like to be invited to department and college events and to assist with mentoring and advising. Many would like to stay in touch with their students, as well as their colleagues. Most retired faculty would like not only support from their former departments but also a space on campus to work in. They would understand if space within the department was not available, but space should be made available somewhere appropriate on campus—even in carrels in the library. Faculty who still want to be active in research are eager for laboratory space, and others need access to special databases to continue their work. Administrators can provide continuing service to retirees by granting them office or laboratory space, continuing support from information technology departments, use of databases, library access, and access to secretarial or lab-assistance support. The most important support that administrators can provide to retirees is to allow them to continue using their institutional e-mail addresses. Many retired faculty expressed displeasure about having their e-mail services cut off immediately upon retirement. Most of these supports are small, cost-effective efforts that can bring immense satisfaction to retired faculty.

Some institutions recall retired faculty for special, part-time teaching assignments. This eases the transition into retirement and allows for the retired faculty member to remain actively involved in the institution. ACE found that a few institutions also have encore career programs, which help facilitate the acquisition of new jobs, volunteer positions, and intellectual and social activities for retired faculty. These encore career programs can be collaborations that the institution has with the community or local government organizations. Such programs allow faculty to retire to a new endeavor, which helps prevent a loss of identity.

More institutions are also creating formal retirement organizations or supporting organized groups of retired faculty to keep them connected to the intellectual life of the institution. Retiree organizations provide news and information, but in addition, they host research seminars at which retired faculty can present new work, provide programs to mentor junior faculty, offer teaching colleges at which retired faculty teach courses for their peers, and coordinate volunteer programs. These organizations also connect retired faculty to their institution by getting them involved in fund-raising and scholarships. Such organizations provide a centralized way for institutions to communicate with retired faculty and to engage them in campus life.

Survey Findings

The data from the institutional and faculty surveys that were part of the awards competition confirmed the themes that had emerged from the other project activities. The faculty survey included 37 questions in the areas of posttenure review and other pre-retirement opportunities, phasing and transitioning supports, campus culture regarding senior faculty, financial planning and medical insurance, and ongoing supports and opportunities in retirement. Key survey findings that relate to the findings from the previous section are highlighted in the following sections.

Institutional Survey

The following list highlights the major findings from the institutional survey, which provided a general landscape of the policies and practices that exist regarding faculty retirement transitions and allowed for ACE to discover what policies and practices were the most widely used.

- 73% of participating institutions had specific criteria in place to determine faculty eligibility for retirement ($N = 26$).
- 65% of participating institutions had a phased retirement program with specific criteria used to determine faculty eligibility for phased retirement ($N = 26$).
- 69% of participating institutions provided medical insurance to retirees ($N = 26$).

Table 2.1 shows the institutions' responses to the question, "In what ways does your institution make a systematic and ongoing effort to communicate

TABLE 2.1

Institutions' Policies, Programs, and Communication Vehicles to Discuss Faculty Retirement

Communication vehicles	*Percentage of participating institutions (N = 26)*
Human resources website	84
Handbooks and pamphlets	80
E-mails/mailings to faculty	76
Orientation for new faculty	52
Frequently Asked Questions web page for retiring faculty	48
University links to state government pension system/human resources websites	44
Ongoing communication/training for department chairs	40
Provost website	32
Other	28
Dedicated retirement office	16
Videos of faculty testimonials regarding faculty retirement transitions	8

its commitment to supporting retirement transitions for faculty members?"
A high percentage of participating institutions rely on the first three communication vehicles—the human resources website, handbooks and pamphlets,
and e-mails/mailings to faculty—but most faculty expect to find information
regarding retirement on the provost's website, as they did for previous career
stages. This disconnect is likely the cause of the lack of communication ACE
noted in earlier project activities. The survey data show that only 32% of
participating institutions communicate about retirement transitions on the
provost's website.

Faculty Survey

Communication
Table 2.1 provides some insight into the high percentage of "don't know"
responses in the faculty survey results. The top items that faculty didn't
know about were as follows:

1. medical bridge program (53%)
2. legacy programs (51%)
3. financial tools (e.g., calculators, comparison charts, and demos) (46%)
4. retirement transition counseling (46%)
5. Employee Assistance Program (45%)
6. availability of tuition remission for partner/dependents in postretirement
   (43%)
7. availability of continued health insurance (40%)

Maintenance of the Faculty-Institution Relationship Postretirement
The survey showed that 75% of faculty would like to remain connected with
their institution in some form after retiring but that 13% indicated no or few
institution-based opportunities for postretirement involvement. Only 12%
answered that they had other commitments that would prevent them from
staying active within their institution (N = 3,243).

Supports With High Satisfaction Rates
Faculty were most satisfied with the following:

1. senior faculty being valued by their junior colleagues (70%)
2. senior colleagues being valued by students (69%)
3. e-mail privileges (63%)
4. library privileges (61%)
5. senior colleagues being valued by administrators (55%)

6. ongoing opportunities to discuss future career at the institution with a department chair or dean (53%)
7. availability of lectures, performing arts, and international opportunities (50%)

Supports With High Dissatisfaction Rates
Faculty were most dissatisfied with the following:

1. office space on campus postretirement (21%)
2. senior colleagues being valued by administrators (19%)
3. ongoing opportunities to discuss future career at the institution with a department chair or dean (16%)
4. timing of the transition into retirement (16%)
5. financial planning independent of retirement fund companies (15%)
6. senior colleagues being valued by junior colleagues (12%)
7. opportunities for mentoring junior colleagues (10%)

Differences by Institutional Type
Faculty at liberal arts colleges were least satisfied with the opportunity to phase into retirement, retirement transition counseling, and financial-planning seminars, but they felt most valued by students, enjoyed their parking privileges, and liked being able to continue to teach and take part in international opportunities.

Faculty at master's large institutions were least satisfied with retirement transition counseling (especially with opportunities to include family members in the sessions), their students' esteem for them, and opportunities to develop a legacy. They liked how their junior colleagues treated them, the opportunities they had to mentor junior faculty, the time they had to phase into retirement, and ongoing access to the library.

Faculty at research institutions were, on average, not dissatisfied with any of the survey items, although they gave low satisfaction scores to retirement transition counseling, availability of continued health insurance, and legacy programs. They were satisfied with parking, ongoing teaching opportunities, and ongoing shared governance.

Faculty Responses to Open-Ended Questions
The faculty survey also contained two open-ended questions: "What are the best things that your institution does to make the retirement transition smoother for faculty?" and "What are some ways in which your institution can make the retirement transition more manageable and smoother for faculty?" Tables 2.2 and 2.3 show the top 10 themes that emerged from faculty responses to these questions.

TABLE 2.2

Top 10 Faculty Responses to the Open-Ended Question, "What Are the Best Things That Your Institution Does to Make the Retirement Transition Smoother for Faculty?"

Response	*Number of Responses (N = 2,017)*
Don't know	672
Phased retirement program	491
Retirement counseling, seminars, and lectures	241
Campus benefits after retirement (office space, access to library, computer support, etc.)	158
Active/helpful human resources office and website	90
Engaged retired faculty community	78
Willingness to work with each individual/flexibility	72
Financial benefits	71
Retiree center	63
Continuing medical insurance and health-care benefits	53

TABLE 2.3

Top 10 Faculty Responses to the Open-Ended Question, "What Are Some Ways in Which Your Institution Can Make the Retirement Transition More Manageable and Smoother for Faculty?"

Response	*Number of Responses (N = 1,779)*
Don't know	257
Discuss retirement more, improve communications, or provide more information about options earlier in career	228
Improve health-care benefits	172
Implement or improve phased retirement program	162
Improve retirement workshops, seminars, and counseling options	132
Offer more campus benefits for retired faculty (office space, parking, library privileges, etc.)	114
Create more opportunities for retired faculty to stay involved with the institution	109
Improve financial incentives and benefits	108
Allow retired faculty to teach part-time	86
Acknowledge, value, and respect faculty contributions	75

These survey results have been used by institutions that applied to the awards competition to improve their relationships with senior and retiring faculty. We believe these results reflect trends in faculty knowledge of retirement transitions, and they appear to be consistent with both anecdotes from individual institutions and nationwide surveys of faculty conducted by third parties.

The 2012 Alfred P. Sloan Awards for Best Practices in Faculty Retirement Transitions

The institutions that won the 2012 Alfred P. Sloan Awards for Best Practices in Faculty Retirement Transitions are listed in Table 2.4. The following chapters discuss the programs, policies, and practices that these institutions have implemented on their campuses. These supports can be replicated to ensure that faculty retirement transitions go smoothly, not just for the faculty members themselves, but also for their institutions and their communities. There are some 4,495 higher education institutions across the United States, ranging from public to private, from well endowed to struggling financially, from emphasizing the teaching of undergraduates to focusing on research and the training of future scholars (U.S. Department of Education, 2012). The best practices discussed in the following chapters can be molded to fit specific institutional conditions and faculty needs.

TABLE 2.4
Winners of the 2012 Alfred P. Sloan Awards for Best Practices in Faculty Retirement Transitions

Baccalaureate colleges	Master's large institutions	Doctoral/research universities
Albright College (PA)	Bentley University (MA)	George Mason University (VA)
Carleton College (MN)	San José State University (CA)	Georgia Institute of Technology (GA)
Mount Holyoke College (MA)	University of Baltimore (MD)	Princeton University (NJ)
Skidmore College (NY)	Xavier University (OH)	University of California–Davis (CA)
Wellesley College (MA)		University of Southern California (CA)
		University of Washington (WA)

We are often asked to provide retirement road maps for faculty and administrators, and the following are guidelines that we have developed over the course of this project. These guidelines have been reinforced by multiple site visits and faculty interviews, as well as dialogues with administrators at all levels and at all institutional types. We end this chapter with our best wishes for institutions and faculty struggling to solve this peculiar problem of higher education.

Faculty Road Map for Retirement Transitions

The following list provides advice regarding faculty retirement transitions that we have put together throughout the course of this project aimed toward the faculty view of the transition.

- Start financial planning as early as possible.
- Map out faculty career path and forecast a retirement date.
- Think about what to retire to—look into outside passions and hobbies.
- Take advantage of any institutional phased retirement programs.
- Prepare for a culminating legacy project.
- Partner with a retired faculty member to serve as a mentor.
- Join any available retiree associations or centers.
- Consider an encore career or volunteer position.
- Remain engaged with the institution—attend events; continue using facilities that are available to retirees, such as the library or fitness center.

Administration Road Map for Faculty Retirement Transitions

The following list provides advice regarding the faculty retirement transition that we have put together throughout the course of this project aimed toward the administrative view of the transition.

- Provide financial planning early in faculty careers and incentivize faculty participation.
- Offer as many different financial plans as possible—defined benefit plans, defined contribution plans, and supplemental plans.
- Host life-planning seminars at all stages of the faculty life cycle and incentivize faculty participation.

- Make all retirement transition information easily available by having a one-stop shop online that is easy to locate on the institution's website and that faculty can access from the privacy of their homes.
- Have multiple communication vehicles for policies and programs.
- Ensure that all policies are transparent and available to all.
- Ensure that policies and programs are sustainable.
- Have a phased retirement policy with multiple time frames for phasing (if the state allows it).
- Offer part-time teaching for retired faculty (especially if the state doesn't allow phasing).
- Have a retiree center.
- Have a retiree association.
- Have a retiree college where retirees can teach courses that are open to the community.
- Continue to offer low-cost on-campus benefits and privileges to retirees—for example, access to the library, parking, and the fitness center.
- Offer opportunities for continued involvement—invite retirees to campus events; allow them to take part in commencement and other activities.
- Offer culminating legacy programs.
- Host celebrations of faculty members' work upon their retirement.
- Show support from senior leaders.
- Train administrators on retirement policies and opportunities.
- Conduct assessments of retirement plans.
- Be conscientious of language used when discussing retirement—consider using the term *transitioning* rather than *retiring*.
- Foster a culture that values senior faculty.

References

LaBauve, B. J., & Robinson, C. R. (1999). Adjusting to retirement: Considerations for counselors. *Adultspan: Theory Research & Practice, 1*(1), 8–10.

McLaughlin, J. (2013). *Retirement transitions in higher education.* Washington, DC: American Council on Education.

U.S. Department of Education, Institute of Education Science, National Center for Education Statistics. (2012). *Fun facts: Educational institutions.* Retrieved from http://nces.ed.gov/fastfacts/display.asp?id=84

Van Ummersen, C., Duranleau, L., & McLaughlin, J. (2013). Faculty retirement transitions revitalized. *Change, 14*(26), 1–9.

PART TWO

THE PSYCHOSOCIAL ASPECTS OF THE CULMINATING STAGES OF FACULTY CAREERS

3

BEYOND THE HORIZON

Helping Faculty Navigate the Retirement
Transition in a Small Liberal Arts Setting

Samantha Roy and Andrea Chapdelaine, *Albright College*

Two key aspects of faculty work that distinguish it from many other professions are high intellectual engagement and service to others. Faculty continually pursue new knowledge, advance their scholarly work, and develop new materials and pedagogical approaches for their courses. Faculty's primary role is to support their students' learning, but they also make contributions to their institutions, their professions, and the communities in which they live. The activities that dominate the professional life of faculty members are rewarding and often expand well beyond their job description. Thus, a faculty member's job responsibilities play a central role in his or her identity (Dorfman & Kolarik, 2005). To the extent that faculty perceive retirement as eliminating these activities, they may feel a significant amount of ambivalence toward and even anxiety about retirement. Anticipating the loss of intellectual engagement, contributions to the community, and ties to colleagues and students, as well as established work routines, can be detrimental to personal well-being if not handled properly by the faculty member and the institution (Moen, 1996). Therefore, it is critical that colleges and universities, reflecting the attributes of a close and caring community, provide services and resources to assist faculty through the retirement transition and beyond. By finding ways to alleviate sources of faculty stress, institutions of higher education can help make retirement a more positive and rewarding experience. This chapter focuses on the psychosocial aspect of faculty retirement, particularly within the liberal arts sector, using Albright College as an exemplar of practice.

Liberal Arts Colleges: More Than Just a Place of Work

The segregation of one's work from one's personal life is often less distinct in a liberal arts setting than it is within other institutional types. Faculty seek employment in liberal arts institutions out of a desire to form strong collegial and student relationships and to be part of a vibrant and friendly intellectual community. The degree to which such a sense of belonging develops becomes a critical factor in a rewarding and fulfilling faculty career. Many newly hired faculty must relocate for their jobs, and consequently, the college becomes their source for a new social network and community. Faculty participate in many campus activities (e.g., concerts, plays, sporting events, homecoming) with their colleagues. Faculty often reside on or near the campus, raise their families nearby, and become active members of the surrounding community, binding their personal lives closely with their colleagues and the college. Since most faculty remain at a single institution for the duration of their career, this frequent interaction promotes the development of close and long-lasting friendships. Colleagues thus become a significant part of the faculty member's social network. The Japanese call this kind of emotional attachment *fureai*, or "mutual contact." *Fureai* goes beyond camaraderie or collegiality to mean family oriented; it is the cognitive recognition and emotional resonance of being ingrained in a community.

Fureai also develops from the communal emphasis on providing an intellectually demanding yet supportive environment for students. Liberal arts faculty have chosen to work at such institutions in order to deliver a highly personalized and quality education built on a commitment to nurturing the faculty-student relationship (Greene & Greene, 2000). For faculty a sense of *fureai* develops as a result of the in loco parentis attitude prevalent in such types of institutions. In loco parentis connotes a nurturing relationship characterized by the development of trust between faculty and students. However, this type of relationship leads to the expectation that faculty will be available and accessible to the students whenever needed. To meet this demand, along with all the other expectations for faculty, faculty will often intertwine work life and family life whenever possible. For example, faculty, both male and female, will take their children to student events or have students provide child-care services. These activities further blur the lines between a faculty member's professional and personal roles in terms of their own identity. Therefore, if faculty believe retirement will result in a loss of their identity and their community, they may face retirement with a sense of impending loss. Retirement can sever individuals from what have been critical aspects of their social function for many years. These work relations often comprise much of a faculty member's identity, to the extent that senior faculty might defer considering existential questions of one's identity without such interconnections, which in turn may delay retirement (Baldwin & Zeig, 2012).

Life-Course and Continuity Theories and Retirement

Albright's work on career and life balance, including retirement, is encompassed in the framework of life-course theories and continuity theories that take into account the entire life span. Life-course theories claim that the environment in which one lives (i.e., the family, the neighborhood, the peer groups, and careers) greatly influences the process of development (Moen, 1996) and argue that "social timing is not synchronous with biological timing" (Neugarten & Datan, 1996, p. 99). The timeline and quality of a retirement transition is heavily influenced both by earlier episodes in life (Bronfenbrenner, 1995; Kim & Moen, 2001) and by what other life events are occurring as the person reaches retirement age. Varying life courses have a significant impact on one's decision about when and whether to retire, how to prepare for that retirement, and what to do after retirement.

Atchley's (1989) continuity theory contends that a person's experiences shape the decisions he or she makes and that people tend to make choices by using "familiar strategies in familiar arenas of life" (p. 183). Adults use various roles they have inhabited in the past to navigate and find happiness in new experiences and to maintain external and internal continuity in their lives (Reitzes & Mutran, 2006). Therefore, adjustment to retirement goes more smoothly when retirees take on roles and relationships that are similar to those they are leaving behind in the employed world (Moen, 1996). For example, teaching is often a source of enjoyment for faculty and thus could be a source of internal continuity that facilitates adjustment to retirement. Albright has several faculty members who continue to lecture as adjuncts in retirement; these men and women even offer their services as public speakers to the college's Speakers Bureau. Likewise, a retiree who attends major social functions at the college is drawing upon external continuity. Many retirees at Albright opt to attend the annual retirees' luncheon, the employee holiday party, and baccalaureate and commencement ceremonies. To facilitate external continuity, retirees should be invited to as many events as possible, thereby creating choice about what one wishes to participate in, with whom one wishes to socialize, and spaces one wishes to inhabit.

Helping Faculty Plan for Retirement at a Small Liberal Arts College

Although faculty may be ready to retire from their daily work responsibilities, it is important to recognize, for the reasons described previously, the significance that the professional role has in the faculty member's identity and to find ways to minimize any psychological distress caused by the ending of those daily work responsibilities. Even faculty who are ready to step down from their full-time job may also be interested in maintaining some facets of their job that have contributed to their personal identity and intellectual engagement. Further, faculty often feel a strong sense of ownership and pride in their institution and hence wish to maintain their contributions to its continued success. To ensure ongoing professional and personal well-being, institutions must help faculty nearing retirement to explore and address areas of concern during retirement planning and then must provide the services and programs needed to address these concerns postretirement (Dorfman & Kolarik, 2005; Ferren, 1998). If the institution fails to provide a road map for faculty, they may postpone their retirement owing to ambivalence, even if they feel ready to move away from their current position.

To address the psychosocial aspects of retirement, colleges must offer support that goes well beyond the typical provision of information regarding finances, health benefits, and the like, although those are important and can be significant sources of stress as well (indeed, faculty indicate that financial considerations are the most important aspect of the retirement decision [Dorfman, 2002; Yakoboski, 2005]). There are several ways an institution can help with the retirement process and allay some of the concerns that accompany it in addition to addressing the financial considerations, often without considerable expense for resource-limited institutions. In the following paragraphs we present the steps and structures we have implemented through the resources provided by the Sloan Award for Retirement Transitions and on the basis of information gathered from our late-career faculty regarding their retirement concerns and needs.

We have found the most successful first step is to have the chief academic officer (CAO), dean, or chair invite any late-career faculty to engage in a one-on-one conversation to explore areas of ambivalence and possible ways to address these concerns. It is important for the CAO to acknowledge the faculty member's positive and negative emotions and validate the reasons for those mixed emotions. It is also critical that the CAO reinforce the faculty member's value to the community and the desire to have him or her remain a part of the college community to the extent that he or she wishes. Next, the CAO should present options for continued engagement in the three primary sources of personal fulfillment the faculty member's career has provided: intellectual engagement, service to the community, and social belonging. Some faculty may be reluctant to have such a conversation for fear of being pressed to make a decision on when to retire. It is critical that the CAO, through more public forums, reassure the academic community that these conversations are strictly meant to be exploratory and supportive. Asking faculty who have gone through this process to serve as the CAO's ambassadors to reluctant colleagues may be helpful.

These conversations have proved to be productive for both the faculty member and the institution. For example, in one such conversation, a soon-to-be-retired faculty member expressed a desire to continue offering his study-away course for 3 years after his retirement. This would enable him to travel and conduct research related to that geographical area while also providing an excellent learning experience for the students. Another faculty member, an alumna who is also a gifted speaker, expressed interest in serving as a spokesperson for the college by meeting with alumni and prospective families. Finally, another faculty member agreed to invest time postretirement assisting in the development of a new academic program that would be beneficial to the students and the college.

In addition to encouraging these conversations, we also have held a series of educational sessions for all faculty nearing retirement age that provide information and resources for retirement planning. Research has shown that such support decreases faculty concern about their retirement (Dorfman, 1997; Dorfman & Kolarik, 2005; Fisher & Specht, 1999). Through the support of the Sloan Award, we developed a more expansive retirement seminar, inviting experts on Social Security and Medicare to provide supplemental information resources on these critical aspects of retirement planning. To address psychosocial concerns, we connected with a variety of experts in fields other than finance as follows: a representative from the Employee Assistance Program (EAP) came to discuss counseling, legal, and other services; a member of the local United Way spoke about community volunteer opportunities; and a travel agent showcased group tours and other excursions. We also scheduled a tour of the faculty retirement facilities and reviewed all the college resources available to faculty postretirement (e.g., shared office and social space, library and technology resources, access to cultural events and facilities). In addition to appreciating the wealth of information provided, the faculty felt reassured that the institution was considering their needs and striving to provide resources and support to address those needs. Lastly, providing this information in the form of a seminar allowed for ample discussion time and reinforced feelings of community continuity (Atchley, 1989).

A third facet of providing faculty with postretirement planning information is a comprehensive, timely, and accurate web page devoted to late-career and retired faculty. Faculty who are considering retirement may not be ready to declare that intention and thus should be given tools to plan on their own before they are ready to announce a retirement date. Through the Sloan Award, we created a website that provides such information (www .albright.edu/sloan/Flexibility_Career_Late.html), not only to assist faculty but, again, to reassure them of the institution's support.

One final strategy we are currently developing for faculty retirement planning and transitioning is a mentor program modeled on the one we provide for our new faculty (a 2-year program in which faculty are given both in- and outside-department mentors). Similar to new faculty, faculty nearing retirement are facing unknown territory and thus would benefit from the mentorship of a recently retired colleague. This mentor could advise them as they explore various options and plans for retirement, as well as provide a reassuring and realistic perspective on the positive and negative aspects of retirement. This mentor also can provide critical feedback to the institution, while respecting the faculty member's privacy, on the extent to which allocated resources are meeting retiring and retired faculty members' needs and expectations. Finally, mentorship provides a service opportunity for retired faculty, thus helping meet their desire to provide service to others and maintain the *fureai* of the small liberal arts community. Although the importance of service drops considerably once a faculty member has retired (Dorfman, 2002), providing service opportunities for retirees is desirable, especially among the newly retired.

With limited funding colleges can provide a variety of different programs and resources for faculty such as the ones discussed thus far. These programs and resources are especially effective at facilitating conversation, exploration, and planning, as well as at addressing some of the anxiety and ambivalence that arise when one is planning for retirement. However, having official policies is also important to provide structure and assurance for the faculty members, as well as liability protection for the college. One effective policy that we and many other institutions have adopted is a phased retirement policy. Phased retirement is discussed elsewhere in this book and thus deserves only brief mention here, in the context of addressing the psychosocial needs of faculty retiring from small liberal arts colleges. Having a successful phased retirement policy in place for the past several years, we have found that it benefits faculty by allowing them to experience retirement without immediately and fully "stepping off the cliff." They are still able to engage in the intellectual and social life of the community and make important contributions to the institution and their profession, while also beginning to enjoy a slower pace of life and new pursuits.

One lesson we have learned through the implementation of the phased retirement policy is that it is important for all members of the community to keep in mind that retiring faculty are still participating members of the faculty. A potential negative side effect of phased retirement is that faculty members may feel less empowered as they move toward retirement. They may witness the hiring of their replacements, see decisions made with which they disagree, and even be asked to relocate or clear out research space. One faculty member in her second year of phased retirement recently told the CAO that her colleagues treat her as though she is already retired. Departments may not want to bother the phasing faculty member with service duties, issues that come up within the department, or other tasks. Faculty members phase into retirement for a variety of reasons, and departments and administrators should not assume that phasing faculty wish to be uninvolved.

Conversely, we have also found that sometimes, despite best intentions, a faculty member is drawn into more responsibilities than agreed upon. For example, a faculty member in phased retirement volunteered to teach additional courses to cover the unexpected leave of another department member. The CAO and department chair should ensure that faculty in phased retirement are not being asked to take on more service than is commensurate with the reduced workload. Colleagues and administrators should be sensitive to these possible unexpected outcomes of phased retirement and identify ways to alleviate their potential negative impact. With regard to raising community awareness, we now include information and training sessions for department chairs on these and other retirement matters. As noted previously, providing a mentor during the phased retirement years can be helpful. Finally, the CAO should encourage and initiate conversations with faculty in phased retirement as much as possible to ensure that the phasing is meeting their expectations.

The Role of the Faculty Community During Retirement Transitions

In addition to understanding the psychosocial aspects of retirement, liberal arts colleges can further facilitate successful retirement transitions by garnering the support of the academic community as a whole. It is helpful to recognize that faculty retirements affect everyone, not just the person who is retiring. Engagement is important for those left behind, who are likely to experience some ambivalence and anxiety about the retirement as well. Recently, at our institution, one department was facing the retirement of half of its faculty in the span of a few years. In total the retiring faculty represented nearly 200 years of service to the institution. The faculty as a whole was tasked to develop a bold vision for the department, building on the opportunities arising from this momentous change in departmental composition and leadership. The faculty members who were not retiring experienced great difficulty in developing such a plan, largely owing to the anxiety created by the significant change. Simultaneously, it was challenging for the retiring faculty—given their many years of dedication to building a high-quality, vibrant academic program—to fully cede the future of the department to the newer faculty. The department eventually did produce an action plan, but it required significant intervention from both colleagues outside the department and the administration. These dynamics are evident across the liberal arts landscape, to the extent that even a single retirement can be a sea change for small departments—a department's research strengths will disappear and new ones may emerge, curricular revision will ensue, and new goals and strategies will develop.

At liberal arts colleges the curriculum, its known strengths, and even the intangible feel of an institution are largely a reflection of the faculty. As we navigate another large wave of faculty retirements, administrators and faculty are encouraged to engage in open dialogue about the impending changes and their impact on the institution. Current faculty should be encouraged to identify ways to engage retired faculty in the governance of the institution, while also ensuring the voice and will of newer faculty are heard. Simultaneously, providing professional development to younger faculty to help prepare them for increasing leadership demands may alleviate some concerns of the retiring faculty about whether the institution is in good hands. Nonretiring faculty should also be given access to services to allow them, if needed, to cope with the feelings of loss they may experience as they say farewell to a valued colleague and, often, a close friend. Employee-provided counseling services, community-building social events for faculty, and simple recognition and validation of that loss are all means to address these concerns.

People born into different generations hold different beliefs about retirement and life as a retiree. A life-course and continuity approach to retirement will allow for these distinctions to evolve over the course of time (Moen, 1996). The distinctive characteristics of small liberal arts colleges that reflect their academic vibrancy, opportunities for service, and a strong sense of community are often those factors that contribute greatly to a faculty member's long and rewarding career in the professoriate at such institutions. Those very characteristics can also make retirement an event that draws upon and is celebrated by the whole community. By recognizing sources of psychosocial discomfort for faculty and responding to them in ways that reflect a close and caring academic community, liberal arts colleges can create an intimate and meaningful retirement transition for their valued faculty.

References

Atchley, R. C. (1989). A continuity theory of normal aging. *The Gerontologist, 29*(2), 183–190.

Baldwin, R. G., & Zeig, M. J. (2012). Making emeritus matter. *Change: The Magazine of Higher Learning, 44*(5), 28–34. doi:10.1080/00091383.2012.706508

Bronfenbrenner, U. (1995). The bioecological model from a life course perspective: Reflections of a participant observer. In P. Moen, G. H. Elder, & K. Luscher (Eds.), *Examining lives in context: Perspectives on the ecology of human development* (pp. 599–618). Washington, DC: American Psychological Association.

Dorfman, L. T. (1997). *The sun still shone: Professors talk about retirement.* Iowa City: University of Iowa Press.

Dorfman, L. T. (2002). Stayers and leavers: Professors in an era of no mandatory retirement. *Educational Gerontology, 28*, 15–33.

Dorfman, L. T., & Kolarik, D. C. (2005). Leisure and the retired professor: Occupation matters. *Educational Gerontology, 31*, 343–361.

Ferren, A. S. (1998). *Senior faculty considering retirement: A developmental and policy issue* (New Pathways: Faculty Career and Employment for the 21st Century Working Paper Series #11). Washington, DC: American Association for Higher Education.

Fisher, B. J., & Specht, D. K. (1999). Successful aging and creativity in later life. *Journal of Aging Studies, 13*(4), 457–472.

Greene, H., & Greene, M. (2000). The liberal arts: What is a liberal arts education and why is it important today? In H. Greene & M. Greene (Eds.), *The hidden ivies: Thirty colleges of excellence* (pp. 11–21). New York: HarperCollins.

Kim, J. E., & Moen, P. (2001). Is retirement good or bad for subjective well-being? *Current Directions in Psychological Science, 10*(3), 83–86.

Moen, P. (1996). A life course perspective on retirement, gender, and well-being. *Journal of Occupational Health Psychology, 1*(2), 131–144.

Neugarten, B. L., & Datan, N. (1996). Sociological perspectives on the life cycle. In D. A. Neugarten (Ed.), *The meanings of age: Selected papers of Bernice L. Neugarten* (pp. 96–113). Chicago: University of Chicago Press.

Reitzes, D. C., & Mutran, E. J. (2006). Lingering identities in retirement. *Sociological Quarterly, 47*, 333–359.

Yakoboski, P. (2005). *Trends and issues: Findings from the retirement confidence survey of college and university faculty.* New York: TIAA-CREF Institute.

4

UNDERSTANDING RETIREMENT FROM A DEVELOPMENTAL PERSPECTIVE

The Case of Mount Holyoke College

Caroline S. Clauss-Ehlers, *Rutgers, The State University of New Jersey,*
and Lynn Pasquerella, *Mount Holyoke College*

Changes in retirement policies and practices in the latter quarter of the 20th century, resulting from compliance with the 1986 amendment to the Age Discrimination in Employment Act (ADEA), have occurred on a national level and across industries, including higher education. These changes have culminated in ad hoc 21st-century practices that may not always be effective in meeting the postsecondary industry's need for continual renewal of the faculty and curriculum (Allen, Clark, & Ghent, 2005; Daniels & Daniels, 1989; Leslie, 2005). This chapter examines how shifts in faculty retirement trends and related policies affected one liberal arts college and describes this college's efforts to support late-career faculty as they transition into retirement. We provide an overview of retirement practices as they relate to higher education, beginning with the last quarter of the 20th century and continuing to the present. Next, we discuss contemporary developmental approaches to retirement, incorporating psychologist Erik Erikson's theory of life-cycle events (Erikson, 1968). We then illustrate, through a case study of increasing retirement supports at Mount Holyoke

College, strategies that help faculty in making the transition. Finally, we conclude our case study by describing policies our institution has recently put in place that can be replicated on other campuses. Together, this overview and case study provide a compelling reason for campuses to adopt a developmental perspective of faculty retirement transitions (McLaughlin, 2013; Van Ummersen, Duranleau, & McLaughlin, 2013).

Retirement: Then and Now

Changes in employment law since the 1980s have prohibited colleges and universities from establishing mandatory retirement ages, leading many faculty to delay retirement well into their seventies. Before Congress passed the amendment to ADEA outlawing compulsory retirement in 1986, colleges and universities were able to enforce the mandatory retirement age of 70 for faculty, although some faculty retired earlier (Ashenfelter & Card, 2001). Writes Leslie (2005) of the 1986 sea change, "Colleges and universities can no longer tell faculty when they must retire. Instead, faculty can now tell their institutions when they will retire" (p. 5). Although colleges and universities had until 1993 to prepare to implement the ADEA amendment, the planning for the transformation seems scant in hindsight. In response to the impending legislation, Daniels and Daniels (1989) presented a compelling question—one that continues to be timely in today's climate: "What is an appropriate retirement age for college faculty?" (p. 36). The Daniels and Daniels study was the first to provide data and insights about voluntary retirement in a higher education context and was influenced by key legislative changes that affected retirement and the options available to faculty. Daniels and Daniels's then-current data indicated that college faculty retired later than employees in other categories (Mulanaphy, 1984). Thus, the elimination of mandatory retirement, coupled with the likelihood that faculty would retire later than before, predictably led to quandaries for college and university administrators, academic departments, and individual faculty (Ashenfelter & Card, 2001).

Administrative and Departmental Concerns

Many administrators in higher education are concerned about the trends in the percentage of faculty who are in tenured or tenure-track faculty positions. Even before the elimination of mandatory retirement, there was concern about the aging of the professoriate. Doyle (2008) claims, "In 1988, 35 percent of faculty in public comprehensive institutions were older than 55. By 2004, this figure had increased to 46 percent" (p. 58). Faculty under 35 employed in non-tenure-track positions in public comprehensive institutions rose from 30% to

70% between 1988 and 2004. By 2004 faculty between the ages of 35 and 44 in non-tenure-track positions comprised 50% of positions (Doyle, 2008). Although these data are certainly not representative of all institutions, they do suggest a system whereby older, more senior faculty have tenured positions and younger faculty often do not. As Doyle argues, when faculty retire now, they leave a system that is increasingly devoid of younger professionals in the tenure-track ranks.

The potential lack of faculty renewal has implications for teaching, student interaction, and role modeling. It also has implications for new research developments—if fewer faculty hold the kind of tenure-track and tenured positions in which their ideas and innovations can be developed over time, then academic disciplines wherein major discoveries are made later in life may be shortchanging themselves of future scholars. In some other fields, notably the humanities and certain languages, faculty are finding themselves deterred from retiring because they, or their line, may not be replaced in their department. While the wholesale replacement of tenure-track positions with contingent faculty is less of an issue at selective liberal arts colleges, such as Mount Holyoke, than it is at larger universities, it is still the case that faculty across the country are worried about sustaining their disciplines in the face of cutbacks and consolidations, which may also act as a deterrent to retirement.

Doyle (2008) identifies shared governance as another administrative concern associated with retirement. In institutions of higher education, *shared governance* means faculty are involved in decision making for the institution. For some institutions only those faculty with tenure or in tenure-track positions have the privilege of participating in shared governance, influencing decisions about promotion and tenure, hiring, and other significant institutional issues. Given an aging faculty that is not necessarily being replaced with tenure-track lines for new scholars, how does the shared governance structure sustain itself in institutions where those associated with tenure are the only participants in this process?

Finally, department heads are concerned about the trajectory of an academic department when multiple simultaneous retirements result in not having enough faculty to keep the discipline robust (or even current). Although phased retirement mitigates this potential gap by allowing the transition to occur gradually, a department (and its corresponding institution) may still experience a sudden shift in membership as often a department chair can do little to plan ahead for faculty departures.

Individual Faculty Concerns

Faculty also voice concerns about retirement, noting both positive factors that make them want to stay and negative factors that deter them from leaving.

For many faculty the ability to continue to engage in "stimulating mental activity and opportunities for meaningful interaction with colleagues and students [is] of perhaps equal or even greater importance" than financial concerns, such as inflation, when they consider retirement (Daniels & Daniels, 1989, p. 37). Writes Leslie (2005),

> Since many faculty . . . are so fully engaged socially and psychologically in their institutions and professional activities, "cold turkey" retirement is both feared and difficult to manage. Phasing provides a transition both from this consuming involvement and to whatever may come next in a major shift in one's life course. (p. 7)

While retirement decisions are influenced by a combination of variables, the two most prominent factors identified in the literature are "adequate retirement income" and "poor health" (Chronisterand & Kepple, 1987; TIAA-CREF, 1988, as cited in Daniels & Daniels, 1990, p. 75). Shrinking retirement accounts in the wake of the recession have also led to concerns about whether there will be enough retirement income in the future should investments continue to decrease. A related concern that encompasses both financial and health factors is health-care coverage. Specifically, the decision about age of retirement may be influenced by whether the individual is eligible to receive Medicare. Even if the individual is eligible, Medicare may not provide sufficient coverage for specific health-care needs or for the individual's spouse, who may have been covered by the institution's health policy. Thus, both financial and physical health can weigh heavily on faculty as they contemplate retirement.

A Developmental Approach to Retirement for 21st-Century Faculty

This chapter takes a developmental approach to the latter career stages, including retirement. A *developmental approach* is defined as recognizing the "predictable physical, mental, and social changes over life that occur in relationship to the environment" (Gladding, 2011, p. 9). Gladding (2011) defines *events* in the life cycle as times throughout life when people reach another level of development. Retirement, then, is a life-cycle event during which the individual interacts with the environment to make a decision about work status, usually involving the decision to leave a position of employment. One theory that is useful in understanding the developmental nature of retirement transitions is Erikson's (1968) theory of psychosocial development. His eighth stage of psychosocial development—integrity versus despair—occurs between 55 and 65 years of age until death. Integrity versus despair explores the extent to which individuals reflect upon their past with a feeling of satisfaction—a sense that they lived a valued and meaningful life. Individuals who feel that they are valued and have lived a meaningful life achieve a sense of integrity, or what Erikson would call wisdom, at this stage. Individuals who do not achieve integrity feel varying degrees of despair. Those who look back on their life with despair see a dearth of meaning; they do not have a sense that they lived in a way that indicates value and worth.

Bradley and Shenk (2003) describe "push-pull interactions" that influence faculty retirement decisions. Push factors are those variables that influence the choice to maintain employment, such as job satisfaction, financial need, and desire to maintain a connection with an academic community. In contrast, pull factors are those variables that are motivators for retirement, such as desire for free time, time with family, and the need to manage health issues. It is critical to acknowledge that faculty who retire from their lives as campus-based professors may later engage in other types of work activity. A developmental perspective accounts for faculty concerns about maintaining a sense of community and contribution as they approach retirement.

The response to Daniels and Daniels's (1989) question about the optimal retirement age is "It depends." It depends because each faculty member has different considerations, life experiences, expectations, responsibilities, and needs when thinking about retirement. Faculty are concerned with staying engaged—on campus, in their professions, with students, and with colleagues. At Mount Holyoke faculty engage in a dialogue about the transition to retirement over several years before actual retirement so that they are well prepared to consider their choices and make decisions that work for them. Critical components of this conversation include transparent retirement options, educational outreach, and resources for financial and other relevant information. Mount Holyoke College is developing workshops specifically for faculty nearing retirement in which questions regarding finances, insurance, health-care options, and opportunities for continued involvement at the college are addressed by human resources, dean of faculty staff, and the retirement benefits manager.

We highlight phased retirement as one way to address the question of when to retire. Phased retirement allows faculty the opportunity to reflect on their careers during their transition into retirement while maintaining a sense of community and contribution. Formal phased retirement programs provide a transitional mechanism that supports this developmental phase while addressing personal needs and financial considerations. Mount Holyoke College's formal phased retirement program is further discussed later in this chapter.

The importance of engaging in a dialogue about the transition to retirement is increasingly critical as faculty consider their own future economic security, professional contributions, and personal goals within the context of dramatic changes in higher education, both nationally and in individual institutions. Faculty are concerned about how they will negotiate financially in a world in which life expectancy means on average 25 years in retirement. They also struggle with the reality that faculty retirements may put their departments at risk, given that replacements are not automatic and that in the absence of a critical mass, entire disciplines may face elimination. Moreover, unlike in the past, today it is often more expensive to replace retiring faculty with new faculty, who require greater start-up packages in a competitive recruitment and retention environment. Thus, faculty may be reluctant to do what they believe is in their own best interest out of a sense of collegiality and dedication to their institutions (Smathers, 2004).

Case Study: Mount Holyoke College

These emotional realities make outreach to faculty all the more important. Thus, in 2009 Mount Holyoke undertook an aggressive effort to inform faculty of the resources available to them during the transition to retirement, a period during which they could continue to contribute to the intellectual and creative vibrancy of their departments. Mount Holyoke began by including a discussion of faculty retirement policies and options in the annual department chairs' training sessions. The then dean of faculty and his staff began an extensive review of the college's policies governing familial and personal leave and dedicated more time to discussions about work-life balance and other policies Mount Holyoke has in place to support faculty at different phases of their careers.

Mount Holyoke has offered a voluntary phased retirement plan for faculty since 2004, although the number of faculty exercising this option has grown significantly in the past few years, owing both to the demographics of the faculty and, we believe, to increased public conversation and flexibility in administering the policy. The phased retirement option can be elected over a period of up to 4 years beginning between the ages of 58 and 71. Faculty are afforded the opportunity to make a formal commitment to move to part-time work and to full retirement within 4 years of the initial contract. Faculty in phased retirement receive a salary that is typically 50% of their previous year's salary. The percentage of annual salary increase is the same for these faculty as for full-time faculty at the same rank and equivalent salary level. In addition, faculty in this plan may draw amounts from their pension accumulation at any time during their phased retirement. The college also continues to make contributions to group health and life insurance plans equivalent to those for full-time faculty. Contributions to the pension plan and to the college's group disability plan are made on the basis of actual salaries, that is, the reduced phased retirement salary.

One of the primary incentives for transitioning faculty to enter this program in recent years has been significant flexibility regarding teaching loads, research expectations, and sabbatical leave. The faculty member and the dean of faculty consult with the department chair to develop a work plan for the term of the phased retirement program. The components of this program usually include part-time teaching, but many plans also highlight scholarly research, professional activities, on-campus consulting, or administrative work. At the completion of each year, the faculty member is able to propose changes to the activities planned for the following year. In addition, faculty members in phased retirement remain eligible for sabbatical leaves, which are available to faculty every seventh semester.

Mount Holyoke shows its appreciation and respect for retiring faculty's continuing contributions by offering a host of other benefits throughout the period of phased retirement. These include eligibility for children's tuition benefits for study at either Mount Holyoke or other institutions; the ability of spouses, domestic partners, and children of early retirees to attend individual courses on campus under the same terms as full-time employees; the retention of e-mail accounts, office space, and laboratory space; complimentary tickets to theater and dance performances; parking privileges; access to athletic and library facilities; participation in discount insurance programs; and lifetime membership at the Willits-Hallowell Conference Center, an on-campus venue for workshops, scholarly meetings, and social gatherings.

In 2010 the President's Commission on Work-Life Balance sought to further standardize best practices in career flexibility. Several of the task forces that emerged from this initiative, including those on professional development, workload management, and dependent care, have charges central to the concerns of prospective retirees. Incorporating the needs of retiring faculty into policies and practices directed at all faculty prevents the marginalization of those considering or engaged in the retirement process. In this way, faculty at all stages of professional development are encouraged to think about the best means of achieving a healthy balance between their careers and lives outside of work. Ongoing conversations about next steps help avoid additional psychological distress that can occur during life's transitions (McLaughlin, 2013; Van Ummersen et al., 2013).

Retired faculty are also offered opportunities to continue to teach first-year seminars or other courses as they wish. The Office of the Dean of Faculty has tried to make sure that faculty do not see retirement as a one-way journey off campus. Mount Holyoke's phased retirement program has been a promising strategy for getting faculty to transition into retirement. While some faculty delayed entering phased retirement because of the financial crisis in 2008, the last couple of years have seen a resurgence of interest. In the spring of 2013, 19 faculty were in phased retirement and another 5 were negotiating the terms of their retirement planning (out of a total tenured and tenure-track faculty of 185).

Honoring the Legacy

Faculty, like other professionals, often think of their legacy as they transition to retirement. At Mount Holyoke, *legacy* refers to the contribution made by the retiring faculty member to academic and social/local communities. As faculty embark on the journey to retirement, honoring legacies provides an important way to acknowledge the contributions they made during their careers and demonstrates to the community the importance of senior faculty. There are many ways to honor a faculty member's legacy, including scholarly publications that describe the person's work and vision (Murrell, Ryan, & Bergfeld, 2011; Winfield, 2003), discussions about the impact of mentoring relationships (Lechuga, 2011; Mansson & Myers, 2012), and acknowledging the influence of the faculty member on students (Patterson, 2009).

As other colleges and universities receiving American Council on Education (ACE)/Sloan awards have discovered, engaging retiring faculty as continuing members of an intellectual and scholarly community brings benefits both to those faculty and to the institution as a whole. Mount Holyoke supports research and creative projects by emeritus faculty in an ad hoc but generous manner when appropriate. Mount Holyoke also honors faculty legacies through a transitioning grant for faculty in phased retirement that allows faculty to complete a body of work in their final years at the college. For instance, in the past several years, the Office of the Dean of Faculty has supported the costs of publication and permissions for illustrations for two books by emeritus faculty (Eugenia Herbert's *Flora's Empire: British Gardens in India* and John Varriano's *Wine: A Cultural History*), provided money to travel to archives abroad for research, and sponsored debut performances of musical compositions by retired faculty.

The Role of Transitioning Grants

Since the fear of losing a lifetime of work and connection to an institution can deter faculty from retiring, Mount Holyoke has begun to provide funding to faculty nearing retirement so that they can complete capstone scholarly and creative projects. With grant funding from the Sloan Award for Best Practices in Faculty Retirement Transitions and in partnership with ACE, Mount Holyoke will make three rounds of capstone awards for scholarly or creative projects to faculty in phased retirement. Awards ranging between $5,000 and $7,500 will support a host of projects that faculty want to complete. The first round of awards in spring 2013 supported four faculty projects, ranging from a social psychology professor's global study of equality in family work (with contributors from 28 countries around the world) to a religion professor's publication of a book and primary documents based on a lifetime's study of the Shakers. The capstone mechanism further underscores the college's developmental perspective as it provides resources for faculty members who intend to finalize their work during this life transition. The capstone honors their contributions to both Mount Holyoke and their disciplines.

Conclusion

As we move further into the 21st century, our demographic landscape continues to change. People are living longer and retiring later. We recommend that retirement be viewed as a dynamic, developmental process that marks a new stage in a faculty member's life. Phased retirement programs such as Mount Holyoke's allow retirees to experience this stage as a transition rather than a sudden change, providing some balance for the push-pull factors influencing individual decisions. Acknowledging this process is particularly important given research that has shown professional considerations (e.g., maintaining connection to an intellectual community) are as important as financial factors in retirement decisions among faculty. Mechanisms such as Mount Holyoke College's ACE/Sloan capstone awards honor faculty contributions and provide opportunities for retiring faculty to renew their connections to scholarly work that may have been long deferred given the responsibilities of teaching and advising.

Our recommendations for facilitating successful faculty retirement transitions are as follows:

- Institutions explore the possibility of offering flexible phased retirement programs.
- Institutions clearly publicize retirement options.
- Institutions honor retiring faculty through various legacy programs.

References

Allen, S. G., Clark, R. L., & Ghent, L. S. (2005). Managing a phased retirement program: The case of UNC. *New Directions for Higher Education, 132,* 47–60.

Ashenfelter, O., & Card, D. (2001). Did the elimination of mandatory retirement affect retirement flows? *American Economic Review, 92,* 957–980.

Bradley, D. B., & Shenk, D. (2003). *Examining the faculty retirement process.* Paper presented at the 56th Scientific Meeting of the Gerontological Society of America, San Diego, CA.

Chronisterand, J. L., & Kepple, T. R., Jr. (1987). *Incentive early retirement for faculty: Innovative responses to a changing environment* (ASHE-ERIC Higher Education Report No. 1987-1). Washington, DC: Association for the Study of Higher Education.

Daniels, C. E., & Daniels, J. D. (1989). College and university pension plans and retirement policies: Current status. *Benefits Quarterly, 5*(2), 28–39.

Daniels, C. E., & Daniels, J. D. (1990). Voluntary retirement incentive options in higher education. *Benefits Quarterly, 6*(2), 68–78.

Doyle, W. R. (2008). The baby boomers as faculty: What will they leave behind? *Change, 40*(6), 56–59.

Erikson, E. H. (1968). *Identity: Youth and crisis.* New York: Norton.

Gladding, S. T. (2011). *Family therapy: History, theory, and practice* (5th ed.). Upper Saddle River, NJ: Pearson.

Lechuga, V. M. (2011). Faculty–graduate student mentoring relationships: Mentors' perceived roles and responsibilities. *Higher Education, 62*, 757–771.

Leslie, D. W. (2005). The costs and benefits of phased retirement. *New Directions for Higher Education, 132*, 61–71.

Mansson, D. H., & Myers, S. A. (2012). Using mentoring enactment theory to explore the doctoral student—Advisor mentoring relationship. *Communication Education, 61*(4), 309–334.

McLaughlin, J. (2013). *Retirement transitions in higher education.* Washington, DC: American Council on Education.

Mulanaphy, J. M. (1984). *Lessons on retirement: A statistical report of the 1982–83 survey of retired TIAA-CREF annuitants.* New York: Educational Research Division, Teachers Insurance and Annuity Association, College Retirement Equities Fund.

Murrell, D. F., Ryan, T. J., & Bergfeld, W. F. (2011). Advancement of women in dermatology. *International Journal of Dermatology, 50*, 593–600.

Patterson, D. A. (2009). Your students and your legacy. *Communications of the ACM, 52*(3), 30–33.

Smathers, D. G. (2004). A new role for emeritus faculty. *Phi Kappa Phi Forum, 84*(4), 38–39.

Van Ummersen, C., Duranleau, L., & McLaughlin, J. (2013). Faculty retirement transitions revitalized. *Change, 14*(26), 1–9.

Winfield, J. B. (2003). Reflections on Henry G Kunkel as a mentor in clinical investigation. *Lupus, 12*, 245–248.

5

WORKING IN COMMUNITY

Flexible Programming to Support Fulfilling Postretirement Careers

Nathan D. Grawe, *Carleton College*

W hen academic leaders discuss ways to manage demographic change in the professorial ranks, the conversation most frequently turns to high-profile programs such as phased retirement or severance. There is little doubt that these "headline" programs are important tools for assisting faculty through the transition to emeriti roles. Yet, in a series of conversations with recently retired faculty at my small liberal arts college, emeriti consistently argued that of approximately equal importance to them was a collection of small, flexible, and personalized policies that supported them as they developed new identities as scholars beyond the employment relationship. In particular, they emphasized the ways in which the tightness of our close-knit community—and its overlap with the Northfield community in which Carleton is nestled—allowed for a range of interesting manifestations of the postretirement academic scholar, all of which were nurtured by the college to the benefit of both emeriti faculty and the institution. This chapter includes many examples of how Carleton College has worked with retiring faculty to define personalized, flexible paths to postteaching careers. Ultimately, our experience reminds us that faculty do not primarily think of themselves as *working* at our institutions. Rather, they view their decades of service as building a community of scholars (including, of course, their students). Thus, the transition to retirement is as much about a question of scholarly identity as it is a financial and contractual crossroads.

Carleton College shares many of the community-minded characteristics commonly associated with small liberal arts colleges. With just over 1,800 students on campus who are taught by around 220 faculty, Carleton exemplifies the slow, personal, intense, and expensive method of education associated with the classical undergraduate liberal arts education. The sense of community born of our small size is further amplified by our nearly universal reliance on full-time, tenure-track faculty. Tenured and tenure-track faculty engage students in small classes (averaging around 17 students each) and regularly meet with students one-on-one or in small groups during office hours. All students are required to complete an integrative capstone experience in their majors, which most often takes the form of a senior thesis with intense faculty oversight.

The close-knit nature of our community seen in the student-faculty relationship also extends to faculty relationships with each other, staff, and administrators. Although we occasionally hire faculty with prior experience (but never with tenure), the vast majority of our faculty are hired early in their life cycle, and they tend to remain at Carleton for the remainder of their careers. As a result, more than 30% of current faculty have worked at the college for 20 or more years. This typically long length of service, along with our small size and a strong and consultative faculty governance process, ensures faculty members repeated opportunities to work with colleagues from all corners of the campus on significant, institution-wide initiatives and policies.

Our 9:1 pupil-to-teacher ratio and reliance on regular, full-time faculty produce predictable budgetary consequences. With a bit more than 40% of our total budget composed of salaries and benefits for faculty and staff, ours is a labor-intensive economic model. When compensation is considered in relation to the budget net of financial aid, this proportion rises above 50%. As a consequence, retirement or nonretirement decisions have substantial implications for the institution. For example, two faculty members deciding to delay retirement by just 2 years could eat up all planned operating budget increases for a year.

As at many institutions, the age distribution among regular Carleton faculty brings particular focus to this issue. The National Center for Education Statistics' 2004 *National Study of Postsecondary Faculty* reported that 8.6% of faculty were 65 years or older and another 26.3% were between the ages of 55 and 64 (U.S. Department of Education, 2004). The study showed that faculty at Carnegie-classified baccalaureate–liberal arts institutions, such as Carleton, were slightly less "gray" than the national average. As approximately 3.5% of our faculty are 65 years or older and 23% fall between 55 and 64 years of age, Carleton fits the pattern. As obvious as the economic implications noted previously may be, it is equally evident that this demographic composition has important implications for future plans to bring new scholars with new teaching and research interests to the college. In this context, for as much as we do not wish to lose senior faculty expertise and wisdom before it is time, we also want to be attentive to supporting faculty when they are ready to move through the retirement transition.

Like many similar institutions, Carleton has long collaborated with faculty to prepare practically for retirement. The college's TIAA-CREF retirement program includes a 10% institutional match connected to a mandatory faculty contribution of 2%. A recent comparison with 23 peer institutions showed this rate of institutional investment to be approximately average. (Peer schools contributed between 7% and 11%. Unlike some peers, Carleton does not vary its rate of contribution by age, rank, or years of service.) In addition, the benefits package includes reimbursements for early and late-career financial planning consultation. Since 1996 the college has offered a phased retirement option to faculty with at least 20 years of service, providing part-time teaching assignments for reduced salary for up to 3 years. During the phasing period faculty members are eligible for full benefits, although benefits that are proportional to salary, like the retirement benefit, are prorated according to the reduction in salary. Among the most visible portion of Carleton's efforts to support retirement transitions, phased retirement has been very popular. In recent years more than 85% of retiring faculty have taken advantage of the program, and of those, over 80% have chosen to phase over the maximum 3-year period.[1]

Although this high uptake rate makes clear that phased retirement plays an important part in faculty retirement transitions, we wanted to understand more deeply why and how this was so in order to think through how we might better meet the needs of retiring (or near-retiring) faculty. To that end I completed interviews with recently retired faculty as part of a comprehensive review of our retirement transition practices. These interviews made it immediately clear that there was nothing "retiring" about our faculty members' postemployment scholarly careers. The reduction in workload offered by phased retirement was certainly not merely a less abrupt transition to purely leisurely pursuits. Freed from teaching, committee and department service, and any external pressure to publish with high frequency in disciplinary journals, retired faculty felt empowered to take on new, often risky, academic projects.

Faculty were not "retiring" from the campus either. Although some took advantage of their newfound locational freedom to travel and do on-site research (Minnesota winters even encourage such plans), all the retired colleagues I spoke with reported important, continuing connections to the college community through friendships and investment in the success of individual academic programs and the institution. Northfield's community is small enough that many retired faculty live within walking distance of campus and continue to use the library, attend talks, take part in departmental and college-wide social events, engage in town-gown conversations about college initiatives, and exercise in the arboretum or gym.

In my conversations with retired faculty, it was clear, however, that despite continuing scholarly pursuits and maintaining campus connections, the end of formal employment marked an important shift in a faculty member's relationship to the college community. After decades of service as faculty, many retirees reported that the process of establishing a new scholarly sense of self-identity was a serious challenge. They shared that in addition to accommodating the predictable physical consequences of growing older, phased retirement provided space and time to conceive of and create a new sense of relation to the academic profession, the campus, and our small-town community. Critically for many, the reductions in teaching and service obligations were insufficient on their own to assist faculty through the transition; they noted the importance of a wide array of small helps provided by the college—often in the form of flexible, individualized support—that allowed them to move successfully into roles as senior, postemployment scholars. The discussion that follows describes the routine and individualized ways the college has worked to assist retiring faculty as they reconceive relationships to the campus community, the scholarly community, and the local Northfield community.

As at many liberal arts colleges, Carleton's small size fosters deep faculty engagement in governance. We do not have a representative faculty senate, for instance, because our faculty is small enough to hold full faculty meetings. After 4 or 5 years, it is rare for faculty not to know all their colleagues, regardless of department. Similarly, close relationships develop between faculty and staff, from reference librarians to snack bar employees. Given the intimate character of our campus, it would be quite unnerving were faculty to feel cut off from that community upon retirement. At the same time it is clear that the relationship must evolve to allow current faculty to lead their departments and the institution. The college fosters healthy, continued emeriti connections in ways small and large. For example, emeriti maintain their e-mail addresses and privileges at the library and recreation center. They are invited to campus and department events. To create a space for retired faculty to maintain their connections to each other, the college provides modest financial support for an emeriti group (and a similar group of retired faculty spouses) that meets monthly to discuss a wide range of topics from new college initiatives to personal health-care decisions. Newly retired faculty noted the value of this group as a resource to discuss a host of issues from the mundane ("How do I navigate Medicare?") to the profound ("How do I maintain an identity as a teacher-scholar without a classroom?").

In addition to these broad efforts to foster continued relationships with the campus community, Carleton has also sought to create paths to more individualized connections. We have surveyed emeriti, inviting them to indicate ways they may want to continue their involvement, including the following list of suggested possibilities:

- tutoring students
- mentoring students on academic success
- mentoring junior faculty
- mentoring faculty who are moving into administrative roles such as chairing, leading an academic initiative, or entering the dean's office
- leading focus groups/conducting interviews as part of a special project assigned by the dean
- completing a special project assigned by the dean (e.g., comparing Carleton policies with those of our peers)
- organizing an event such as a student research celebration
- visiting alumni groups
- serving on student fellowship selection committees
- hosting international students (mentoring, inviting them to dinner, etc.)

This list, which was developed in consultation with the emeriti group, intentionally includes projects that are short-lived or periodic so that they might work around snowbird travel to the south in winter.

Not surprisingly, not every retired faculty member indicated an interest in more in-depth service. But those who did volunteer proved very helpful to the college. One area of particularly powerful service was mentoring. For example, one recently retired colleague who had previously served as a dean provided useful mentoring to two faculty members as they entered significant administrative roles. In one case he offered specific knowledge about the workings and organization of a staff department, while in the other he offered more general insights into the development of leadership skills. In a less formal way, several emeriti provided similarly invaluable counsel to a new president as he learned about the campus culture and issues that lay ahead.

Retired faculty have also offered their expert advice to departments and programs. For example, a recently retired faculty member served as a consultant to an internal program review. Drawing on decades of experience in a similar interdisciplinary program, the emeriti colleague guided conversations about a fundamental redirection to the curriculum and the program's identity. Yet another retired colleague, at the request of the dean, facilitated a department's conversations about questions that had the potential to divide current faculty members. Retired faculty have also made contributions to staff hiring committees. With decades of service they bring a distinctly long-term view to these important deliberations. In one recent example an emeriti colleague served on the search committee for the vice president of external relations. Another, through years of academic research and active engagement, brought invaluable disciplinary expertise to the search for a new Japanese garden specialist.

Finally, emeriti have played critical roles in off-campus study emergency management. Approximately 70% of Carleton students study abroad and nearly two-thirds of those study on a Carleton-run program. With around a dozen programs in the field in any given year, it is perhaps not surprising that twice in the last decade, faculty on those programs experienced significant family medical issues that required us to send a replacement faculty member to take over the program for a short stint. Because other current faculty are inevitably tied up with regular teaching duties, none were able to travel to take over the program. In both cases emeriti who had previous experience on the program were able to travel on very short notice and provide the needed support.

All the preceding examples show the role emeriti can play in serving the immediate campus community. But at liberal arts colleges, the strong sense of community often extends across time to include alumni. Emeriti play an important role in creating this sense of extended community. Supported by our alumni relations office, emeriti provide featured lectures at alumni group gatherings around the country and at reunions. A good number of retired faculty have led lifelong learning travel seminars for alumni. While the benefit to the alumni office is clear (these faculty are, after all, the teachers whom middle-aged alumni associate with the college), emeriti also spoke positively about opportunities to get back into the classroom with Carleton students—even if that classroom turned out to be on the other side of the globe and the students had more than a few gray hairs.

As important as continuing a relationship with the college community is, my conversations with retired faculty also uncovered a deep appreciation for the small ways the college facilitated evolving relationships between retired faculty and the local community. Along with St. Olaf College, Carleton is located in Northfield, Minnesota, a small town of around 20,000, including about 5,000 students and 1,000 employees of the two liberal arts colleges. Because the town is 40 miles from the urban centers of Minneapolis and St. Paul, roughly one-third of faculty commute while the other two-thirds live in town, nearly always within walking or biking distance of campus. The academic and civic communities are predictably interrelated so it is difficult to find a meaningful civic body—from the historical society to city council to church boards—that does not have at least one faculty member or faculty spouse/partner among its leadership.

While emeriti make significant individual contributions to many local organizations, they noted with appreciation two specific means by which the college facilitated their contributions to the intersection between the campus and town communities. First, many emeriti expressed gratitude for the use of Carleton spaces for the Cannon Valley Elder Collegium (CVEC). Devoted to fostering lifelong learning, CVEC offers roughly one dozen seminars each term with 10 to 25 student participants engaging in each. In addition to enrolling regularly in CVEC courses, former faculty are often recruited to lead seminars in the collegium. By allowing CVEC to use the occasional open classroom for class meetings, the college effectively supports emeriti as they maintain their self-identities as teachers while simultaneously aiding CVEC in creating a more vibrant Northfield.

Second, such community-campus overlap provides great benefit to Carleton as it works to be a good neighbor to those who live in the residential area adjacent to the campus. Our residential neighbors have created a formal organization—the Northfield Eastside Neighborhood Association (NESNA)—to foster thoughtful land use and zoning, sponsor neighborhood-wide social events, develop safety initiatives, and facilitate collaboration with the city and institutional neighbors like Carleton. Many emeriti continue to live in the neighborhood adjoining the campus, and their involvement in NESNA can yield substantial benefit to both the neighborhood association and the college. In particular, their intimate knowledge of the college's mission and practices makes emeriti especially effective partners as we look to live well together. For example, Carleton appointed a retired faculty member who is a member of NESNA leadership as cochair (with a current staff member) to a college task force charged with studying the campus parking policy and practice and offering possible solutions to minimize inconveniences to neighbors. The result was a report that was informed by the needs of the college and its many commuting employees but still reflective of the residential essence of the neighborhood.

At liberal arts colleges where institutional missions place great emphasis on intensive teaching, one advantage of retirement for many is the opportunity to devote greater time and energy to research. Faculty often reach retirement with a desire to continue making contributions to the academic disciplines to which they have devoted decades of service. Recognizing this ongoing intellectual commitment in emeriti lives, Carleton has found ways to support continuing scholarship and artistic production. For example, we have offered faculty office space for the year or two immediately following their retirement to give them a place to work and write. (The office space is typically outside the emeriti member's academic department. While this slightly reduces access to some department-specific resources, it also provides a healthy spatial change for both the retired faculty member and the department as new faculty leaders emerge.) In addition, when faculty retire with unused resources in their professional development accounts, rather than reallocating those funds to other purposes, the dean has chosen to put them in a pool to support emeriti scholarship and artistic production. When feasible, we provide financial management of emeriti grants.

While the emeriti I spoke with appreciated these standard policies, they shared at much greater length observations about the value of more idiosyncratic support. From their stories it was clear that creativity and flexibility in scholarly support are necessary because postemployment intellectual lives are often more diverse than their pre-retirement counterparts. In part this is true because retirement offers considerably more options for how and where scholarship and artistic production take place. But it is also important to recognize that the later years of the faculty life cycle are often deeply marked by personal factors that heavily influence intellectual plans. Whereas one's life and career circumstances may lead one retiring colleague to look for a bridge to a new postemployment scholarly agenda, another might rather complete a culminating project that represents an intellectual victory lap. Still others may see professional service as an important end-of-career contribution. As a result we have found that it is beneficial for both the faculty and the institution in facilitating smooth faculty retirement transitions for the dean to meet with retiring faculty (often multiple times) to talk at length about the individual circumstances, needs, and opportunities that might inform the college's support.

A few examples demonstrate the wide range of ways in which retiring faculty have sought support from the college as they transitioned through retirement. Among current faculty a large majority of professional development money is spent on travel to research sites, research materials, and expenses associated with conference presentations that prepare work for publication. Not infrequently, retiring faculty seek similar support as they bring major research projects to completion. Indeed, the additional freedom of phased or full retirement often allows greater opportunity for on-site research. One recent retiree received funds to cover participation at two conferences toward the end of a book project studying the connection between virtue and the creative process. Another received airfare to return to the overseas site of his doctoral research in support of a book on Peace Corps activity in Nepal. The college further provided subvention funds for the publication.

Although these types of support are routine in nature, their mechanics sometimes change to reflect the new emeriti role. For instance, a retiring musicologist received support for research materials and conference travel for a continuation of his pre-retirement research agenda. Because many of the materials were recordings, the faculty member and the dean agreed to buy the recording acquisitions through our music library. This allowed the money to simultaneously support the faculty member's continued scholarly engagement and build the college's collection.

Some emeriti transition projects take on a more capstone feel, in some sense representing a culmination of a life's work. Over the course of his career's scholarly activity, an emeriti faculty member discovered and curated a significant number of letters written by and to three generations of a 19th-century family of French politicians. With the help of information-technology and library staff, college-provided server space, and support for digital scanning, the retiring faculty member built a digital archive to preserve the letters for future scholars. Another retiring faculty member used the time freed up by phased retirement to edit a digital Festschrift composed of works written by students of hers who had gone on in the discipline. The college supported the project by providing for copyediting and server space connected to the department's webpage.

While the transition projects taken on by many emeriti represent continuations of ongoing scholarship, others find it meaningful to open a new chapter of service. For example, one recent retiring faculty member agreed to serve as the editor of a significant disciplinary journal. To take on the task, he needed administrative support and a bit of storage for back issues. The dean was able to find a few hours per week in an administrative assistant's schedule and an unused attic space to meet those needs. Another had played a critical role in establishing a nation-leading interdisciplinary program at Carleton. So that others might learn from the process that led to the creation of the pathbreaking program, he sought support to write a history of its inception.

Still others have put their efforts of service toward the enhancement of education in less developed countries. In one case, upon retirement from Carleton an emeriti faculty member became the chair of a new department in the inaugural year of Bhutan's first private college. Carleton supported his vision of establishing a first-rate educational institution in this developing country by providing airfare. Another retiring colleague had played a central role in the design and establishment of our environmental studies program. After completing his service to Carleton, he sought external grant funding to support the development of new active-learning science education programs for schools in Southeast Asia. In this case the faculty member was able to secure significant financial support from a granting agency as long as the college agreed to serve as the financial administrator.

I have been asked to reflect on the cultural and structural features of Carleton that have led to our openness to flexible, individualized retirement transition supports. As an empirical social scientist, I am intensely aware that my thoughts flow from a sample size of one and so must be weighed with considerable caution. But with that caveat made explicit, some features of Carleton may be important to understanding how we have come to our current practices. First, it is likely that our small size matters. As noted previously, individualized retirement planning is only possible if the dean can understand the retiring faculty member's specific needs. Although intense conversations at the point of retirement decisions are critical, in our intimate community long-developed relationships between the dean and senior faculty grow naturally out of college service. It is likely that the length and depth of these relationships are critical to making the end-of-career discussions effective and useful. Second, we benefit from a long-standing tradition of shared governance. While administrators must and do at times make decisions that might not receive a majority of votes if put to the full faculty, important matters from budgets to academic policy are routinely handled by committees in which faculty (and staff) typically outnumber administrators. Even when administrators hold final decision-making authority, such as in the allocation of tenure-track faculty lines or tenure and promotion, we have established formal channels for extensive faculty input and advice. While respect for retiring colleagues demands that retirement transition planning decisions are made in confidence by the dean without committee input, the transparent and shared governance structure that marks broader decision making on the campus encourages trust in the institution's equitable approach to individualized retirement support.

Finally, the college is generally blessed by collegiality. For example, faculty routinely lend their efforts to cross-disciplinary curricular initiatives out of a recognition that students' needs often transcend our more narrow disciplinary silos. In fact, during a recent December break (under our trimester calendar, courses are not in session between Thanksgiving and New Year's Day), over half of our faculty participated in at least 1 of around 10 workshops put on by our interdisciplinary curricular initiatives. While our culture of collegiality is clearly connected to the faculty's fierce commitment to the college's liberal arts mission, the root causes of this culture are not very clear. Our size might contribute by allowing many faculty to participate in broad governance conversations. Or perhaps the part real–part satire that is "Minnesota nice" shapes our interactions. Whatever its cause, this culture allows for the kind of individualized retirement transition planning described previously without undue concerns over identical (as opposed to equal) consideration across faculty members.

To close, I want to underscore the primary motivations behind Carleton's broad and flexible approach to supporting the retirement transition. By supporting engagement within three concentric communities—the campus, the town, and the wider academy—Carleton has found inexpensive but critical means to support faculty as they make the transition into their new identities as emeriti scholars. As the many preceding examples make clear, the college derives substantial benefit in the process. Not only do we continue to profit from the scholarly and artistic output of our faculty, but we also are able to tap their decades-long store of institutional knowledge and equally lengthy relationship with our local community. Because of our sensitive and nuanced approach to retirement transitions, we are a stronger intellectual community with greater contributions to the academy, we experience a better town-and-gown relationship, and we enjoy deeper connections to our alumni.

But as real as these benefits are, ultimately these are not the reason we have pursued flexible practices to support a healthy transition to emeriti status in our community. At a fundamental level supporting faculty through this often-difficult transition is the morally proper way to treat cherished community members. This is especially true given the incredible length of the relationship between the faculty member and the institution. While the challenges of academe continually change, we know that in each generation our faculty members have walked with, and often led, the college through serious challenges. Whether navigating the social transitions of the 1960s, the inflationary period of the 1970s, the double-dip recession of the 1980s, or the financial crisis of the present decade, these challenges have been overcome with personal flexibility, sometimes-painful cooperation, and (often) personal and financial sacrifice. Ultimately, our faculty aspire to create a culture in which each member weighs seriously the needs of students, departments, and the institution as a whole as he or she considers teaching, scholarship, service, and even retirement plans. In this light flexible and accommodating retirement support, which we find practically useful in building interconnected campus and local communities, is also the right and proper response to such service.

Author Note

This chapter has benefited from feedback given by Beverly Nagel and Steven G. Poskanzer and from ideas included in a talk given by Poskanzer at a July 11, 2011, American Council on Education (ACE) Panel on Faculty Retirement.

Note

1. Phased retirement is not, in practice, early retirement. Fully two-thirds of phasing faculty retired after age 66. Although the number of nonphasing faculty is too small to draw firm statistical comparisons, the average age of phasing retirees is actually more than a year older than their nonphasing peers.

Reference

U.S. Department of Education, Institute of Education Sciences, National Center for Education Statistics. (2004). *NSOPF: 2004 National Study of Postsecondary Faculty*. Retrieved from http://nces.ed.gov/surveys/nsopf/

PART THREE

INSTITUTIONAL STRUCTURES THAT SUPPORT THE CULMINATING STAGES OF FACULTY CAREERS

6

PLANNING A GRACEFUL EXIT TO RETIREMENT AND BEYOND

The San José State University Way

Amy Strage and Joan Merdinger, *San José State University*

If one does not know to which port one is sailing, no wind is favorable.
—*Lucius Annaeus Seneca*

There's a trick to the "graceful exit." It begins with the vision to recognize when a job, a life stage, or a relationship is over—and let it go. It means leaving what's over without denying its validity or its past importance to our lives. It involves a sense of future, a belief that every exit line is an entry, that we are moving up, rather than out.
—*Ellen Goodman, January 1, 2010*

We would be hard-pressed to think of words of wisdom better suited to the challenges and opportunities that our senior faculty encounter. Since the mandatory retirement age was abolished in 1994, decisions pertaining to the timing of and planning for retirement have rested more squarely in the laps of faculty themselves. Although campuses typically devote extensive resources to helping faculty launch their careers, they have yet to direct much support, beyond financial matters, to helping them bring those careers to a close. The programs we highlight in this chapter reflect the commitment of San José State University (SJSU) to providing opportunities for faculty members to identify personal goals and secure the information and support they need to achieve them as they move through the significant transition from full-time employment to full-time retirement.

Starting Points and Guiding Considerations

Like snowflakes, no two faculty members are exactly alike. When and how they choose to retire is an extremely complex and personal decision, and how extensively and effectively they prepare for the transition varies enormously from one individual to another. The programs SJSU offers to support faculty members throughout this process are designed to accommodate a wide range of needs and personal circumstances. The considerations we raise in this section may well resonate with faculty and administrators at other campuses.

1. *To disclose, or not to disclose?* Some faculty members feel comfortable— even eager—talking about what comes next. In contrast, others are intensely private. Whether they are not ready to acknowledge for themselves the coming to a close of their teaching career or are concerned about how others will respond or how their status will change, they do not want to tip their hand, as it were, until they are ready. At a recent board meeting of our campus's Emeritus and Retired Faculty Association (ERFA), for example, one member described sharing his intentions "with great enthusiasm, and with everyone who would listen," as he sought input from colleagues about the projects he planned to undertake once he retired. One of the other board members present that day shook her head, smiled wistfully, and recounted going to great lengths to "keep [her] plans quiet," lest she be seen as a "lame duck, . . . no longer invited to the table" when important conversations about the future of the department took place. Another board member acknowledged regretting having divulged her plans to retire as soon as she did, adding that "once the cat was out of the bag," conflicts with her calendar were the lowest priority as groups tried to schedule meetings. As a result, even though colleagues "did a nice job keeping [her] informed about decisions taken," she gradually felt that she was "sitting on the sidelines, out of the loop."

Faculty who are loath to come forward and share their plans to retire may be the most difficult to reach and support. For them, ready access to individuals with whom they can speak in confidence or to resources that they can access privately (e.g., online) may prove particularly useful.

2. *Struggling to compare the upside and the downside of retiring.* Many faculty are torn about whether to "stay or move on." Some are drawn to the opportunities they imagine in life postretirement, but at the same time they are reluctant to abandon unfinished projects. Others acknowledge the stresses and day-to-day frustrations they experience at work, but they also worry they won't find anything as fulfilling or meaningful to occupy them once they leave their jobs. Some resist because, although they would like to pursue other interests, they worry about their finances or that various benefits will disappear.

Efforts to help these faculty articulate the parameters of their ambivalence, connect with the appropriate resources, and explore their options more intentionally can provide the reassurance they need as they move closer to retirement.[1] Faculty who feel compelled to hold their cards closer to the vest are more likely to feel additional stress as they grapple with their indecision on their own.

3. *Clean break or gradual exit?* Some faculty members want a clean break, whereas others prefer a more gradual separation, decreasing their time and professional responsibilities on campus over a span of several years. Fortunately, an increasing number of campuses are offering options to suit a variety of preferences. Data reported in the most recent nationwide survey of faculty retirement patterns conducted by the American Association of University Professors reveal that nearly one-third of responding institutions (32% of 567 institutions) offer faculty some kind of phased retirement option (Conley, 2007). Fully one-third of these programs were launched within the 5 years leading up to the survey, and over 10% of them became available within 1 or 2 years of the survey. As such programs proliferate, so have studies documenting their advantages and costs (e.g., see Clark & Ma, 2005).

The California State University (CSU) system offers faculty three retirement options, including traditional outright retirement and two phased retirement plans. The two plans are included in the collective bargaining agreement between CSU and the California Faculty Association (CFA), the union that represents all faculty in the CSU system. Deciding which retirement or phased retirement option is the best fit requires weighing a variety of factors, including financial as well as personal and contextual considerations. On our campus, of a total of 115 faculty who have retired since the 2007–2008 academic year, two-thirds ($n = 77$) have opted for a phased retirement. During the past 3 years, the proportion has risen to three-quarters ($n = 56$ of 74 faculty). In this chapter we describe an online tool faculty can use to help them compare financial projections for the three retirement pathways.

4. *How much to change at once?* Some faculty members plan to start a new chapter once they retire. They anticipate leaving their university lives behind—perhaps even relocating physically—and filling their postretirement days with activities and experiences completely different from what they had been doing, year in and year out, often for decades. Others don't want such dramatic change, imagining instead a period during which they will divest themselves of the more onerous and tedious parts of their faculty work life and be able to devote more time to those aspects of their professional lives that have brought them the greatest satisfaction. For many, however, despite thoughtful planning, for one reason or another, their lived experience turns out to be quite different from what they had envisioned. Some discover that the people

and activities they encounter once they begin their new life turn out not to be as engaging or interesting as they had anticipated. And some who opt for a phased retirement may be less successful than they had hoped in "filling their dance card" (as one department chair on our campus refers to faculty academic assignment) with only those responsibilities they had hoped to preserve.

Resources that can help faculty develop greater self-knowledge, personal efficacy, flexibility, and resilience are particularly valuable here. Again, individuals who are more open to sharing their thoughts and plans ahead of time may be more successful in accurately assessing what will turn out to be the right path or in making the necessary midcourse adjustments.

5. *Grappling with the issue of one's legacy in a changing world.* For many senior faculty, a significant part of their professional identities revolves around seeing themselves as leaving something lasting to their institution. Whereas some may have the resources and desire to make one or another kind of monetary contribution (e.g., some type of institutional gift or endowment), many others strive to make their mark more directly or more personally by helping to nurture the next generation of faculty (Bland, Taylor, Shollen, Weber-Main, & Mulcahy, 2009). Thus, a more elusive but no less significant consideration is the challenge presented by the culture change seen over the last few decades on university campuses across the nation, most notably at institutions where teaching has traditionally been a priority and a point of pride.[2] For example, fully a third of the senior faculty who participated in a professional growth and renewal retreat program on our campus indicated that their greatest wish was to mentor junior colleagues and help them through the tenure and promotion gauntlet. While heartening in many respects, this generosity of spirit is not unproblematic, as the nature and demands of the faculty role have evolved significantly since they themselves launched their own careers. How valuable, for example, could their counsel be for current junior faculty if they themselves came of age at a time when expectations for scholarly productivity were far more modest than they are now? How relevant could their insights about teaching effectiveness be if they spent their careers perfecting the art of lecturing whereas now faculty are feeling pressed to adopt more student-centered and technology-enhanced pedagogical methods? And with radical changes just now being made to the state-employee pension plan, assumptions that soon-to-retire faculty could safely make at the outset of their careers about their pensions no longer apply for newly hired faculty. Thus, advice that senior faculty may be inclined to share with their younger colleagues, although well intentioned, may be counterproductive at this point. Efforts to help these faculty identify what they can share that would be of greatest value could go a long way to helping both the retirees and the junior faculty they seek to assist.

Programmatic Support for Faculty Retirement Transitions

In this section we focus on three specific elements of our campus-wide efforts to support faculty retirement transitions—two are part of the slate of offerings pertaining to the preparation and planning stage of retirement, and the third is part of our slate of offerings pertaining to the adjustment to retirement stage. We describe these resources and the evidence that they assist our faculty as they make the transition into retirement, and we consider how they might be adapted for use on other campuses.

Support for the Preparation and Planning Stage

Career-Planning Retreats
During the 2008–2009 academic year, as part of a sabbatical project titled "Stayin' Alive," one of the authors (Dr. Strage) interviewed several dozen midcareer and senior faculty to better understand the factors (personal characteristics, professional circumstances) that differentiate faculty who saw themselves as thriving from those who saw themselves as stagnating. Three key themes emerged from the study: "Vital" faculty members were more likely to be able to articulate specific professional goals ("I know what I want to accomplish, and I have a good sense of what I need to do it"), they were more likely to feel a sense of control ("I make my own luck"), and they were less likely to be derailed or discouraged by challenge or failure ("Just because it's hard, or just because I've never done it, or just because it's new doesn't mean I can't figure it out").

The following year, with the support of an Alfred P. Sloan Award for Faculty Career Flexibility to our campus, we put into place a program to assist faculty members at this stage in their career, as they sought to "stay alive." At the heart of this program, the Office of Faculty Affairs and the Center for Faculty Development cosponsor daylong professional growth and renewal retreats for groups of 15–20 midcareer and senior faculty, most of whom are, technically, eligible to retire (California Public Employees' Retirement System [CalPERS], 2013). In preparation for the retreat day itself, participants are asked to write a brief statement about why they are interested in being a part of the retreat and to read and submit reflections about selected written materials.[3] These premeeting assignments serve several functions: they provide the retreat facilitator with a better sense of the strengths, needs, and goals of the participants; they establish a common framework for participants to begin to think about their own roles in guiding their career trajectories; and they establish a point of departure for the group. Throughout the day, the group works through a series of topics, including discussions of sources of work-related enjoyment and frustration as well as potential areas of professional growth and renewal. Not surprisingly, given the focus of the retreat as well as the chronological age and career stage of participants, themes of generativity and stagnation (Erikson, 1968), of mastery and learned helplessness, of motivational orientation (Dweck, 1999, 2006), and of agency and communion (Bakan, 1966) are typically evident in the day's conversations. Faculty share experiences of feeling "stuck," "productive," "lost," "purposeful," "adrift," "open to change" or "afraid" of it, "on top of their game" or "overmatched," and "disconnected" and of "craving and welcoming professional communities." It has been heartening to note how quickly fellow participants intervene and proffer compelling counterevidence when retreat participants confess to grappling with the concern that their expertise is outmoded or that what they have to offer is of little current value. As the day draws to a close, participants are asked to respond in writing to a series of prompts, commenting on one or two insights from the day as well as one or two specific plans or goals for the upcoming year. Some of the participants end the day sufficiently buoyed, reenergized, and refocused that they reconsider plans for imminent retirement. Others end the day on a high note, with a clearer picture of what they want to leave behind as their legacy. All emerge grateful for the chance to talk candidly, to be affirmed by those who share their experiences, to learn from those whose university "journey" has been quite different from their own, to reconnect with old friends, and to finally match the names and faces of colleagues they have never actually met despite having worked on the campus for decades. Three to four months later, the facilitator meets individually with retreat participants, to check in and to learn how goals articulated during the retreat are being achieved or revisited.[4]

The Pre-Retirement Reduction in Time Base / Faculty Early Retirement Program Calculator

As noted previously, along with our sister campuses, SJSU has in place two phased retirement options: the Pre-Retirement Reduction in Time Base (PRTB) program and the Faculty Early Retirement Program (FERP). Both provide faculty with a gentler and more protracted transition to retirement, but the financial consequences of opting for one or the other program are likely to be quite different, and the option likely to provide a more desirable income stream, in both the short term and long term, varies as a function of a number of variables related to one's employment history within the CSU system.

The PRTB program is available to all tenured faculty members who have reached the age of 55 and are no older than 65 at the time of entry into the program. Applicants to the program must have been employed in the CSU system for at least 10 years full-time, and the last 5 years must have been in continuous full-time employment. For tenured faculty who meet those conditions, the PRTB program provides a reduction in time base to two-thirds time, one-half time, or one-third time for a maximum period of 5 years. While in the PRTB program, faculty receive a reduced paycheck based on their new reduced appointment (two-thirds salary, one-half salary, or one-third salary). During the 5 years of the program, both the participant and the university pay into the retirement system at the same rate as they did during the faculty member's full-time employment. A significant benefit of this program is that the faculty member in PRTB receives up to 5 full-time years of retirement service credit rather than the reduced credit that would have been earned if the faculty member had taken personal leave or a permanent work-load reduction unrelated to the PRTB program. Health, dental, and other appropriate benefits available to full-time faculty are available to participants in PRTB. At the conclusion of the program, PRTB participants may elect to enter the FERP at half the time base established while in the PRTB program. Faculty who take advantage of these two programs can be in transition from full employment to full retirement for up to 10 years.

To participate in the FERP, a faculty member must be 55 years old or older (unlike the PRTB program, the FERP has no age cap). Faculty who are in the FERP have a time base of 50% at the same rank and salary rate as they had in their pre-retirement tenured status. As a result faculty members in the FERP have two sources of income: (a) a monthly retirement check from the state retirement plan, CalPERS; and (b) a monthly paycheck for half time at the pre-retirement salary rate from the university. When CSU system faculty receive raises, faculty participating in the FERP receive raises of the same percentage but on the basis of their university FERP salaries. Medical benefits are provided to faculty in the FERP through CalPERS; the dental plan provided to all faculty members is also available to FERP participants. For the duration of the program, which is no more than 5 years, faculty participants retain their status as tenured faculty members, at the rank they had at the time of retirement, and FERP participants are required to perform normal responsibilities, duties, and activities, including participating in governance activities. With the appropriate permissions, FERP faculty may serve on recruitment committees; on departmental-level retention, tenure, and promotion committees; and as a principal investigator on grants and sponsored projects. Although this is not a usual occurrence, FERP faculty have served as department chairs.

Drawing on funds from our 2008 Alfred P. Sloan Award for Faculty Career Flexibility, we developed a user-friendly online calculator to enable faculty to estimate the financial implications of each of three financial scenarios: (a) retirement only, (b) the PRTB option, and (c) the FERP option. Although the PRTB program and the FERP had been in existence since the

1970s, there was no easy way to calculate the short- and long-term financial outcomes of choosing one program over the other. In addition, our campus had few participants in the PRTB program, whereas the FERP was used by a large number of retiring faculty. An important way of publicizing the PRTB program was to show the benefits of participating in the program by comparing it with the FERP, which was already well known by the faculty.

To create a calculator that could be used by tenured faculty throughout the CSU system, beginning with those from our campus, who were considering entry into either of the programs, we recruited a faculty member from the College of Business, Dr. Marco Pagani. It took a year and a half for him and a graduate student, working part-time, to create the mathematical spreadsheets that populate the calculator. The calculations, which are estimates, rely on financial information provided by CalPERS that is in the public domain. After the calculations were completed, we worked with a campus web developer to place the calculator on an interactive university webpage in March 2011. Both quantitative and anecdotal data suggest that our faculty find this tool useful. According to the *Sloan Awards Faculty Benchmarking Report* (American Council on Education, 2012), faculty from our campus were twice as likely to report being "satisfied" or "very satisfied" with the financial planning tools available to them (41.5%) than were faculty from all master's large institutions (20%) or from all other participating institutions (19.5%). We continue to receive positive informal feedback from faculty about the calculator and its usefulness. A number of faculty have shared with us that the information the calculator provided has helped them come to important financial conclusions about retirement and transitioning into retirement. We continue to promote the use of this calculator as part of a more systematic Financial Literacy for Faculty effort that we are in the process of developing.

Support for the Adjustment to Retirement Stage: A Multifaceted Welcome Wagon for Newly Retired Faculty

In 1986 a group of emeritus faculty met and formed the SJSU Emeritus Faculty Association (EFA). In 2010 the organization broadened its scope, amended its name to the ERFA, and welcomed faculty who were retired but did not hold the title of emeritus to its ranks. It is now a vital organization with over 300 members, engaged in a variety of activities designed to support retired faculty as well as the university. Its goals include helping emeriti and retired faculty to maintain a continuing and fruitful association with the university; keeping them informed of university affairs and developing means to facilitate their participation in university life; securing and enhancing their status, rights, and privileges; encouraging them to continue their scholarly and professional activities; providing social, recreational, and educational programs; and contributing to achievement of the university mission by such means as may be determined by association members. Members pay modest annual dues (currently $24 per year), which are used to fund a variety of programs and activities. All members are encouraged to suggest potential activities and to assist board members in bringing them to fruition. The organization maintains connections with its membership through a newsletter and through e-mail missives.

A significant initiative begun over a decade ago is the biographies project: every new member is invited to complete, with the assistance of a current member, a brief biographical sketch. The exercise of preparing one's narrative statement can be a valuable opportunity for reflection on one's career and a step in the process of settling in to this next phase. Perusing the entire set of biographical sketches and the photos people have included provides a number of valuable insights for faculty contemplating their own changing status. First, the sketches capture the variety of paths being pursued by retired faculty, now that they have moved on. Second, the sketches provide information about what retirees opted to single out as their most significant professional accomplishment or what they hoped would be their legacy. Third, the photos included in the sketches provide important, if subtle, clues about how the retired faculty now see, or at least chose to portray, themselves; for example, some have opted for formal portraits in professional attire, whereas others have chosen snapshots of themselves pursuing hobbies or surrounded by grandchildren. And fourth, these biographies can help faculty contemplate what has become of many of their former colleagues as they try to envision what their own lives will be like once they cross over into ERFA status. We have also begun creating podcasts of brief interviews with retired faculty, in which they talk about their own transition to retirement—what was easy, what was difficult, what was unexpected, and what they wish they had known earlier in the process. These podcasts are posted on both the ERFA and Center for Faculty Development websites for both retired and active faculty to view at their leisure.

Conclusion

Demographic trends across the nation are clear: over half of faculty members currently holding university appointments are eligible to retire. As a result our collective challenge in higher education is to assist senior faculty to plan for a graceful exit and a meaningful connection to home campuses as they transition from full-time work to full-time retirement. At SJSU we acknowledge the individual nature of that transition for each faculty member; the dilemma of disclosure/nondisclosure; the ambivalent feelings about retirement; the differences between a clean break from the university or a gradual, phased departure; and the hope for a personal legacy and a sense of accomplishment for a life's work.

Taken together, the resources we have described in this chapter—the professional growth and renewal retreats, the calculator, and the ERFA welcome wagon—have proved to be effective tools for our faculty as they chart their new direction and set sail for the next port, armed with a sense of future. Each is relatively easily replicated or adapted to other universities, and each is relatively inexpensive to develop and sustain.

Author Note

The development of many of the programs described in this chapter was funded by two generous awards made to San José State University: a 2008 Alfred P. Sloan Award for Faculty Career Flexibility and a 2012 Alfred P. Sloan Award for Best Practices in Faculty Retirement Transitions. We are grateful for this support. We are also grateful to several individuals at the university whose efforts have contributed to the success of these programs: Angee Ortega-McGhee and Melanie Kwan from the Office of Faculty Affairs and Dr. Marco Pagani from the College of Business.

Notes

1. Resources might include a wide variety of people (campus benefits office personnel, emeriti faculty, student assistants to help them wrap up projects) or online resources and readings. See Foster, Naiditch, and Politzer (2011) for a more detailed discussion of faculty ambivalence about retiring and potential institutional responses and supports.

2. This cultural sea change may also prompt senior faculty to consider retiring sooner than they had originally planned, as they may come to find themselves less current and out of step with campus innovations.

3. Sample readings have included Carol Dweck's *Mindset* (2006), Howard Gardner's *Five Minds for the Future* (2009), and Tom Rath's *Strengthfinder 2.0* (2007).

4. See Strage and Merdinger (2010) for a more detailed description of the faculty retreat program.

References

American Council on Education. (2012). *Sloan Awards faculty benchmarking report: San José State University*. Washington, DC: Author.

Bakan, D. (1966). *The duality of human existence: Isolation and communion in Western man*. Boston: Beacon.

Bland, C. J., Taylor, A., Shollen, S. L., Weber-Main, A.-M., & Mulcahy, P. (2009). *Faculty success through mentoring*. Lanham, MD: Rowman & Littlefield Education.

California Public Employees' Retirement System (CalPERS). (2013, January). *Your CalPERS benefits: Planning your service retirement* (PUB1). Sacramento, CA: Author.

Clark, R. L., & Ma, J. (2005). *Recruitment, retention and retirement in higher education: Building and managing the faculty of the future.* Northampton, MA: Edward Elgar.

Conley, V. (2007). *Survey of changes in faculty retirement policies.* Washington, DC: American Association of University Professors.

Dweck, C. (1999). *Self-theories: Their role in motivation, personality and development.* Philadelphia: Psychology Press/Taylor & Francis.

Dweck, C. (2006). *Mindset: The new psychology of success.* New York: Random House.

Erikson, E. (1968). *Childhood and society.* New York: Norton.

Foster, J., Naiditch, L., & Politzer, L. (2011). Motivating reluctant retirees in higher education: Interviews with college administrators and senior faculty. *Research Dialogue (TIAA-CREF Institute), 103,* 1–24.

Gardner, H. (2009). *Five minds for the future.* Boston: Harvard University Press.

Rath, T. (2007). *Strengthfinder 2.0.* New York: Gallup Press.

Strage, A., & Merdinger, J. (2010). *"Stayin' Alive": Professional renewal for mid-career faculty.* Paper presented at the American Association of University Professors, Washington, DC.

7

DEVELOPING A LEGACY

Janette C. Brown, *University of Southern California*

This chapter provides an overview of University of Southern California (USC) legacy programs that enhance faculty transitions to and through the retirement years. These programs help our faculty create their academic heritage, that is, the tangibles or intangibles transmitted to their academic heirs. Legacy projects abound in each of USC's 18 schools; this chapter focuses on university-wide programs.

The USC Emeriti Center, the USC Emeriti Center College, and the USC Living History Project preserve, promote, and help support the creation of faculty legacies. This chapter explains how these programs evolved, what resources were necessary, and how they play a vital role in USC's culture regarding faculty retirement.

The University of Southern California's Retirement Support

USC has fostered a culture of inclusiveness, interdisciplinary collaboration, and partnership that values faculty, staff, students, and alumni. The metaphor we use to describe this culture of reciprocal caring is the Trojan Family. USC also values entrepreneurial spirit and welcomes all ideas. Many opportunities exist to secure resources for implementing good ideas. This, in turn, enables professors to leave a legacy in many different ways.

Our legacy programs can succeed only because they are built on a firm foundation of retirement support. USC supports faculty before, during, and after retirement, enabling faculty to more easily create legacies for future generations. USC supports include the following:

- income support
  - matching contributions of up to 10% of faculty members' salaries for their retirement accounts
- information
  - transition-to-retirement seminars explaining retirement options, Social Security, Medicare, legal and estate planning, and programs/services through the USC Emeriti Center, USC Emeriti Center College, and USC Benefits Administration
- continuation in the academic community
  - policy allowing faculty to work for up to 3 years at 50% time with full benefits as they transition to retirement
  - policy encouraging retired faculty to return to service to teach one or more classes or to do research or service with compensation and assignments (less than 50%) agreed on by the individual and the school
  - USC Emeriti Center services
  - retiree Gold Card, which provides special privileges, discounts, and services for those who have worked at USC for at least 10 years prior to retirement
  - USC Emeriti Center College, which provides opportunities for teaching, learning, mentoring, and research stipends
- health care
  - USC Senior Care, a "Medigap" retirement health insurance for retirees over age 65, offered at cost

University of Southern California Faculty Satisfaction

In 2012 the American Council on Education (ACE) conducted a nationwide survey of faculty. The results illustrated USC's culture of respect for faculty contributions. Of all institutions surveyed, USC generated the highest satisfaction scores compared to all other institutions surveyed in the following categories:

- legacy programs
- culminating projects
- retirement transition counseling
- ability to phase to retirement
- plan for staying connected with department and other parts of the academic community after retirement (ACE, 2012)

Further indicators of faculty satisfaction were found in responses to the open-ended survey question, "What are the best things that your institution does to make the retirement transition smoother for faculty?" USC faculty responses were higher than faculty responses from all institutions in the ACE survey in two areas: (a) encouraging retired faculty to remain actively involved in the institution and (b) having a retirees' center for information and programs. ACE particularly acknowledged USC for (a) the USC Emeriti Center; (b) the USC Emeriti Center College, which sponsors a speakers' bureau, offers small research grants to retired faculty, and provides opportunities to teach and attend enrichment courses; (c) the USC Living History Project, which records faculty legacies; and (d) the Trojan Encore program, which promotes part-time work and on-campus volunteer service, leveraging retirees' unique skills and experience. USC has also been instrumental in assisting other universities in improving the retirement experience for their faculty and staff through the Emeriti Center's leadership role in the international nonprofit the Association of Retirement Organizations in Higher Education (AROHE), which is housed at USC.

USC Emeriti Center programs that promote faculty legacies include the following:

- USC Living History Project
- Guided Autobiography course
- USC Lifetime Achievement Award
- Paul E. Hadley Faculty Award for Service to USC
- Emeriti Center Endowment
- Benefactor Recognition Program
- Inamoto Japanese Cultural Programs
- Lilia Li Trust Chinese Cultural Programs
- Emeriti Center resource publications written by retiree committees
- Retiree profiles posted on the USC Emeriti Center's main webpage

Also see Appendix A.

USC Emeriti Center

Understanding a university's culture, values, and stakeholders and engaging respected university leaders (retired or not) as champions for the cause are the keys to creating a retiree center that can help initiate and foster faculty legacies.

History

The USC Emeriti Center was established in 1978, during the era of mandatory retirement, to provide much-needed support and services to faculty and staff before and after retirement from USC. Until 1978 it was USC's Benefits Office that kept the records and provided pre-retirement services. In 1975 the university established the USC Leonard Davis School of Gerontology, the first of its kind in the country, and built the Andrus Gerontology Center, and the time was ripe for the creation of an emeriti center. The first dean of the newly created Davis School of Gerontology, James Birren, himself a world-renowned gerontologist, welcomed the idea of an emeriti center and allocated space for it.

Dr. James Peterson, a sociologist and gerontologist, led the Emeriti Center in providing more comprehensive retirement assistance for faculty who were 65 years old, the mandatory age for retirement at that time. Peterson and other leaders provided resources and support for retirees and integrated themselves into the USC administration by helping to create and implement new retirement policies, while serving as understanding advocates and arbitrators for retiree causes.

Respected retired faculty led the Emeriti Center—James Peterson (1979), J. Tillman Hall (1989), and Paul Hadley (1996)—and in 1990 the Emeriti Center College was established as part of the center. Dr. Paul Hadley directed the college and was the founding president of AROHE, which was formed in 2002. Hadley's vision and management experience helped grow the Emeriti Center in important ways (see example in Appendix B).

The Emeriti Center's original mission was to serve as the focal point for faculty and staff who were nearing retirement or had retired. It illustrated the university's appreciation for, concern for, and continuing interest in retirees by providing service and support functions to individuals and to the university. The center retains this core mission and continues to be part of the Office of the Provost.

Purposes

At its founding in 1978, the Emeriti Center's goals were as follows:

- to provide pre-retirement and postretirement planning and counseling
- to utilize retired faculty and staff expertise in various services to the university and community
- to provide service and support to retired faculty and staff
- to provide or accomplish research, development, and administration in the area of retirement policy and practices
- to serve as a two-way communication link between the university and retired faculty and staff
- to provide opportunities for continuing intellectual growth and enhancement of the skills of the retired

The USC Emeriti Center, supported by the Office of the Provost, offers retirees and pre-retirees educational programs, services, resources, activities, and service opportunities that are multidisciplinary, multigenerational, and multicultural. It also acts as the office of record for retired faculty and staff; maintains retiree records, e-mail accounts, directory listings, and donor records; and manages events, publications, websites, and, in conjunction with the Benefits Administration, transitions-to-retirement sessions. The center is directed by the Executive Committee, composed of the executive director and retiree leaders. The committee makes important decisions for the center and for Emeriti Center College programs, initiatives, and services that support the university.

To honor faculty legacies, the center sponsors the USC Living History Project, which has produced video recordings of retired USC faculty and staff since the mid-1980s. Many of these recorded interviews have been posted online on the USC YouTube channel and are listed on the Emeriti Center website. In addition, short biographies of all retirees are posted on the center's website. The center offers two retiree service awards annually—one for retired faculty service to the university (in the name of Paul Hadley, emeritus professor) and one for retired staff service to the university (in the name of J. Tillman Hall, emeritus professor)—as well as opportunities for interdisciplinary projects and publications benefitting retirees, the university, and the community.

On behalf of the university, the Emeriti Center provides the retiree Gold Card, which grants free on-campus parking; library privileges; discounts; and continued membership in the University Club, which is a hub for faculty lunches. Gold Card privileges make it easy for retirees to visit campus for activities and volunteer service and stay part of the academic community. Another center program, Trojan Encore, engages retirees for volunteer and paid part-time positions. The Emeriti Center Benefits and Resource Committee empowers retirees to work with campus partners to advocate for benefits and create programs for both retirees and the entire campus community. Finally, the Emeriti Center hosts wellness events and other consumer educational programs that are also open to the community and alumni, manages regional socials, and arranges lifelong learning programs for retirees in their local communities.

Funding

In the early days the Emeriti Center functioned with funds secured from large foundations, retiree donations, and the Provost's Office. Funding for the Emeriti Center grew incrementally over the years. In the beginning retired faculty pursued funding through nonprofit foundations and fundraising, but gradually they started to conduct major fund-raising activities to partially subsidize staff salaries. Appendix B shows a letter documenting the transition to full funding and establishment of the Long Range Planning Task Force, which was instrumental in the transition. By 2006 the university provost approved the hiring of a full-time Emeriti Center executive director, and with a support staff funded by the provost, the Emeriti Center was open five days a week.

The first paid part-time executive director for the center was approved and funded by then-provost Lloyd Armstrong. The center became fully funded owing to the support of the next provost, C. L. Max Nikias, now the university president, who responded enthusiastically to the proposals of a retiree committee led by respected leader Professor Robert Biller. The provost increased the Emeriti Center budget three years in a row. Annual fund-raising continues, and planned gifts and grants help fund projects and increase endowments.

Culture

The Emeriti Center takes the university's Trojan Family culture a step further by using "Colleagues for Life" as its motto in all publications. Since the center's inception, the word *emeriti* has been used to describe honorable service. The center has always been the home for emeriti faculty, retired faculty, and retired staff. It supports the work and activities not only of the USC Emeriti Center College but also of both the Retired Faculty Association (RFA) and the Staff Retirement Association (SRA).

The Emeriti Center has established itself over the decades as a vital part of the USC culture. It has helped to ease the transition to retirement by involving retirees in programs, activities, educational seminars, intergenerational exchanges, and more. Emeriti Center programs and services are focused on USC retirees, but they also benefit current faculty and staff, students, alumni, and the community at large. The satisfaction of USC retirees has risen with every passing decade because of the center's attention to retiree interests and needs and also its close relationships with faculty, staff, students, alumni, and offices and schools across multiple USC campuses.

Faculty and staff need to know that they are going to be treated well once they retire. They also need to know that there are many meaningful opportunities to stay connected and contribute in retirement. This knowledge adds to a feeling of well-being, making retirees more likely to stay connected with and to support the university. Because USC faculty know that the university cares about them and that there are valuable services, programs, opportunities, and resources for them, they tend to respond with planned gifts and donations, mentoring, teaching, volunteering, collaborative research, and speaking well of the university to others. Because USC treats retirees well, this sends a signal to newly recruited senior faculty and administrators; they are valued by the university and will have special opportunities and privileges when they retire.

Successful Strategies

The Emeriti Center leaders' strategies for success in securing support, whether for funding, space, or approval of an initiative, include the following:

- identifying and encouraging leaders with distinguished reputations and far-reaching relationships to lead organizations, projects, or committees
- securing the support of highly respected faculty and administrators and using them as champions for the cause
- establishing a dedicated departmental budget and mission focused solely on retirees (Glazer, Redmon, & Robinson, 2005)
- having retirees involved in governance and programming (Glazer et al., 2005)
- understanding the university's culture and stakeholders in order to design programs and services that are most valuable for them
- conducting surveys to collect important data for decision making and project development
- being aware of the current atmosphere in order to identify potential administrative concerns
- allowing time to elapse between requests for different types of support, including staffing, funding, space, equipment, and contacts
- spending time documenting valuable and important accomplishments
- publicizing or presenting accomplishments whenever and wherever possible

A larger campus presence was established in 2003 by producing a successful 25th anniversary event for the center, which included a professional video, a development publication, and a strategic planning retreat.

Reasons for Success

As it is in any organization, experienced leadership is a key element of the Emeriti Center's success. During the first few decades of the Emeriti Center's existence, retired faculty leaders provided excellent leadership for the center and the Emeriti Center College. As respected and widely known campus leaders, they facilitated cooperation and support and encouraged group collaboration to provide the necessary retiree support programs. Emeriti Center committees have included both current and retired faculty and staff from many disciplines and departments. The interdisciplinary and intergenerational groups worked together and shared their wisdom, knowledge, and experience for the common good. Without this collaborative spirit, neither the center nor the college would be as successful as it is today.

Retired faculty and staff associations also contributed to the success of the Emeriti Center and College. These organizations connected retired USC faculty and staff to the university and to the center. The board president of each association sits on the Emeriti Center's Executive Committee. The president of the RFA is also a full voting member of the Academic Senate, and retired faculty serve on a number of university committees.

The Emeriti Center collaborates and partners with USC offices and schools to tap expertise for various programs. The Provost's Office, Center for Work and Family Life, Human Resources Administration, Benefits Administration, Alumni Association, Career Center, Retirement Plan Administration, Davis School of Gerontology, School of Social Work, and Continuing Education are all partners with the center. Along with many other campus colleagues, office and school staff provide resources that enable the Emeriti Center to continue its work.

The Emeriti Center and Emeriti Center College have also been successful because they recognize and illustrate the importance of USC retirees. They provide opportunities for retirees to contribute in significant ways. Their contributions enhance not only the lives of retirees, but also the lives of many others. Finally, the center and college have been successful because of their strong desire to promote and uphold the Trojan Family spirit.

The USC Emeriti Center College

The Emeriti Center College is the academic arm of the Emeriti Center. It was founded with two consecutive $50,000 grants from the Rose Hills Foundation in 1990 through Dr. J. Tillman Hall. The Emeriti Center College was built upon Hall's belief that "what you don't use, you lose" and aimed to identify and advance the continuing intellectual interests of its retirees. It strived to arrange lectures, teachings, consultations, and research through which mature scholars could "keep their minds vigorous, their knowledge expanding, and their skills sharp" (Fassbinder, 1994).

The college facilitates the service of scholars to society, helping to disseminate accumulated knowledge and wisdom through lectures, short courses, and occasional publications for retired colleagues and the general public. Every year the college sponsors between 200 and 400 presentations in the community, including lectures, discussions, and multigenerational forums. Many retired faculty and staff teach or take courses to share their knowledge or participate in new learning experiences. Retired faculty can also apply for small research grants to continue their scholarship in retirement.

The principal activities of the Emeriti Center College include the following:

- providing panels on critical issues to allow retirees to participate in discussions on controversial topics of public concern
- providing speakers for social, professional, and academic service groups; schools; and senior centers
- providing pre-retirement seminars for city agencies and educational institutions
- offering part-time teaching assistance in the various fields of specialization at USC and other academic institutions
- arranging colloquiums with distinguished scholars in order to benefit their retired colleagues
- initiating and supporting neighborhood programs such as USC's famed Neighborhood Academic Initiative, by enabling the parents of urban secondary school students who are enrolled in USC programs to meet with retired faculty and staff

Today, the college also operates a speakers' bureau, offers campus and regional enrichment classes, manages the intergenerational Forum on Global Change, and sponsors a book club.

The USC Living History Project

The USC Living History Project (http://emeriti.usc.edu/programs/living-history-project) is a cherished university resource that honors faculty and staff and contributes to the historical legacy of the university. Recordings capture individual stories that together offer a tapestry of perspectives describing university history.

The Emeriti Center established the USC Living History Project in the 1980s in honor of H. Dale Hilton. This project is responsible for producing more than 60 recorded interviews of important USC faculty and staff, documenting their contributions to the university and the university's evolution over time. The USC Living History Project highlights retired faculty and staff who are the living embodiment of the historical evolution of the university (Fassbinder, 1994). Their minds are the repositories of the past, and their talents have helped to create the current university. The interviews are eclectic remembrances of major campus events from the 1940s to the present: the evolving academic environment, administrative restructuring, and research and teaching accomplishments. Most video interviews have been posted on the

USC YouTube channel (www.youtube.com/user/USC). The archival-quality recorded interviews have USC library catalog numbers assigned by the university archivist.

Original funding for the project came from private donations. When this funding was fully used by 2005, a retired administrator transferred to the Emeriti Center a USC endowment established in her son's honor. Funding now comes from the USC Living History Endowment, the USC Emeriti Center, and sometimes various USC schools.

The endowment underwrites approximately two to three interviews per year. A committee of current and retired faculty and staff decides on the interviewees and facilitates scheduling, recording at a studio run by students of the USC School of Cinematic Arts. The edited recording is sent to the interviewer, the interviewee, the university archivist, and USC Communications for posting on YouTube.

Guided Autobiography

Not only is Guided Autobiography, established by Dr. James Birren in the 1970s, a legacy in itself, but it is also a way for current and retired faculty and staff to create their own legacies. The first dean of the School of Gerontology, Birren is acknowledged as one of the founders of the field of gerontology. He was instrumental in finding space for the USC Emeriti Center in 1978, and his research in the 1970s on cognitive change and aging led to the Guided Autobiography course (www.guidedautobiography.com). He endowed Autobiographical Studies in the USC Davis School of Gerontology to ensure that his Guided Autobiography method of using thematic life histories would be promoted and taught continuously.

Guided Autobiography classes for current and retired faculty and staff, as well as university students (the class is an academic for-credit course), help ease transitions to and within retirement. In the class, participants write thematic self-histories for themselves and posterity. After taking the class, some participants have even gone on to teach the class in more casual, not-for-credit venues, such as retiree organizations and churches. The classes provide a multigenerational venue for activating memories and intuitive thinking that in turn causes participants to rethink their lives. They provide stepping-stones for planning a more purposeful and interesting life, encourage a hard look at life's branching points, and help illuminate a person's life values.

USC Retired Faculty Association

Established in 1949, well before the Emeriti Center, the RFA (http://rfa.usc .edu) has more than 1,100 members, 784 of whom actively support the RFA through their annual contributions. The association aims to connect retired faculty to USC and to each other. Joining with the USC Emeriti Center, the Staff Retirement Association, Emeriti Center College, alumni, and USC's faculty and staff, the RFA actively supports the university's mission. The RFA preserves its legacy by supporting Caldwell Scholarships for undergraduate USC students from local inner-city schools with annual donations and activities for the scholars. In addition, RFA leaders are active on university committees, advocate for faculty, mentor students, contribute to neighborhood initiatives, sponsor lectures, and lead Emeriti Center and College initiatives.

The Trojan Encore Program

The term *Trojan Encore* is applied broadly to any USC voluntary or paid part-time work accomplished by a USC retiree, either formally or informally. The Trojan Encore Program (http://emeriti.usc.edu/programs/trojan-encore) enlists retired faculty and staff to contribute to the academic community in ways that go beyond being re-called to teach a class. The program registers retired faculty and staff willing to volunteer and work in part-time or short-term positions. Creating this program for paid positions required a university policy change. The program allows a retiree to post a curriculum vitae or résumé on the Trojan Encore website and provide a schedule for when he or she is available to work. Academic units seeking volunteers or part-time personnel can access the list of retirees and interview them for positions.

New Trends and Implications for Higher Education

As institutions of higher education begin to appreciate retiree populations as valuable campus assets, new retiree centers can become vehicles for retirement transitions and for important services, resources, legacy projects, and connections in retirement. Research conducted by AROHE indicates that the number of retiree organizations on college campuses is increasing. The 2012 AROHE survey indicates that most retiree organizations on North American campuses are retiree associations (75%); the remainder (25%) are established campus centers (Anderson & Brown, 2012). Over the past 4 years, the number of campus retiree centers has increased. USC was the first North American university to create a retired faculty association (in 1949) and the second to officially establish a retiree center (in 1978).

Because of greater life expectancy and the rapid growth of the population over age 65, supporting retirement transitions and developing legacies have become even more important. The encore career movement, inspired by Marc Freedman and his nonprofit organization, Encore.org, is taking hold in the United States (Freedman, 2007). This movement emphasizes meaningful and important work for the greater good in the second half of life. These ideas may affect higher education as retirees living well into their eighties and beyond provide meaningful, productive, and inspirational legacies for universities and society.

Conclusion

A major factor for successful retirement transitions is the existence of a campus retiree center that can offer faculty ways to stay connected to their university postretirement. A center is an office of record and a place where retired faculty can go for support, opportunities to contribute, programs, resources, referrals, and important connections. A center can efficiently connect campus units and serve many schools with an interdisciplinary and collegial atmosphere that honors faculty and staff contributions and offers multiple opportunities to stay connected. A center can also connect and support faculty and staff associations as well as an emeriti college. And a center can facilitate the development of legacies for faculty and for the institution by engaging faculty during the final campus years, letting them decide how to come to terms with what they want to define as their legacy (Perlmutter, 2012).

The steps for establishing a center, retiree association, or retiree program include the following:

- Assess the institution's culture and understand its stakeholders.
- Secure committed, well-known, prominent, and respected volunteers as leaders.
- Search for funding from the institution, foundations, and volunteers.
- Institutionalize programs by having prominent leaders promote the cause, develop good relationships across campus, sponsor valuable events, and publicize programs in digital and printed publications.
- Clarify to university administrators how a strong emeriti center yields benefits, not just for the retirees, but also for active faculty by facilitating their transition to retirement.

The importance of creating campus-based retiree centers, emeriti colleges, and retiree associations cannot be emphasized enough. For those institutions wishing to create a retiree organization, AROHE is a nonprofit dedicated to assisting them. A subsequent chapter provides information about AROHE and a case study of one institution that developed a retiree organization. By creating retiree organizations, institutions can demonstrate their commitment to supporting faculty and staff before, during, and after retirement. These organizations help faculty to feel more comfortable transitioning to retirement, and as a result, faculty are more likely to give back to the university and the larger community in their encore stage of life.

References

American Council on Education (ACE). (2012). *Alfred P. Sloan Awards for Best Practices in Faculty Retirement Transitions: Research institutions report for the University of Southern California.* Washington, DC: Author.

Anderson, R., & Brown, J. C. (2012). *Differences between centers and non-centers among retiree organizations in higher education in North America, 2012.* Unpublished paper.

Fassbinder, J. (1994). *The Emeriti Center and the Emeriti Center College.* Unpublished paper for GERO #499 Directed Research Study.

Feldman, F. L., Scales, R., & Stallings, R. (2008). *USC Emeriti Center: 2007 situation and circumstances survey report.* Retrieved from the USC Emeriti Center website: http://emeriti.usc.edu/files/2011/06/Situation-and-Circumstances-Report-20072.pdf

Freedman, M. (2007). *Encore: Finding work that matters in the second half of life.* New York: Public Affairs.

Glazer, S. D., Redmon, E. L., & Robinson, K. L. (2005). Continuing the connection: Emeriti/retiree centers on campus. *Educational Gerontology, 31*(5), 363–383.

Perlmutter, D. D. (2012, March 18). In search of a professor's legacy. *The Chronicle of Higher Education,* 18, A9–10

USC Emeriti Center. (2011, July). *After the death of a loved one.* Retrieved from https://emeriti.usc.edu/files/2011/06/EmeritiAfterDeath.pdf

USC Emeriti Center. (2012). *My confidential documents.* Retrieved from http://bit.ly/USCEmeritiRecord

USC Emeriti Center. (n.d.). *Colleagues for life: Sharing knowledge and experience.* Retrieved from http://emeriti.usc.edu/files/2011/06/Emeriti.web_.pdf

Appendix A: Faculty and Staff Legacy Examples

1. The Emeriti Center is partnering with the Provost's Office in a proposal to erect a half-dozen faculty history stations in prominent places on campus with text and photos honoring the achievements of outstanding retired and deceased faculty in all the scholarly fields of the university. The plan is that one of the history stations will reside outside the main administration building, which sees significant traffic from the university's officers, trustees, and key friends. This station will honor the legacy of the most noteworthy faculty, while the other stations will be located close to the schools where the faculty taught and conducted research.

2. Since 2002 retired faculty have been able to apply for small research grants to continue their scholarship and extend their legacy (http://emeriticollege.usc.edu/research-fund). Thanks to support from the Kenneth T. and Eileen L. Norris Foundation, for the past 10 years, grants of up to $2,000 have been available through the Emeriti Center College to assist retired faculty with expenses related to research and publication. Grants also may be used to fund undergraduate research assistants. One, two, or three grants may be awarded up to the total available funding of $2,000 per year. Previous grant recipients may reapply after 3 years. As this funding is used up, endowment interest, donations, and the transfer of an endowment by the provost will continue the support offered by the Emeriti Center College.

3. The Emeriti Center's Benefactor Recognition Program allows individuals to honor faculty and staff on specially engraved nameplates on two large benefactor plaques at the Emeriti Center. The program was created in the 1980s by J. Tillman Hall and Norman R. Fertig with support from the Albert and Elaine Borchard Foundation. Colleagues who wish to honor someone make a tax-deductible gift of $500 or more and identify their honoree. The engraved plates include the names of both the honoree and the honored. A letter of recognition is sent to both honoree and donor, and their names and the dates of the recognition are posted on the Emeriti Center website (http://emeriti.usc.edu/about/benefactor).

4. The Emeriti Center Inamoto Endowment funds the Inamoto lecture series, which has promoted understanding between Japanese and Americans since the late 1990s. Lectures and other presentations honor the memory of Professor Emeritus Noboru Inamoto, who taught at USC from 1953 to 1986. Born in Canada and schooled in Japan and the United States, Professor Inamoto devoted his life to fostering better understanding between the people of his two adopted countries, the United States and Japan. After his marriage his wife, Barbara, joined him

in this work, and it is her $30,000 endowment gift to the Emeriti Center that supports the Inamoto programs. Proceeds from Professor Inamoto's book, *My Three Homelands*, published in 1994, also support the USC Emeriti Center's Inamoto Fund.

5. A special contribution to the USC Emeriti Center endowment through a planned gift from Professor Lilia Huiying Li has provided funds to support the center's Chinese cultural programs. The USC Emeriti Center received a $110,000 charitable remainder annuity trust gift from the estate of Professor Li, wife of Professor Emeritus George O. Totten III. The trust was set up on behalf of the Emeriti Center and was funded in 2009, after both Li and Totten passed away. Li's trust provides for ongoing learning events for USC retirees, faculty, staff, students, alumni, and the greater community. When the trust was signed in 1992, Paul Hadley, then Emeriti Center director, indicated the significance of this gift, which recognizes the long-term role of the Emeriti Center and Emeriti Center College in the intellectual and international life of the university and furthers USC's role in developing peaceful communication among the major entities of the Pacific Rim. Li was a lecturer, writer, journalist, and special correspondent. Her principal concern was the search for peace between Taiwan and the People's Republic of China.

6. A number of faculty have endowed chairs, professorships, library funds, and centers. In addition, they have established scholarships before or after retiring from the university and continue to contribute to many causes for which they feel a strong commitment (http://about.usc.edu/faculty-distinctions/named-chairs-and-professorships).

7. The USC Emeriti Center webpage highlights retiree profiles (under the heading "Life After Retirement"), which illustrate retirees' work at the university and their lives in retirement. USC retirees are busy with many interesting and purposeful activities, and the USC Emeriti Center website is a place to inform others about their many years of service to the university. Retired faculty and staff postings rotate at the bottom of the Life After Retirement webpage. They each include a photo and information about the retiree's work before and after retirement. The short vignettes serve to inform and inspire.

8. The USC Emeriti Center offers a catalog of useful publications for retired faculty, including *After the Death of a Loved One* (USC Emeriti Center, 2011), *My Confidential Documents* (USC Emeriti Center, 2012), *USC Emeriti Center: 2007 Situation and Circumstances Survey Report* (Feldman, Scales, & Stallings, 2008), and the USC Emeriti Center brochure (USC Emeriti Center, n.d.).

Appendix B: Establishment of the Long Range Planning Task Force

January 6, 2000
Dr. Martin L. Levine
Vice Provost, Faculty Affairs
LAW 306B MC 0071

Dear Dr. Levine:

The persons listed have constituted a Long Range Planning Task Force to consider the future of the Emeriti Center programs, including the Emeriti Center College. Our deliberations have acquired a special importance because of the imminent retirement of our present administrative personnel, with the exception of the Director of the College, Dr. William Faith. We have tried to follow Provost Armstrong's instructions that the primary mission of the Emeriti Center should be to render human services to faculty and staff retirees in order that they may remain active members of the University family.

In order to fulfill this mandate, we have divided the assignment into two broad segments: 1) the Emeriti Center, which maintains records, serves as advocate, and administers services and benefits, including the Transitions Retirement Education Series, to which University employees, as well as retired staff and faculty, are invited; and 2) the Emeriti Center College, which provides intellectual service to our retirees and to the community.

In considering these objectives, we have posed a number of questions which the Task Force is deliberating and on which your guidance will be both appreciated and necessary.

1. Given the present level of staffing, with only part-time personnel and a group of volunteers, how can we perform these services effectively?
2. How shall we reconstruct our staffing?
3. How can the Emeriti Center, including the Emeriti Center College, communicate its mission and services more effectively to a) the University administration and campus community, b) faculty and staff who are within range of retirement, c) existing retirees, and d) USC alumni and the wider community?
4. Are there additional services, intellectual and administrative, that we should provide?

Since you are the designated representative for the Provost in matters related to the Emeriti Center, we feel that you are key to communicating with Provost Armstrong. Your advice is essential and critical as the Emeriti

Center determines its future. Accordingly, we request that you receive either this entire group, or a designated subcommittee, to discuss these matters.

Yours very sincerely,
Paul E. Hadley
    Director, Emeriti Center

PEH:mbs

William Faith	Anthony Lazzaro
Frances Feldman	Taylor Meloan
Norman Fertig	Janis Romero
Eli Glogow	Harriet Servis
Walter Graf	Madaleen Smith
Paul Hadley	William Thomson
Tillman Hall	Nancy Warner
Howard Hansen	Teri Ziegler
Dale Hilton	

8

PHASING INTO RETIREMENT

Vicki LaFarge and Patricia Foster, *Bentley University*

Like many institutions seeking to address faculty retirement, Bentley University established a phased retirement policy for tenured faculty in 2004, hoping to assist faculty in their transition to retirement. Although the then-new program represented progress in the institution's approach to retirement and retirement planning, few Bentley faculty initially used the phasing options. Instead they continued to move immediately from full-time employment to retirement. A restructuring of the program in 2008 that increased and emphasized flexibility resulted in significantly greater faculty participation. This flexibility allowed retiring faculty in conjunction with department chairs and the academic administration to craft a phased retirement plan that is beneficial to all parties. In 2012 the Alfred P. Sloan Foundation, through an awards program administered by the American Council on Education (ACE), recognized Bentley's program for the flexibility it provides to faculty, their academic departments, and the university by awarding Bentley a 2-year grant. This chapter presents the historical backdrop to our program, explores its evolution—including initial faculty reluctance to use the program and reasons for the 2008 restructuring—and discusses present-day deficiencies and benefits. It concludes with a summary of plans for improvements.

Background and History

Higher education institutions nationwide have a large number of faculty nearing retirement age, in part because of the influx of faculty members in the 1960s and 1970s, the elimination of mandatory retirement in 1994, the tenure system, and the significant economic downturn that began in 2008. Although the contribution of older faculty to an institution remains significant, the disproportionate percentage of such faculty presents two major dilemmas for most institutions. First, senior faculty often command the highest salaries, thus placing pressure on institutional budgets, and second, retention of older faculty may limit the ability of a university to employ recently graduated faculty who can infuse campuses with new perspectives.

Bentley University's faculty demographics reflect the national trend.[1] In September 2012, for example, more than half (51.9%) of full-time faculty (tenured, tenure track, and lecturers) were 56 years of age or older. In contrast, only 4.3% of full-time Bentley faculty were under 35 years of age. Table 8.1 details the age ranges of the Bentley faculty.

Given this demographic scenario, Bentley's senior leadership recognized the need for a formalized faculty retirement plan, and by academic year 2002–2003, several factors coalesced to serve as catalysts for the program's development. First, a perception, based to some degree on reality, existed among faculty that faculty members were negotiating individual retirement plans and packages, resulting in inequities among prospective and current retirees. In response, the Faculty Senate began discussing the need for a more consistent and transparent retirement package. Second, in part because of an extremely generous postretirement medical plan, Bentley's health-care costs were becoming increasingly burdensome for the institution. The university needed to develop a plan to contain these costs, while still recognizing

TABLE 8.1
Age Range of Bentley Faculty

Age	Number of faculty	Percentage of total faculty
<35	12	4.3%
40–36	26	9.4%
45–41	29	10.5%
50–46	33	12.0%
55–51	32	11.6%
60–56	38	13.8%
65–61	57	20.7%
70–66	35	12.7%
75–71	14	5.0%
	276	

the institutional contributions of retiring faculty. Third, Bentley offered a two-tiered retirement benefit under its 403(b) plan wherein faculty earning more than $60,000 were given a higher contribution rate (at 12%) than faculty making less than that figure (at 8%). There was a general consensus that this inequity should be eliminated.[2]

These considerations were critical in spurring collaboration among the Faculty Senate's Salary and Benefits Committee, the academic administration, Human Resources, and the Board of Trustees to develop Bentley's phased retirement plan. The plan and the collaborative process used in its development reflect Bentley's institutional history and culture. Founded in 1917 as the Bentley School of Accounting and Finance, Bentley began its transformation from an urban commuter school to a residential, suburban, regional business college with its move in 1968 to its current suburban campus outside of Boston, Massachusetts. It launched two doctoral programs in 2006 and became Bentley University in 2008. At the time the phased retirement program was introduced, a significant number of current senior faculty either had served at Bentley before its relocation or had joined the university soon afterward. They had been integral in the school's development, taught alumni members of the Board of Trustees, and helped to shape Bentley's system of governance. Moreover, faculty tended to stay at Bentley for their entire career. They were highly invested in and valued by the institution. Close collaboration among faculty, administrators, and the board to create a program that recognized the contributions of long-serving faculty thus reflected a cultural norm.

During the first few years after the 2004 policy adoption, few Bentley faculty used the phasing options. Instead, they continued to move immediately from full-time employment to retirement. To some degree this was a result of low awareness among faculty and academic departments of the various options. Although discussed in the Faculty Senate and included in the Faculty Manual, the new program was not heavily advertised and no specific programming was developed around the phasing option. This might have been the result of several changes in Bentley's administration (e.g., new president, deans, department chairs) that occurred at about the same time. Another factor contributing to low program use might have been the strict interpretation and application of the policy, with no exceptions made to address individual circumstances or the varying needs of academic departments.

In 2008, with advice from Bentley's general counsel and in coordination with the associate deans and the Human Resources Department, the university initiated a more flexible approach to the phased retirement program. To some extent this modification was driven by institutional changes in expectations about faculty workload. Teaching, scholarly activity, and institutional service had traditionally been expected of all full-time faculty at Bentley. The majority of faculty, except those with significant service obligations, such as chairing academic departments or serving on the Faculty Senate, had a six-course-per-year teaching obligation. As Bentley evolved from an institution primarily focused on excellent undergraduate teaching to one also focused on faculty scholarship, the need to reconsider faculty workload allocations became apparent. Recognizing that at various times throughout their careers faculty might wish to focus energy and attention differently, Bentley had previously developed a profile system that allowed individuals the flexibility to emphasize one of three academic spheres (teaching, scholarship, or service), consistent with departmental and institutional needs. Bentley faculty are therefore able to negotiate and be evaluated on a profile (teaching, scholarly, service, or standard) that reflects their particular emphasis. When the university implemented the system, many faculty adopted a scholarly profile, which included increased expectations for scholarship along with a reduced teaching load of four (and in a few cases two) courses per year rather than six. In addition, Bentley had offered four-course-per-year teaching loads to tenure-track faculty in support of the scholarship needed for them to achieve tenure. As faculty with scholarly profiles began to consider retirement, it became obvious that a strict interpretation of faculty workload being equivalent to six courses per year during the phaseout period provided no incentive to take advantage of the phased retirement option. For example, a faculty member with a scholarly profile and a four-course teaching load who opted for a 3-year phasing period at full salary would still have the obligation to teach the same course load (two-thirds of the six-course standard load). On a 2-year phased retirement plan at full salary, the same faculty member would be obligated to teach three courses per year, making it more difficult to schedule a full semester away from the university. Under a strict interpretation of the policy, therefore, a faculty member with a scholarly profile was more likely to opt for a 1-year phasing period (or none at all), giving both the retiring faculty member and the department less time to plan for and adjust to the departure.

The more flexible implementation of the phased retirement program reflected the underlying premise of the profile system and the long-held Bentley view that faculty contribute more than the number of courses taught, articles written, or committees assigned. Contribution involves a combination of all such activities. Faculty, while expected to achieve in all areas, may differ in the emphasis of their contribution. A more flexible approach to implementation of the retirement phasing program recognizes this and allows faculty to continue to contribute during the phasing period.

How Bentley's Program Works

The Bentley University flexible retirement policy allows full-time tenured and tenure-track faculty who are at least 60 years of age and have at least 10 years of service to phase into retirement over 1, 2, or 3 years.[3] During the phased retirement period, the faculty member is considered a full-time member of the university and of his or her department, maintains his or her tenure status, and is eligible for all full-time status benefits.

The program works as follows:

1-Year Phasing

For full compensation, faculty members agree to engage in some combination of teaching, service, and scholarship activities of benefit to them and the university that is equivalent to teaching one course per semester. In practice, the majority of faculty members opting for a 1-year phasing process use it as a time to complete a legacy project (e.g., a research project or book) or to provide service to the university, perhaps working on a curricular innovation rather than teaching.

2-Year Phasing

The faculty member works half-time for full compensation for 2 years. The faculty member is eligible for an annual merit increase if the university gives merit increases in those years, and can apply for summer research grant support. Many faculty retiring via a 2-year phasing process conduct their teaching and on-campus service activities during one semester and have few, if any, institutional commitments during the other semester. Many continue their research agendas throughout the year.

3-Year Phasing

The faculty member works two-thirds time for full salary or one-third time for two-thirds compensation over 3 years. The individual is eligible for an annual merit increase if the university offers such increases in those years, and can apply for summer research support. As with the 2-year phasing process, many faculty focus their teaching or service activities on one semester.

Eligibility

Any faculty member who is at least 60 years of age with at least 10 years of full-time tenure-track or tenured service at Bentley is eligible for phased retirement. Generally, the phasing process must begin at least 6 years after the last full-year sabbatical and 3 years after the last 1-semester sabbatical. However, faculty with 20 or more years of full-time tenured or tenure-track service are eligible 4 years after their last full-year sabbatical and 2 years after their last 1-semester sabbatical. As a result long-serving faculty who are considering a sabbatical to pursue projects important to them and to Bentley are not discouraged from doing so because of the potential impact on their ability to take advantage of the phased retirement option.

Faculty generally must apply to their dean by February 1 of a given year for a phased retirement start date of September in that same year. This date allows the academic department time to take the phasing agreement into account as part of the development of the fall teaching schedule. The faculty member and dean negotiate the specific terms of the agreement, consistent with the guidelines. Human Resources and the general counsel then review the agreement, and the provost provides ultimate approval.

If more faculty apply for retirement phasing than a department can accommodate in a given year, priority is based on a combination of criteria that includes length of service, including tenure-track and tenured service, and length of time since the last sabbatical.

Postretirement

At the end of the phasing period, the faculty member relinquishes his or her tenure and retires from Bentley. At the discretion of the dean and the faculty member's department, retired faculty may teach at Bentley; if they do so, they serve technically as adjunct faculty but have permission to use their pre-retirement titles. During retirement, compensation for teaching is 33% above the Bentley average pay for adjunct professors. Retired faculty members may apply for summer research grants for 3 years after retirement; access the library, athletic center, faculty/staff dining room, and other facilities; participate in commencement ceremonies; share office space (if available) with other retired faculty; obtain free tickets to Bentley's performing arts series; and retain a number of other benefits. Retired faculty members also retain their Bentley laptop, Bentley e-mail access, and laptop technical support for any Bentley-related issues.

More Flexibility, More Usage

Since the 2008 revisions to the retirement program, Bentley has exercised considerable flexibility in determining how to implement the phased retirement policy, with the goal of ensuring benefits to both faculty and the university. Because faculty workload is more than just the number of courses taught per year, the activities that technically constitute a half or two-thirds load may vary to meet the needs of individual faculty, their department, and the institution. These pursuits are determined through discussion among the retiring faculty member, the deans and associate deans, and the department chair.

One faculty member with a 2-year phasing agreement taught the entirety of the phasing period teaching load (six courses, or one-half of the standard load) and maintained some service commitments in the first year of phasing. In the second year this person continued with some service commitments but did not teach. The arrangement allowed the faculty member to remain integrally involved in the delivery of a new core course during the first year of the 2-year phasing period. The design of the phasing plan benefited the department by keeping an experienced teacher in the classroom during an important course introduction. By the second phasing year, the course was established and additional faculty members were trained to deliver the course, so it was less critical to have the retiring faculty member in the classroom.

As part of a 2-year phased plan, another faculty member opted to teach three courses in the fall semester for each of the 2 years (one-half of the standard load in each year). However, the departmental need for three courses in the fall semester changed after the agreement was made. Therefore, rather than requiring the retiring individual to fulfill the three-course teaching load across both the fall and spring terms, the department substituted a curriculum development project for one of the three courses in both phasing years. This fulfilled a critical departmental need and allowed the retiring employee to have the spring semester free from university commitments.

On a 1-year phased retirement plan, a senior faculty member agreed to maintain an active role in one of Bentley's accrediting bodies. This allowed her to travel extensively (which would have been impossible with the one-course-per-semester teaching load normally part of 1-year phasing) and fully represent Bentley in the accrediting organization.

The teaching load for another faculty member taking a 3-year phased retirement was reduced from four courses per year (two-thirds of the standard six courses per year) to three courses to allow the faculty member to complete a book in progress. The combination of research for the book and teaching was considered to be two-thirds of this individual's load. This arrangement allowed the faculty member to maintain a full salary and complete an important book project. It allowed Bentley to have an experienced instructor in the classroom and to benefit from the publication of the faculty member's legacy book project.

While adhering to the basic benefits and structure of the original retirement phasing plan, Bentley allowed greater flexibility in its implementation, which resulted in mutually productive and satisfactory phasing periods, such as those described. The phased retirement option is now used more extensively, with 17% (n = 11) of eligible faculty involved as of spring semester 2013 in some phase of the flexible retirement process: five on 3-year phased plans, four on 2-year phased plans, and two on 1-year phased plans.

Program Benefits and Faculty Feedback

The flexible implementation of our phased retirement program offers benefits to both Bentley and its retiring faculty. Any phased retirement obviously aids in the retirement adjustment process and allows faculty to transition gradually into retirement rather than making an abrupt shift. The added advantage of the flexible implementation of phased retirement is that faculty can design a transition that fits their particular combination of interests and needs on a 1-, 2-, or 3-year schedule. As illustrated previously, one individual might focus on teaching, another on research, and another on serving as a Bentley representative to an accrediting agency.

As the phased retirement option has evolved and awareness among faculty has grown, reactions have been exceptionally positive. Interviews with individuals engaged in various stages of phased retirement have provided insights into their experience with the program.

A professor and former department chair currently in the final year of a 2-year phased plan described how he chose this option to optimize his needs and those of his department. Because he was serving as department chair, he knew that the department needed time to find and train a replacement. From a personal standpoint, he wanted to "retire gradually." For 2 consecutive academic years, this faculty member has taught in the fall but not in the spring. "Personally, I was interested in seeing what it would be like to have the free time and also practice living on a lesser income," he said. The faculty member found that adjusting to being away and living on a reduced salary was not a problem. However, were he to do it again, he said, he would prefer a 1-year phased plan for two reasons: First, it has been emotionally challenging to come and go, to slowly break away from professional and personal friendships, and to be greeted by colleagues on campus after a long period away with, "You're still here? I thought you retired!" He likened it to "the long good-bye." Second, because his teaching focused on a highly technical field, he needed to revamp his courses in order for them to be current. Therefore, his free term was consumed with work, just to keep current in a rapidly evolving field. "In a technical business, the market will impose change on you. This burned me out a little," he said.

This same faculty member felt strongly that formalizing the phased retirement policy has been a benefit to all and noted that the formalized program eliminates stress and confusion related to the retirement planning process. He also believed it is a fair and equitable policy. While he applauded the deans, associate deans, and provost for their personal involvement and assistance with his process, he recommended that pre- and postretirees have access to more information, possibly including a workshop on postretirement medical and technology benefits. For example, he noted, "I'm actually unsure of my benefits around computer use." He recommended that Bentley offer a more formalized program for long-serving nontenured faculty. He believes that his most useful nonmonetary retirement benefit will be continued access to the library.

An associate professor in a different department also opted for a 2-year phased retirement plan. However, departmental needs enabled her to teach full-time in the first year of phasing and to treat the second phasing year as a terminal sabbatical. This faculty member solicited advice from many peers in making her decision and believed that the biggest factor influencing option preference was her age. She felt that younger faculty were more comfortable with a longer phasing period and that older people were "ready to go." She expressed high satisfaction with the retirement plan and the personal information she received from peers and senior administrators, noting, "The associate deans were wonderful." For her, this personalized attention was as important as formal workshops, online information, or printed materials. Since she will relocate to a different part of the country after retirement, she is unconcerned with postretirement benefits beyond electronic access to library functions.

An emerita professor and former department chair chose a 3-year phased retirement process, which is now complete. Since this individual served on the Faculty Senate's Salary and Benefits Committee during development of the phased retirement program, she had unique insight. She described her retirement transition as a continuum, allowing her to remain active in her research and at Bentley while also enjoying time for other activities. This year, for instance, she is engaged in research and grant proposal development in a university research center. This professor believes that the phased retirement option is critically important for faculty's ability to maintain intellectual engagement. The system is beneficial to Bentley because "if retirees remain connected to the institution, they will provide financial support, pass on resources, and share intellectual knowledge with junior faculty." She concludes, "We have a foundation in place. Some people want a little longer time to leave and others want to go quickly; this meets these needs. It lets people wind down and wrap up."

The flexible phased retirement program is also perceived positively by faculty who are not yet specifically considering retirement, but who are in what might be termed the *pre-retirement phase* of their careers with retirement 5 to 10 years in the future. For example, one faculty member in this career stage noted that the phasing option provides "peace of mind and a sense of security" because it allowed him to consider a variety of options for managing the retirement process. For another, the flexibility of the program reflects the "culture and values" of the institution, which places value on the "varying ways that faculty contribute to Bentley throughout their careers." This faculty member went on to say, "Traditionally, our faculty stay at Bentley for their entire careers. They make a tremendous intellectual and emotional investment in the institution and are very connected to Bentley." The option for faculty to retire more gradually rather than to leave more abruptly "just seems to fit who we are."

Program Challenges

Despite Bentley's success in implementing the phased retirement policy, program challenges exist. For example, a recent meeting with department chairs revealed that the policy was not well understood by this important constituency and that they did not feel well prepared to discuss retirement options with their department members. The chairs also believed that awareness of the plan is not high among faculty. In effect, a program recognized externally for the benefits provided to faculty does not enjoy high internal recognition. Because pre-retirement programming at Bentley has been largely individual and focused on benefits-related issues, opportunities for faculty to discuss retirement options and implications in a regular, larger forum that includes psychosocial aspects of the retirement process have not been available on a regular basis. It has become clear that retirement and Bentley's phased retirement plan are not a part of any larger community discussion.

In addition to identifying communication gaps related to the phasing program and retirement in general, Bentley recognizes that there has been little explicit focus on mechanisms to connect retired faculty more closely and explicitly to the institution. Although some retired faculty members maintain connections through adjunct teaching and continued research, other mechanisms, such as a retiree group, retired faculty events, or structured opportunities for retired faculty to present ongoing research, have been unavailable. One retiring faculty member indicated that there is some confusion about the nature and degree of technical support that retired faculty members receive from the university; clarifying this postretirement benefit is a priority for the university. Finally, conclusions about the success of the phased retirement program as well as about the needs of faculty pre- and postretirement have been drawn largely from anecdotal information rather than focused research.

Next Steps

Upon receiving Sloan grant award notification, Bentley established a steering committee to address the program's challenges and weaknesses discussed throughout this chapter and to oversee the immediate administration of activities resulting from the grant. Specifically, we have developed a plan to conduct research among potential and current faculty retirees, refine retirement program policies, improve and expand communication related to faculty retirement planning, and develop new retirement programming initiatives. The steering committee includes the associate dean of academic affairs, the executive director of human resources, the senior human resources business partner, and the academic affairs grant and budget administrator. The university's general counsel is an ex officio member of the committee. Bentley has also established an advisory committee composed of pre-retirement and postretirement faculty who act as resources and a sounding board for the steering committee.

Research

The first step in improving Bentley's faculty retirement program is research. The Human Resources Department and Office of Academic Affairs have worked jointly to conduct a literature review, obtaining extensive data on best practices in higher education retirement programs. Human Resources is currently conducting two surveys, one of prospective faculty retirees (all faculty 50 and over) and another of all recently retired faculty members, to obtain data about their perceptions of the retirement program and, where applicable, their personal experience with the retirement process. The university will also conduct focus groups and one-on-one interviews as part of the research process. As for the surveys, we will select participants by e-mailing all faculty 50 and over. Bentley's Institutional Review Board reviewed and approved survey tools for all research.

Phased Retirement Program Enhancement

Information gathered through the research will enable Bentley to refine and clarify the current phased retirement policy and to identify areas for enhanced programs for retiring and retired faculty. Potential changes might include better coordination of sabbaticals with phased retirement, clarification of the plan's retirement notification status provision, clarification of postretirement technology privileges, changes to the retiree perquisites package, introduction of a retirees' association, and creation of a retiree mentoring program. In addition, the university will consider policies and practices related to retirement of lecturers, many of whom have long tenure with the institution and are integral to our educational mission.

Improved and Expanded Communication and Programming

Bentley recognizes the immediate need for improved and expanded communication about the phased retirement policy. To address this need, Human Resources will develop a retirement planning timeline and checklist for those anticipating retirement, as well as other materials developed for faculty who are in the pre- or postretirement phase. Plans are also under way for a dedicated website to house all the materials and to address all aspects of retirement planning and postretirement concerns. The present plan is to link the site to the Human Resources Policies and Procedures page, where faculty search for information about benefits and related programs.

Although checklists and other materials will enhance faculty knowledge about the retirement plan and process, programming (i.e., workshops) can supplement this knowledge and allow faculty to explore more fully the complete range of retirement-related issues. As previously noted, one identified need is for department chair education about managing the retirement planning process within departments, with particular emphasis on how chairs should approach retirement planning discussions from legal, personal, and practical perspectives. Another need is for workshops targeted at faculty considering retirement and for their spouses and partners. These would include information and discussion not only about the retirement plan, benefits, and financial planning for retirement, but also about retirement's impact on lifestyle. Additional programming could also be developed for retired faculty and staff.

Conclusion

Bentley's flexible phased retirement program provides our faculty with the opportunity to design a transition that fits their unique combination of interests and needs on a 1-, 2-, or 3-year schedule. Anecdotal evidence indicates that the program is appreciated by and beneficial to retiring faculty. Bentley's president, provost, and other senior administrators are committed to the current program and improvements resulting from the Sloan grant funding. Our hope is that the new strategies and program enhancements made possible through our grant will garner even greater satisfaction among Bentley faculty and retirees, resulting in a committed and connected pre- and postretirement community.

Notes

1. As a business university, Bentley University educates creative, ethical, and socially responsible organizational leaders by creating and disseminating knowledge within and across business and the arts and sciences. The vision of this business university is to distinctively integrate business and the liberal arts and to provide international leadership in business education and research. With 276 full-time faculty in September 2012, Bentley offers undergraduate degrees in 11 business disciplines and 9 arts and sciences fields, 3 MBA programs, 7 master of science degrees, and PhD programs in business and accountancy to approximately 5,500 undergraduate and graduate students.

2. The Bentley Faculty Senate's Salary and Benefits Committee crafted new plans to address the retiree medical benefit and the 403(b) program. Both reforms were approved by the Board of Trustees and introduced before the phased retirement program was finalized.

3. Faculty on tenure track at Bentley must come up for tenure after a maximum of 6 years. It is therefore possible that a senior lecturer who has converted to a tenure-track position might fulfill the eligibility requirements of age and length of service while still a tenure-track faculty member. In practice, this has not been the case.

9

STARTING A RETIREE ASSOCIATION AT A SMALL LIBERAL ARTS COLLEGE

Terence E. Diggory and Susan A. Kress, *Skidmore College*

S kidmore College has been paying close attention to the retirement transitions of tenured faculty for a number of years. In the following summary, we describe the context for our efforts and the process we followed in starting our own retiree association, which includes both faculty and staff and which draws on elements of the three kinds of associations defined by Sue Barnes and Janette Brown in chapter 15 (retiree associations, retiree centers, and emeriti colleges). We hope that our work may provide a starting point, and indeed a model, for liberal arts colleges with similar ambitions.[1]

Skidmore College

Skidmore is a small liberal arts college located in the foothills of the Adirondack Mountains in Saratoga Springs, New York. In 1922 New York State chartered Skidmore College as a 4-year, degree-granting institution. In the nine-plus decades since, we have transformed ourselves from a regional women's college of 1,200 students into a highly selective, coeducational institution with a national reputation and an enrollment of 2,400 students. The college has close to 900 employees. Many faculty and staff members remain in the area after retirement, as do a significant proportion of Skidmore students after graduation, testifying to the strength of the local and college community.

Retiree Planning at Skidmore

Skidmore College has shared the growing national concerns regarding the retirement of tenured faculty. In particular, the most recent economic downturn, which was developing into a full-blown recession by 2008, delayed retirements and contributed to a growing number of faculty members at the college over the age of 55. Few dispute that some outstanding faculty should remain in their positions as long as possible, but the health of an institution is best sustained when there is a reasonable balance of faculty at various ranks and at different degrees of distance from their graduate school experience. Accordingly, institutions like Skidmore that once were more concerned about the orientation and mentorship of new faculty at the beginning of their careers are now equally concerned about supporting and mentoring faculty moving into retirement.

The Skidmore focus on retiree transitions has been part of a comprehensive approach to faculty development. Since the mid-1990s the college has put in place several programs in support of faculty approaching retirement. By 1995 Skidmore had developed a phased employment program, open to all employees. The Office of Benefits and Labor Relations offers private and family consultations for those planning retirement and, starting in 2008, organizes an annual seminar to educate potential and actual retirees about key aspects of retirement. For some time Human Resources has also hosted occasional lunches and receptions for retirees and lists retirees in the annual *Faculty and Staff Directory.* Beginning in 2006, the vice president for academic affairs hosted an annual event in honor of currently retiring faculty to which all faculty and staff retirees in the area were invited.

Retirees at Skidmore are accorded certain privileges and benefits. As the *Skidmore College Faculty Handbook* notes, "All full-time faculty who retire are accorded emeritus status and are invited to attend and participate in official activities of the College, to use the Scribner Library, Computer Services, and laboratory facilities, when available, and the College's fitness and recreational facilities." Skidmore employees have the opportunity to take courses free of charge, a benefit extended to retirees as well. Moreover, retirees may attend an annual 7-week series of lectures, delivered by current Skidmore faculty (and by retirees), designed for mature learners, aged 55 and older.

In turn, retirees provide significant benefits to the college. Retired faculty have been approached to mentor either department chairs or other faculty members, and on occasion, a retired faculty member might be invited to return to teach a course or even to chair a department or direct an office on an interim basis. That such arrangements are ad hoc and informal reflects the close-knit culture of a small liberal arts college community.

By 2008 it was clear that one of the most pressing challenges for the academic administration to address was faculty retirement demographics. Thanks to the generosity of the Andrew W. Mellon Foundation, Skidmore received a bridge grant to support adding lines in specified departments for a limited period to ease the anticipated clusters of retirements. Some of the larger questions posed by the grant proposal included the following: How could the college do a better job of orchestrating individual retirement transitions? How could the college continue to benefit from the wisdom, institutional memory, and capacities of retirees? How could retirees benefit from a continuing attachment to the college?

A Legacy Project

In fall 2008 former dean of the faculty and professor Phyllis Roth was in her first year of phased employment and proposed to take up a project to benefit the institution. Given the institution's interest in supporting the full range of faculty needs from orientation through retirement and beyond, it was agreed that Roth would focus on the mutual benefits of the continuing connection of retirees with the college. Her final report on October 7, 2010, included recommendations for improving communications generally, developing a dedicated e-mail list for retired faculty, and clarifying that retirees could apply for positions posted on the Human Resources website.

Retiree Initiative Fund and Planning Group

When Phyllis Roth retired in May 2010, her colleagues sought an appropriate way of honoring her. Her recent research on the relations between the college and retirees typified the spirit of her contributions to sustain the Skidmore community; thus, the idea emerged to solicit contributions to an endowed fund named in honor of Roth that could be used to implement programs for retirees. Roth's English Department colleague, Terry Diggory, supervised the solicitation along with the college's Office of Advancement.

The following description was provided to potential donors:

The Phyllis A. Roth Retiree Initiative Fund
In grateful recognition of Phyllis Roth's extraordinary contributions to Skidmore College, her friends and colleagues have established a fund in her name to promote continuing vital relations between the College and all its retirees. In her role as Dean of the Faculty, Phyllis took a special

interest in advancing the cause of faculty development. Recently, she has extended that interest to the community of all retirees through a study of the resources they might need or provide to the College and to each other. This fund might support, for example, occasional social gatherings, group excursions, informal reading groups or book review presentations, guided tours of new facilities, demonstrations of new technologies for searching for information on everything from practical living resources in the community to sophisticated research tools. In turn, the fund might support developing a variety of volunteer activities on campus, such as assisting in Admissions or mentoring new employees in a variety of areas.

In contrast to the other retiree organizations described by the Association of Retirement Organizations in Higher Education (AROHE) in Appendix 10 of the 2005 *AROHE Start-Up and Development Kit*, Skidmore's organization did not begin with a committee that then developed a mission statement and sought funds to implement it. Rather, Skidmore began with the sense of a mission that Roth's research helped crystallize.

During the fall of 2010, conversations among Phyllis Roth, Terry Diggory, Susan Kress (vice president for academic affairs), and Barbara Beck (director of human resources) indicated that all categories of retirees should benefit from the Retiree Initiative Fund, in keeping with Skidmore's community ethos. Accordingly, a minimal organizational structure, the Retiree Initiative Planning Group (RIPG), emerged with the initial purpose of advising the college on the use of the funds. Although membership of RIPG has fluctuated during the brief period that has elapsed since that time, the number of participants has remained fairly constant, at about eight, with a mix of faculty and staff members. Sadly, the group suffered the loss of Phyllis Roth when she died from cancer on March 25, 2012.

A crucial addition to RIPG meetings has been the representation of Academic Affairs by Patricia Rubio, associate dean of the faculty for personnel, development, and diversity, and of Human Resources by Terri Mariani, training coordinator, and David Spokowski, assistant director for benefits and labor relations. Coordination with Academic Affairs has proved essential in matters relating specifically to faculty retirees—for instance, the establishment of Emeritus Faculty Development Grants. Close cooperation with Human Resources is a natural outgrowth of the decision that Skidmore's retiree initiative should serve all categories of retirees. Activities that Human Resources had already offered for retirees, such as luncheon gatherings and receptions, provided a base for plans that developed further with input from RIPG. Communication with retirees has been facilitated through address lists maintained by Human Resources, including the two e-mail lists: one for all retirees and one specifically for faculty. Human Resources also maintains a webpage for retiree information, which is due to be enhanced on the basis of recommendations from RIPG. Meeting space for the group has been provided in a conference room maintained by Human Resources.

Beyond the occasional use of this conference room, RIPG has not yet advocated for such spaces for retiree use as have enhanced the presence of retiree associations on some other campuses. For larger gatherings RIPG has had to compete with demands from other users on campus. At the same time retirees have special needs—accessibility, for example—that make some spaces less suitable than others. Space on or near campus, suitable for both large gatherings and informal drop-ins, designated specially for retiree functions would undoubtedly promote further interaction among retirees and encourage their continuing identification with the college. RIPG is watching for the right opportunity to request such space.

Cooperation with administrative offices, such as Human Resources, Advancement, and the Dean of the Faculty, has enabled RIPG to function effectively without itself taking on a complex administrative structure. The group has remained informal, with participation solely on a volunteer basis. Terry Diggory has served as convener of the group, but there are no officers or bylaws, and decisions are reached by consensus. Since the group stands only in an advisory relation to the Phyllis A. Roth Retiree Initiative Fund, which is maintained as part of Skidmore's endowment, there are no tax implications such as those that apply to retiree associations at some other institutions. Retirees pay no dues in order to benefit from programs planned by RIPG; upon retirement they automatically become "members" of the retiree cohort.

In developing an agenda, RIPG has been fortunate in being able to build on a strong foundation for retiree relations that was already part of the Skidmore culture. Thus, while Human Resources had an established practice of hosting events for retirees, RIPG simply became a means of ensuring retiree input in planning such events. Meanwhile, the list of retiree privileges has continued to grow (e.g., free tickets for retirees for campus events that are free to current employees).

Given RIPG's informal status, a question necessarily arises about the extent to which RIPG represents retiree interests. The group has responded to this question in two ways. First, it has sought more formally representative channels for particular functions. For instance, the Faculty Development Committee, an elected body within the college governance system, has agreed to award grants for professional activities by retired faculty, in a process parallel to that employed for current faculty. Second, RIPG has reached out to retirees for their suggestions about programs and resources that they would find beneficial. The principal instance of such outreach so far is a survey of all retirees conducted in the summer of 2012 (RIPG, 2012).

Retiree Survey

The survey was conducted online using SurveyMonkey, a convenient program that provides useful tools for tabulating results and a user-friendly interface (in a few cases, hard-copy survey forms were supplied to retirees who requested them). Repeated invitations (three e-mails and one letter) to participate were sent to all retirees for whom Human Resources had an address. The survey collected 107 responses, of which 51% were from faculty and 49% from staff; most of the respondents had retired between 2000 and 2009, and the majority of the respondents (84%) lived within 50 miles of campus. The overall response rate (53% of total invitations sent) can be considered good in light of typical survey experience.

The goals of the survey were to assess the level of interest among Skidmore retirees in remaining connected to Skidmore and to determine the most attractive types of interaction. Both faculty and staff retirees expressed strong interest in staying connected via e-mail lists, mailings, the website, and *Scope* (the Skidmore alumni magazine). The most favored website locations were the calendar of events and campus news. Retirees noted that they would welcome a more informative retiree webpage with financial and estate planning information, news of retiree achievements, opportunities for participation in Skidmore classes, travel and lecture opportunities, and a tips and ideas exchange.

We learned that retirees especially enjoyed attending Skidmore performing and visual arts events and, to a lesser extent, appreciated the retirement and recognition luncheon and sports events. For retiree-specific events, respondents expressed high interest in the president's reception, informal lunches, tours of new facilities, and special interest groups. Suggestions for workshop topics included travel, new technologies, Medicare and other health issues, elder law, and senior living.

So far, RIPG has found the survey useful in brainstorming enhancements to the retiree webpage and in planning events. In some cases the survey indicated significant disparity in the interests of faculty and staff, but the RIPG sees its task as providing programs of interest to each constituency, not only programs appealing to both.

Opportunities and Challenges

Skidmore joined AROHE in the spring of 2012. RIPG's survey of Skidmore retirees was prompted in part by advice in the 2005 AROHE *Start-Up and Development Kit*, and Terry Diggory consulted with Janette Brown, AROHE executive director, about sample survey instruments.

In October 2012 Susan Kress attended the AROHE conference in Chapel Hill, North Carolina, and brought back to RIPG a report of the national conversation represented there. Kress's subsequent election to the AROHE board for 2013–2015 ensures that Skidmore will continue to benefit from and contribute to that conversation. The board hopes that Kress, the only representative of a small liberal arts college on the board, will be able to bring the concerns of such colleges to the attention of AROHE and that the association will be able to reach out more broadly to those liberal arts colleges so that best practices can be shared.

External support for retirement programs at Skidmore in a quite different and most valuable form arrived in June 2012, when the American Council on Education (ACE) in collaboration with the Alfred P. Sloan Foundation selected Skidmore as one of 15 institutions, and five liberal arts colleges, to be recognized with a $100,000 award for innovative practices in policies and programs supporting faculty retirement transitions. The public endorsement by ACE/Sloan of Skidmore's work across the college on behalf of retirees will certainly strengthen our efforts to improve programs and to share our experience with other institutions. As we move forward with planning, we will use the results of the ACE/Sloan baseline surveys, as well as our own survey of retirees and informal polls, to make the best use of the opportunities afforded by the award.

One challenge that Sloan funds are helping us meet is the crucial issue of communications among and with retirees. The Sloan award will be used to improve web design and to pay for the creation of new webpage materials. Our goal is to make the website attractive, informative, and interactive, a virtual gathering space. But retiree needs are diverse in ways that pose challenges to website design. Ideally, the website should serve employees who are in transition toward retirement as well as those who are already retired. We recognize too that the period of retirement includes its own transitions through various stages, each of which may present different needs and find expression in different forms of relation to the college.

In other areas as well, the inclusive scope of RIPG's mission to serve all categories of employees has presented both a challenge and a stimulus to new ideas. For instance, the establishment of Emeritus Faculty Development Grants has led to the question of offering grant opportunities to retired staff. What sort of projects might retired staff undertake that would be analogous to the professional development conventionally recognized for faculty? How would such projects be identified with the college, as is typically the case when faculty publish or exhibit their work? An elected Faculty

Development Committee reviews applications for Emeritus Faculty Development Grants, but no similar body exists in the case of staff. RIPG consists solely of volunteers and has encountered some difficulty in recruiting volunteers from all employee categories. But the prospect of funding projects by retired staff would make more tangible the college's commitment to retirees in all employee categories and might itself stimulate wider interest in RIPG and its activities.

While it is still very much a work in progress, the inclusive retiree association that is emerging at Skidmore College can claim both solid accomplishments and considerable promise as a model applicable to other institutions, particularly small liberal arts colleges. The informal organization allows functions to evolve organically as part of college culture, and of course, certain functions (such as the Emeritus Faculty Development Grants) can be instituted in formal structures as the case may require. The strong voice of faculty in college governance resonates in plans to support retired faculty, while the goal of serving all retirees, both faculty and staff, stimulates creative programming of benefit to all. Ultimately, it may even enhance relations among current faculty and staff, who are encouraged to see themselves as long-term colleagues, both on the job now and after retirement in the future.

Note

1. As part of our effort to uncover the best practices regarding retiree associations at other liberal arts colleges, we polled the Northeast Deans, an association of 32 liberal arts colleges in the Northeast: Bard, Barnard, Bates, Bowdoin, Bryn Mawr, Bucknell, Colby, Colgate, Connecticut College, Dickinson, Franklin and Marshall, Gettysburg, Hamilton, Hampshire, Haverford, Hobart and William Smith, Holy Cross, Lafayette, Middlebury, Mount Holyoke, Skidmore, Smith, St. Lawrence, Swarthmore, Trinity, Union, Vassar, Wellesley, Wesleyan, Wheaton, and Williams. Our query was worded as follows: "Skidmore College is in the preliminary stages of forming a retiree association. We would be grateful to learn whether you have such an association at your college. If you do, would you please direct us to the appropriate website and let us know as well what advice you might have for a similar small liberal arts institution? If you do not, would you let us know whether you have plans to develop such an association in the near future?" We received responses from nine colleges; of those, Wellesley, Smith, and Vassar have associations of varying degrees of formality for emeriti; Lafayette has a faculty committee on retirement that includes both retired and active faculty; and two colleges indicated their interest in offering more support for retirees.

References

Association of Retirement Organizations in Higher Education (AROHE). (2005). *Start-up and development kit: How to start, build and maintain an academic retirement organization*. Retrieved from http://www.arohe.org/Resources/Documents/AROHE%20Start-Up%20Kit%20complete.pdf

Retirement Initiative Planning Group (RIPG). (2012). *Skidmore College retiree survey*. Retrieved from AROHE website: http://www.arohe.org/Resources/Documents/Skidmore%20Retiree%20Survey%202012.pdf

PART FOUR

SENIOR AND EMERITI
FACULTY CONTRIBUTIONS
TO LOCAL COMMUNITIES

10

EMERITI FACULTY AS A VALUABLE INSTITUTIONAL RESOURCE

Mary Lefkowitz and Kathryn L. Lynch, *Wellesley College*

Tenured faculty members at Wellesley College in Massachusetts, with a few exceptions, tend to remain at the college until they retire. During those years most will have devoted considerable time and energy to their teaching and committee work and made lasting friendships with some of their colleagues. So when the time comes for them to retire, they are not simply leaving a place of work; they are also breaking close ties to friends and to an enterprise that has been a major part of their lives for, in most cases, 20, 30, or 40 years. For some faculty merely contemplating a break with the college and community is unthinkable. Others, even when they have other projects and interests, find the process of detaching themselves from what has been for so long a central part of their lives difficult or even painful.

Although in recent years Wellesley College had conscientiously addressed most of the practical issues involved in retirement, it—like most other universities and colleges—had no particular strategies to address the emotional and intellectual issues retirement evokes, at least for some people. What can or should colleges like Wellesley do to allow faculty to remain part of the college community or to continue to contribute in some way, if they wish to do so? In this chapter we first describe what Wellesley has done for retiring faculty in the past and the practical steps the college has taken to recognize and make effective use of their contributions. Then we explain how the institution has begun to address the larger questions raised by retirement.

Wellesley's Efforts on Faculty Retirement

Like many institutions of higher learning, Wellesley College maintains through our Human Resources Office an active series of events and a set of resources for faculty contemplating retirement. Over the past several years, that office has run an expanding set of workshops for the teaching faculty nearing retirement, which have covered such topics as retirement income planning, medical benefits in retirement, estate planning, and lifestyle. All this programming has been evaluated through questionnaires distributed to participating faculty. In those questionnaires we have also asked participants what additional programming they would like, and we are continually looking for new opportunities to serve faculty who stand uncertainly on the brink of this new phase of their professional lives.

Faculty who have attended the sessions indicate that they receive useful information and that they feel more prepared, with targeted questions, to do further research on their own about their options. For example, we have brought a representative of the Social Security Administration to come on campus to present income options, as well as Medicare coverage information, and attendees at these events have reported gaining knowledge that has yielded a tangible benefit to their bottom line in retirement. The college also provides both in-house and outsourced counseling for faculty navigating the transition to Medicare to ensure that their coverage is seamless and targeted to meet their specific needs. Such health-care counseling is especially needed because some of our faculty report that they avoid retiring because their retirement medical options are complicated, costly, and difficult to research in comparison with the ease of employer-provided health insurance.

In addition to providing retirement counseling, the college seeks to make emeriti faculty feel welcome on campus and allows them to continue to use many college resources. Emeriti faculty have free use of library facilities, campus recreational facilities, and campus parking facilities. They can retain their e-mail addresses and use the Help Desk and other campus computer services. They can also apply for research and travel grants for amounts up to the award limit set for other faculty. Scientists with grant money have had access to college facilities to support their research. The Provost's Office has for many years hosted a lunch for retirees in October, at which the provost and deans update the attendees on recent developments. Emeriti faculty are also invited to the provost and deans' annual holiday party in December.

The Evolving Role of Wellesley Emeriti Faculty

But many of the aforementioned benefits are available only to emeriti faculty members who live in the Greater Boston area. The college began to keep in touch with the emeriti who lived at some distance from campus thanks to the initiative of Phyllis Fleming, Sarah Whiting Francis Professor of Physics, emerita, and a former dean of the college, whose extraordinary dedication to her students, her department, and Wellesley College was recognized in the creation of an award endowed by students and colleagues that has been given annually in her name for the past 24 years. Fleming started a newsletter that was mailed out by the Office of the Dean of the College and that now is created digitally by three volunteer emeriti faculty. These emeriti belonged to a group of local retirees and had been meeting informally to see what they could do to help emeriti maintain closer ties to the college. They knew that some of their contemporaries and a few older members of the faculty were reluctant or unwilling to retire, either because they were not certain what retirement involved or because they were not sure what to do with themselves when they did (or both).

During this time an associate dean of the college, Joanne Berger-Sweeney, also made sure that emeriti faculty were specifically informed of the full range of privileges to which they were entitled after retirement, since (as she discovered) none of the privileges had been described to them in the letters that the president's office sent out to faculty in the year that they planned to retire. Berger-Sweeney also saw to it that those benefits were specified in correspondence with current faculty during their final year of teaching.

In 2007 two former associate deans of the college joined the local group of emeriti. They offered to serve as cochairs along with one of this chapter's authors (Mary Lefkowitz) and to help address faculty concerns by encouraging the college to keep in closer contact with emeriti faculty by creating a steering committee and virtual community for emeriti. The cochairs sent out a questionnaire and ballot to all emeriti, who formally elected them as their representatives. The answers to the questionnaire showed that most emeriti were interested in knowing more about particular areas of common interest: medical programs, estate planning, investment planning, and wellness. Mary Lefkowitz had been president of the Wellesley chapter of the American Association of University Professors just before she retired and was aware that some faculty were hesitant to retire because of concerns about medical insurance after retirement, as they would no longer be able to take advantage of the college's group insurance program. Upon investigation, she discovered, somewhat to her surprise, that her expenses were just about the same before and after retirement, at least in a year in which she was relatively healthy.

In 2008–2009 the cochairs of the Emeriti Steering Committee met with the Wellesley College provost in the hope of improving the status of and developing new, additional cost-effective programs for retired faculty. They asked the provost to define, formalize, and expand some of the rights and privileges of emeriti faculty. At this time these rights and privileges were explicitly extended to all emeriti faculty (e.g., previously, only emeriti who had been at the college for more than 20 years were allowed to retain their college e-mail addresses). They also made it possible for emeriti to apply for available library office space ("library studies") and regular faculty funds for travel and research. They requested that the provost expressly ask department chairs to allow emeriti faculty to make reasonable use of department resources (such as photocopying) for their research and that departments invite retired faculty to attend lectures and other departmental events. The provost also authorized a modest budget of $500 for the Emeriti Steering Committee, which allowed them directly to sponsor events for their colleagues on campus and to exist as an official entity within the college. The dedication of this relatively small cache of institutional resources, as it has turned out, has been working to the benefit of the entire institution.

These emoluments were just the beginning of a continuing relationship that promises to return more than it demands. Over the past 4 years, the steering committee has come up with other ways to reach out to emeriti colleagues and older members of the faculty and other services that it can perform for the college. On the basis of conversations with their retired colleagues, members of the steering committee were convinced that most newly retired faculty needed more information about how to manage their TIAA-CREF portfolios, especially after the downturn that began in 2008. Also they discovered that most retirees were eager to get advice about many end-of-life issues, such as Medigap insurance, wills and trusts, long-term care, and retirement communities.

Since several recent retirees already had considerable collective experience in those areas of common concern, the steering committee sponsored a series of talks and discussions, featuring emeriti faculty as speakers, for retired faculty and any other faculty who wished to attend. For example, Howard Wilcox, professor of mathematics, emeritus, held informal seminars on pension investment strategies for senior faculty. Sonja Hicks, professor of chemistry, emerita, gave a well-attended lecture on Medicare and Medigap insurance and an informal talk to the local emeriti about the Affordable Care Act. Karl Case, professor of economics and an internationally recognized expert on real estate, spoke to the emeriti about real-estate values, along with Alison Schechter, a local real-estate executive (and wife of Alan Schechter, professor emeritus of political science). A panel of members of the steering committee led a discussion on end-of-life issues. On the basis of these presentations and discussions, the committee has begun to compile a library of resources to meet these informational needs, which they have made available electronically to emeriti faculty. The library includes basic information about estate planning and how TIAA-CREF pensions are subject to both inheritance and income taxes; a template for a letter of last instructions, containing essential information that ordinarily would not be included in a will; basic information about local retirement communities; a narrative about the disposition of a close friend's estate; and some guidelines about how to deal with a family member's dementia.

Another important aspect of the steering committee's work has simply been to improve communication within the emeriti group. Technology provided a platform to make this possible. Ganesan Ravishanker, Wellesley's chief information officer, spoke to the emeriti about information services available to them and the upcoming transition to the Google Apps platform. After the talk the steering committee set up an emeriti Google group as a place for members to post information of interest to the emeriti community. These posts included announcements of shows and concerts by emeriti; special events sponsored by the steering committee; contact information for emeriti currently in nursing homes or hospitals; and descriptions of such resources as the File of Life, a national program that enables emergency personnel to have access to a patient's medical information. Thanks to the grant from the Alfred P. Sloan Foundation, the Library and Technology Services Department has now been able to provide the steering committee with a private emeriti portal on the college website where emeriti can access documents of continuing interest at their leisure. To ensure that emeriti who are still actively involved in research can keep up to date with what new technologies can offer, a member of the Emeriti Steering Committee has been placed (as a nonvoting member) on the standing committee of the academic council that considers library and technology policy. As a result of this nonvoting appointment, the policy about website access for emeriti has been expanded.

Most important, perhaps, the communications of our steering committee of emeriti faculty have not been limited to faculty members who have already retired. An innovation in programming has been to reach out to and include a group of faculty nearing retirement whom the committee has dubbed (for lack of a better term) *pre-emeriti*. Communication between these two groups has, we believe, worked to ease anxieties and answer questions about retirement, so that when faculty do feel ready to retire many of their questions will already have been answered and they will feel they have a cohort of active retired colleagues they can join. Responding to this need in 2008, when the college offered an attractive retirement package to senior faculty, several members of the Emeriti Steering Committee volunteered to chair open meetings with teaching faculty who were considering retirement. Most recently, a small group of emeriti faculty presented a panel to a mixed audience of current and retired faculty members that covered four topics: "Transitioning to Emeritus Status," "Maintaining Involvement With Students and Research," "Planning a Secure Financial Future," and "Negotiating the Medicare Maze." The handouts from this panel have been posted on the private emeriti portal and a video on the For Emeriti page of the college's main website for future reference and for the benefit of the many faculty who expressed interest in the event but were not able to attend.

Every year the steering committee extends an invitation to all faculty over the age of 50 to subscribe to the emeriti Google group. In November 2012 a special invitation was sent to all faculty who had been at Wellesley for 20 years or more. Some 27 out of 139 members of that particular cohort immediately asked to be included. Many of the pre-emeriti faculty who subscribe to the emeriti Google group have taken advantage of the opportunity to keep up with their retired colleagues through their newsletters, which are posted on the private emeriti portal page. Other college webpages are also increasingly including information for and about emeriti faculty, as we continue to build and expand the public "landing page" featuring the emeriti community. For example, to increase awareness of benefits that relate to emeriti (e.g., newly instituted medical benefits for spouses under age 65), the Human Resources Office now has a direct link on the private emeriti portal page, and all the emeriti faculty profiles can be accessed directly from the public landing page as well as on the webpages of individual departments.

In addition, as part of their continuing desire to remain connected to Wellesley, many of our retired faculty members have proved eager for opportunities to give back, literally and figuratively, to the college, which has led to an initiative to involve them in annual fund-raising. Every year the steering committee writes to emeriti faculty asking for contributions to this unrestricted fund. In fiscal year 2011, the contributions of emeriti faculty exceeded $30,000, and in 2012 that number was $40,000. Emeriti faculty are also active contributors of alumnae presentations and are some of the most sought-after speakers to clubs off campus, assisting the college in staying in close touch with its alumnae base. Recent popular emeriti faculty speakers have included a renowned economist talking about the economics of real-estate cycles; an art historian presenting research on Roman copyists of ancient Greek originals; an architectural historian tracing our campus's changing landscape; a classicist exposing academic fraud; and a political scientist speaking about Madeleine Albright, Hillary Clinton, and "the next generation of leaders from Wellesley College."

The desire to stay in touch, however, does not end at the college's gates. Lifelong teachers, our retired faculty harbor a desire to share their research and experience with others in the larger community. The college's assistant vice president for administration saw an opportunity to connect retired faculty members with an organization with which he had been working called Wellesley Neighbors (http://wellesleyneighbors.org), a "village" of senior citizens in the town of Wellesley. He proposed the idea to this organization that our emeriti faculty might be interested in presenting talks to their group, an idea that has borne fruit in a series of lectures that cover both issues of practical interest to seniors and topics more purely academic in nature. For example, talks included "Academic Fictions and Fantasies," about the effects of financial pressure, social engineering, and postmodernism on ways in which academics view reality; "Planning for the Future," with a focus on end-of-life issues; "Ancient Medical Theories and Their Lasting Impact on Modern Attitudes Toward Women"; "How the Housing Market Went Crazy"; and two other talks on the presidential election and landscape planning. Through these lectures emeriti faculty have provided an additional benefit to the college by strengthening our important relationships with our partners in the town of Wellesley. The Emeriti Steering Committee is now planning to continue this cooperation with Wellesley Neighbors during the 2013–2014 academic year, in a series of three multilecture seminars on individual topics funded by the college's Sloan grant.

Addressing Larger Issues Raised by Retiring Faculty

The steering committee will also be exploring other ways that the college can serve all emeriti faculty in creating an inclusive and supportive environment consistent with our resources. Resources for and involvement of emeriti faculty vary across the different divisions of the college. Especially in the sciences, emeriti remain quite actively involved in department life, planning seminars, substituting in classes when active teaching faculty are traveling, and serving as advisers to departmental committees. The Science Center is also a leader in providing space to retired colleagues. Currently, a bullpen office area in the Science Center is shared by emeriti and research postdoctoral students, and some emeriti faculty have entered into arrangements with their individual departments for access to research space and instrumentation. Emeriti are also allowed to maintain space in laboratories as available; longer-term plans exist for shared research space for research-active emeriti to permit them to work with collaborators or to use with non-tenure-track faculty, postdocs, and lab instructors. Emeriti who continue to work with students are eligible to participate in and receive funding associated with the Science Center summer research program. Retired faculty who continue to work with students and who have either internal or external funding for their research are accommodated to the extent possible with appropriate research space, though finding sufficient space is an ongoing challenge.

Space in other buildings, however, has so far proved even harder to locate than space in the Science Center, and the college no longer has a formal faculty common room or special space where faculty and emeriti faculty might gather. Several years ago the college offered the emeriti a shared space in the main library with a computer and printer, but the steering committee learned from a survey that few if any of their emeriti colleagues would make use of it. In general, people wanted private spaces or access to a common room with other faculty. Shared computers no longer seem necessary, since smartphones and tablets have made access to desktop computers and printers less attractive or necessary. Yet emeriti continue to need working space on campus and common space to be shared across generations of faculty, and such spaces should be considered as part of long-term renovation projects that are currently in the planning phase.

In addition, the steering committee needs to have formal bylaws to ensure that the work that it has started will be continued by soon-to-be retirees. While they are still active, the present group of emeriti can make a further contribution to the college by helping to preserve its institutional history. There is precedent for such involvement: several emeriti helped to write the centennial history of the college, *Wellesley College, 1875–1975: A Century of Women* (1975), and we are planning this year to interview members of the emeriti community for an oral history. Another way for our emeriti to contribute scholarship and other papers to the archives exists through the college's institutional repository, which is prominently featured on the private emeriti portal.

To be sure, most of these initiatives require some institutional resources or the time of some willing person, however modest they may be and (in comparison) however profound the benefits they confer. In listening to our recently retired colleagues, however, we have learned that perhaps the most important changes we can make require nothing more nor less than a quiet paradigm shift in our thinking about what "emeritus status" means. A retiring colleague is not departing from our community during the "transition" to emeritus status; he or she merely stands in a different relationship to our academic community while remaining a lifelong member of it. Emeriti faculty continue to produce scholarly work, represent the college to alumnae, and give lectures at other universities. For that reason they need to be treated somewhat differently from other retired employees, and their names should not be removed from the alphabetical directory on the college website (as was the practice in the past). They will from now on not only be listed in the alphabetical directory but continue to be listed (with photographs and short biographies) as faculty on the webpages of their individual departments so that colleagues in their fields can locate them easily and the college can showcase their work. If they wish to be available as mentors to students or junior colleagues or to serve as representatives of the Committee on Curriculum and Academic Policy on oral examinations for departmental honors, department listings and faculty profiles online will provide a ready way to enable the necessary connections. Just as the research of actively teaching faculty is often featured on the institutional website so also should the work and achievements of retired faculty, who also represent the college to the world.

Most important, we need to take care with how these attitudes are conveyed in our communications with faculty as they move through the transition to emeritus status. We would like to conclude with a simple example from one of our own offices. Until recently, each retiring faculty member received a letter, generated from a template, confirming the retirement date, requesting the return of any college-owned equipment, and referring the retiring colleague to Human Resources for advice on benefits. As one of our new emeriti colleagues pointed out to us, this is the type of communication that should appropriately come directly from the Human Resources Office, which would be in a better position to offer concrete support with arranging the termination of specific benefits and to advise on new benefits providers (and in fact already conveys much of this type of information). Communication from the academic side of the institution should, in contrast, acknowledge the individual faculty member's contribution, often over decades, and lay the foundation for that colleague's relationship with the college in the future, a relationship that can continue to be meaningful and productive. As a new emerita colleague told us in an appropriately unretiring way, "All of us, no matter our fields, are readers, good readers. Over the years, we have written and read an abundance of letters of recommendation for colleagues, students, and alumnae. We know a form letter when we see one." It goes without saying that a form letter is never the way to honor a beloved colleague's contribution to the college community.

As each faculty member makes the move from active teaching to the next stage of his or her life, often after decades of tireless effort as a faculty member, he or she deserves our most informed and sensitive celebration. No matter how busy we are, each of us in our everyday tasks, this moment of leave-taking and new beginnings should be the occasion for the full and sincere appreciation of each individual faculty member's contribution. Anything less not only shows disrespect to our common profession and to our personal connections but also risks squandering a valuable resource.

Author Note

Our thanks to several colleagues who were a great help in compiling the information for this chapter: Marymichele Delaney of the Wellesley Human Resources Office; Ruth Frommer, assistant dean of the college for faculty appointments; Linda Miller, professor of political science, emerita; and Cathy Summa, director of the Science Center. Faculty teaching at all ranks are eligible for emeritus status if they have been teaching at Wellesley College at least half-time for 20 years or more. Tenured faculty members become eligible for emeritus status after 10 years of half-time or greater teaching.

11

LEVERAGING THE TALENTS OF FACULTY MEMBERS TO CREATE AN ENGAGED RETIREMENT ECOSYSTEM AT THE UNIVERSITY OF BALTIMORE

Laura Koppes Bryan, Margarita M. Cardona, and Dennis Pitta,
University of Baltimore, and Beverly Schneller, *Belmont University*

The University of Baltimore (UB) is an urban comprehensive master's university located in the heart of Baltimore and one of the 12 public universities in the University System of Maryland (USM). Until as recently as 2006, the mission of UB was to provide upper-level and professional education, including law school. In 2007 UB began accepting first-year students, and it has been undergoing a transformation since then to offer academic programs and services as a 4-year undergraduate institution as well as graduate and professional programs. UB has consistently attended to the work-life effectiveness and satisfaction of all faculty and staff and in 2008 was granted an Alfred P. Sloan Award for Faculty Career Flexibility. Currently, the University Faculty Senate (UFS) appoints the Faculty Work-Life (FWL) Committee, and there is also a university-wide work-life committee. Numerous best practices and policies have been implemented to encourage retired faculty to continue to engage in the life of the university.

A retirement transition project was undertaken at UB with funding from a second Sloan award focusing on faculty retirement transitions. We were especially interested in keeping retiring faculty involved with the university through community outreach. The specific goals of this project included identifying a systemic approach for engaging retiring faculty, securing support from the administration, and collaborating with the community. Notably, the concept of early engagement—that is, securing faculty involvement in the program well before retirement—emerged as a vital element. This chapter describes our efforts as faculty, staff, and administrators to develop a system that is sustainable and mutually beneficial for the stakeholders, including faculty, the university, its organizational partners, and the outside community.

An Engaged Retirement and Its Ecosystem

Defining *engaged retirement* requires consideration of objectives and potential benefits. Our definition is "activity that develops or uses the skills and interests of faculty to benefit the university, the faculty member, and society at large." Engagement could center on the traditional work of faculty— teaching, research, service, and community outreach. For the purposes of this project, we focused on community outreach. With our definition of *engaged retirement* in mind, we conceptualized an "ecosystem" that would encourage engagement through interactions among faculty, the university, and external organizations that are mutually beneficial and self-sustaining.

An ecosystem is a self-sustaining community of organisms interacting as a whole. In this case the ecosystem is composed of active faculty, cooperative external communities, and the university. To be self-sustaining, the three elements have to share value. The faculty provide value in their expertise and willingness to engage with the community. The community provides and receives value in its collaboration with faculty, which may enhance research and service-learning. The university provides value to its environment and its employees by aiding the community.

Because a large percentage of tenured faculty is approaching retirement both on UB's campus and nationwide (Trower, 2012), we devoted considerable effort to researching the nature and scope of engagement and retirement and the benefits and liabilities of each for the faculty, the university, and the community. Separately, the two terms—*engagement* and *retirement*—each have a body of literature. Most of the academic and trade literature focuses on the financial aspects of retirement. Of interest to this project was research on employees' going back to work for their former organization. Brown, Aumann, Pitt-Catsouphes, Galinsky, and Bond (2010) of the Families and Work Institute found that one in five workers aged 50 or older has a postretirement job today and that 75% of workers aged 50 or older expect to have postretirement jobs in the future. A similar phenomenon is observed in higher education.

Engaged Retirement

The concept of employee engagement has been popular in the business press, but only in recent years have academic researchers examined the nature, antecedents, and consequences of employees engaged in the workplace (Llewellyn, Balandin, Dew, & McConnell, 2004; Saks, 2006; Wilson, Harlow-Rosentraub, Manning, & Carroccio, 2008). Engagement has been found to be important for job satisfaction. The Sloan Center on Aging and Work defines *engagement* as "a positive, enthusiastic and emotional connection with work that motivates an employee to invest in getting the job done, not just 'well' but 'with excellence' because the work energizes the person." Another typical definition is "a period when individuals choose to use their experience to engage in work that makes meaningful contributions to society" (Simpson, Richardson, & Zorn, 2012). Businesses, in particular, recognize the importance of contacts outside the organization and thus support external engagement. External or community engagement could be a mechanism for transitioning faculty to retirement and keeping them engaged with an institution.

The literature is mostly silent on *engaged retirement,* which focuses on the university and involves retired faculty pursuing their interests in a meaningful way. What seems vital to engaged retirement is a confluence of university and faculty interests. Those who do not have sufficient interests outside of the university and the teaching profession will be unprepared to enjoy life after the university. Bond and Paterson (2005) found that

> academics exhibit a strong commitment to engagement and interaction with their communities both in principle and practice; that such interaction often takes place at a variety of geographical levels; and that it is often accomplished under less than propitious circumstances.

Notably, few organizations foster off-the-job interests, and as a result they may have workforces predisposed to engagement in retirement.

During our research several important principles that informed and guided our efforts toward engagement emerged; these principles may also be relevant to other institutions.

Guiding Principles for Engaged Retirement of Faculty

Engagement Is a Strategic Process

Engagement requires early and extensive planning and implementation. Logically, tenured faculty, free from the burdens of the tenure track, will be able to devote their attention to possibilities for engagement, such as mentoring, community projects, university-level committees, and faculty senate. However, early engagement may also be valuable for tenure-track faculty, who may enjoy career development opportunities in research, teaching, and service that could improve their chances of achieving tenure. For postretirement engagement to succeed, early preparation is vital.

Engagement Activities Should Be Beneficial to All Parties

The parties involved in engagement activities are faculty, the university, partner organizations, and the community. For faculty, these activities may provide personal fulfillment and help avoid midcareer issues of direction or commitment. For the university, engagement activities may help provide a visionary strategy for meeting the challenges facing education in the 21st century. Partner organizations receive faculty expertise at no or minimal cost, as well as access to university resources. For the community, faculty engagement may provide solutions to current or emerging problems.

Engagement Requires Extensive Coordination

A university is a complex system of interacting elements. For a university to succeed in achieving its objectives, it must work efficiently and harness efforts toward the same goals. For engagement activities to be useful, they must be consistent with university objectives. Moreover, the university must value and support them consistently. The best way to demonstrate university commitment is by providing the following:

- clear objectives based on visionary university values
- coordination across the university schools to avoid inefficiency and promote synergy
- meaningful faculty rewards consistent with career stage, skills, interests, and performance
- sufficient support for successful implementation, including organizational resources, tenure-track policies that support faculty engagement, and a functioning communication infrastructure to promulgate engagement activities
- metrics to assess success and direct any necessary corrections

- effective cooperation and coordination with the external targets of engagement
- university policies that encourage engaged activities and that are consistent with human resource and governmental regulations
- effective communication with all internal and external audiences about the value of engagement activities

Planning an Engaged Retirement Ecosystem

At UB we approached the issue of engaged retirement by seeking to identify the needs of the faculty, university, and community within the context of the university's mission, vision, and strategic directions, both within its regional community and as part of USM. The complex set of actors and their self-sustaining interaction make up the previously mentioned ecosystem.

Phase 1: Identifying Faculty Interests

Planning began by focusing on faculty roles and investment in the UB community and determining how their needs, interests, and perceptions match those of the university. In most organizations, promoting behavior is easier when individual preferences or interests are known. We conducted a series of faculty focus groups designed and administered by experts. Focus group questions and leader guides were developed to obtain the faculty's input on the following issues:

- current retirement practices
- faculty preferences before and after retirement
- current faculty interests that might serve to inform engagement
- ideas that might aid their profession, their careers, and the external community

Leaders facilitated three faculty groups, each with five members:

1. individuals who retired three or fewer years before
2. individuals who were eligible to retire but chose to remain employed (some faculty were well past the current Social Security retirement age [66 years])
3. midcareer faculty who were 10 or more years away from retirement

The last group was included in the study to address our interest in earlier engagement and career development.

The focus group participants were asked to identify their current or previous roles at UB, the most and least satisfying aspects of those roles, their personal readiness for retirement, and their perception of and thoughts about engaged retirement. These questions were intended to determine the extent to which the experiences faculty had at UB shaped their willingness, desire, and interest in remaining part of the UB community.

Written transcripts were prepared and analyzed for major findings. These findings were shared with the UFS FWL Committee and the Provost's Office. For this effort, experts from University Human Resources were added as ad hoc members to the project team led by the principal investigators (PIs). Recommendations from the FWL were shared with the Provost's Office for review by the school and college deans.

The participants in the focus groups were lightly coached on the types of actions the PIs and the UFS FWL Committee had identified as possible ways to remain engaged in UB postretirement. Participants were initially prompted to comment on whether they might consider teaching part-time, mentoring colleagues still employed, and being involved in recruitment efforts as a UB school or college representative. The participants expressed interest in teaching part-time, tutoring and being part of the Achievement and Learning Center (ALC), and working with students as a mentor on college success skills. They were not interested in recruitment efforts, and one participant stated that junior faculty would probably not want to be mentored by retired faculty, whom they might perceive as offering outdated advice. As for community engagement, participants indicated interest in providing mentoring and tutoring to K–12 schools under a UB umbrella. Others said they would be interested in attending meetings as an observer to stay connected to the school or program from which they retired and in listening to faculty authors present on their scholarship. One person wanted to lead tours of France and Italy for faculty and staff, retired and active.

The focus group participants clearly wanted to remain engaged with UB. Specific comments revealed the faculty's interest in ongoing and active involvement in the university community and the important role that the administration could play in providing opportunities for involvement. Some respondents seemed less connected to UB as their careers progressed, possibly because midcareer and senior faculty had fewer new, energizing opportunities for engagement.

Phase 2: Identifying University Interests

It is important to recognize not only faculty preferences but also those of the university. For engagement to be sustainable, it must be a win-win proposition. Faculty skills and efforts will be vital, but if they do not benefit the university, institutional support may disappear. Before engagement opportunities could be created, we needed to determine the following:

- amount of support the university provided for alumni relations
- amount of support the university provided for university development
- nature and extent of university outreach to the community to improve quality of life, business success, economic climate, and civic engagement
- university's commitment to fostering faculty engagement
- university's resources for implementing an engaged retirement ecosystem

Learning university interests was relatively straightforward. We asked administrators and faculty the following questions:

- What are the university's goals for engagement with the community, local government, and local and regional organizations?
- What are the university's needs in retaining staffing flexibility?
- How important is retaining organizational memory?
- What are the current community outreach efforts?
- What are other important university values?

We also looked at the USM plan titled *Powering Maryland Forward: USM's 2020 Plan for More Degrees, a Stronger Innovation Economy, a Higher Quality of Life* (USM, 2010) and found two complementary goals: (a) advancing Maryland's competitiveness in the innovation economy by building on existing levels of extramural research funding and a culture of innovation and entrepreneurship throughout USM and (b) transforming the academic model with course redesign strategies that help more students understand material, complete their degrees, and become better qualified to join the workforce. These goals identify specific university interests that might support a variety of opportunities for faculty engagement.

Additionally, the university-wide strategic planning coordinating group consists of faculty and administrators from across the campus. This group has as part of its charge (a) coordinating campus dialogue and outreach regarding institutional values, priorities, goals, and objectives and (b) aligning institutional planning with the USM 2020 plan and the state plan for higher education.

In addition to the strategic planning process, UB has instituted a planning effort titled "UB21: Creating the 21st Century University." "UB21 Catalyst" grants are supported by internal institutional funding designed to promote transformative growth through faculty and staff-driven projects and committees. Currently, there are several committees whose efforts shape university interests and innovations, and provide a variety of avenues for creating and supporting postretirement opportunities.

Phase 3: Identifying the Larger Context or System of University and Community Engagement

UB educates leaders predominantly in the greater Baltimore–DC metro areas and throughout the state of Maryland, and, thus, serving the community has always been a priority. The Carnegie Foundation designated UB as a "community-engaged" institution for its extensive service, partnerships, and scholarly activity in its urban neighborhood.

Each of the university's colleges and schools offers significant community outreach opportunities (Figure 11.1). These opportunities include over 30 formalized activities or relationships that benefit Baltimore and the region and range from discrete projects to more encompassing centers and institutes. They involve a number of activities that may be classified as (a) improving the relevance of instruction; (b) applying faculty expertise to benefit the

Figure 11.1. Examples of UB Engagement Activities

- **The Jacob France Institute** (part of the Merrick School of Business) provides opportunities for faculty research benefiting the community.
- **The Schaefer Center for Public Policy** (part of the College of Public Affairs) provides opportunities for faculty research benefiting the community.
- **The Helen P. Denit Honors Program** has performed community service through the local organization Civic Works.
- **UB Community Service Day**
- **Yale Gordon College of Arts and Sciences (CAS)**
  - Faculty from CAS have worked with numerous local Baltimore organizations, including the People's Community Health Center, Station North, the Central Baltimore Partnership, Baltimore Heritage, Artscape (the annual Baltimore arts festival), Baltimore Historical Society, Maryland Historical Society, and Enoch Pratt Free Library.
- **College of Public Affairs (CPA)**
  - CPA maintains a robust set of continuing professional education programs, including Election Judge Training, the Maryland Certified Public Manager (CPM) Program, and the Master Manager Program, conducted with the Baltimore City Public School System. In addition CPA provides a Public Sector Strategic Management for Senior Leadership program, a Certificate in Community Building Strategies, and the Roper Victim Assistance Academy.

(Continues)

Figure 11.1. Examples of UB Engagement Activities (Continued)

- **School of Law (LAW)**
  - LAW maintains the Law Career Development Office, which administers a number of outreach activities, including attorney externships, judicial externships, the EXPLOR Program, and the Pro Bono Challenge Program. There are a variety of clinics and centers, including the Innocence Project; the Civil Advocacy Clinic; the Immigrant Rights Clinic; the Mediation Clinic; the Appellate Practice Clinic; the Community Development Clinic; the Criminal Practice Clinic; Disability Law Clinic; and the Center for Families, Children and the Court. In addition, the tax faculty, who are up to date on the latest changes in the federal and Maryland tax code, offer inexpensive tax clinics for local businesses. The clinics are managed and promoted by UB to support local business and achieve part of the USM plan requirement to boost the economy.
- **Merrick School of Business**
  - MSB created the Center for Entrepreneurial Innovation to assist student and community entrepreneurs with their business plan design, as well as to provide education and contacts with potential investors, government agencies, and businesspeople. Current entrepreneurship faculty who are experienced in mentoring students and helping them develop successful businesses are interested in helping entrepreneurs outside of UB. The center has developed multiple contacts and sources of assistance within the entrepreneurial community. This effort will aid in the USM plan to increase the numbers of businesses in Maryland. In addition, it offers technology advice through its information systems faculty. MSB also offers technology education aimed at the community in the form of a nationally recognized technology camp for qualified area high school students for an intense weeklong program to showcase technology and foster student mastery of new developments.

community, government, primary and secondary education, and business; and (c) interacting with other organizations to further development of knowledge for the profession. These existing activities developed over time as a result of faculty interest, input from the community, and university strategic decisions.

In addition to community outreach programs and opportunities hosted internally, UB has significant contact with USM, the city of Baltimore, and organizations within Baltimore and the state of Maryland. UB has relationships and joint programs with a number of other USM schools, including Towson University, Coppin State University, the University of Maryland–Baltimore, as well as with universities around the world. UB has stressed cooperation with our partner schools in curriculum development, maintenance of accreditation standards, and research.

Phase 4: Identifying Current University of Baltimore Retirement Practices

In 2008 UB received an Alfred P. Sloan Award for Faculty Career Flexibility for its Balance That Works Program, which promoted flexible career paths for faculty and encouraged retired faculty to remain involved with the university through volunteerism, scholarly contributions, and other activities. Some of the existing UB retirement policies were implemented as a result of this award. UB published a comprehensive guide to institutional policies and resources regarding retirement, titled *Policy for Engaged Retirement and Privileges of All Retired Faculty* (University of Baltimore, 2010c), which highlights several ways faculty can remain involved after retiring.

Engaged Retirement Policy

The Engaged Retirement Policy aims to maintain the close relationship between an active faculty member and the university and includes a substantial list of benefits. Retired faculty have access to university e-mail and computer accounts; can use library, athletic, parking, and dining facilities; are invited to select university events (e.g., community service day, convocation, alumni events); and are entitled to any applicable faculty discounts to university cultural activities. They may also mentor students and faculty, serve on committees, and teach classes for compensation. UB offers emeriti faculty clerical and financial support to help them travel to conferences and the opportunity to keep a named chair position and have dedicated and private office space, which is unusual for an urban campus. The university's Human Resources Office also maintains a time line tool that helps faculty plan their retirement transition.

Phased Retirement

Faculty now have the right to request a phased transition to retirement. The policy is compliant with state of Maryland and USM policies and allows faculty to

> reduce their workload for up to a three (3)–year period, from 100 percent to 75 percent or 50 percent and will be compensated on a prorated basis. (Fifty percent time is the minimum standard under Maryland law for employee eligibility for health care benefits.) During their Phased Retirement, faculty members will remain eligible for prorated merit raises and cost of living adjustment (COLA) as may be approved by the State and USM. (University of Baltimore, 2010a, p. 1)

This phased retirement arrangement instructs deans to attempt to accommodate a faculty member's request, subject to the needs of students, other faculty, and funding availability.

Emeriti Status

UB has clearly articulated procedures to grant emeriti status to faculty in their final year at the university. Emeriti status conveys the same privileges enjoyed by retired faculty as set forth in UB's Engaged Retirement Policy. *Policy for Emeritus and Emerita Faculty* (University of Baltimore, 2010b) treats "engagement" as a relationship between the faculty member and the university. It tends to focus on activities typical of current faculty and the internal workings of the institution.

Other Initiatives

As part of the current Sloan award, we are pursuing additional initiatives that will enhance the engagement of retired faculty. One initiative is dedicating a campus space for a retired faculty lounge that will include workstations and computers. A second initiative is the development of a work-life website that will include retirement policies and practices. A third initiative is the establishment of a grant program that would provide retirees with funds for community engagement projects.

Phase 5: Developing a Plan for an Engaged Retirement Ecosystem

As described earlier, UB is highly engaged with its external community, or ecosystem. One element not addressed in current retirement practices and policy is the relationship among retired faculty, the university, and the community at large. The project PIs, along with others on campus, believe that retired and soon-to-retire faculty have much to give to the university's mission as a public, regional institution of higher education through community engagement. We propose an engaged retirement ecosystem with self-sustaining fluidity among the university, faculty, and community. Growing this ecosystem will require the following steps.

Stakeholder Buy-In

One of the most important elements of a successful engaged retirement ecosystem is recognition of mutual benefits for all stakeholders. As described earlier, UB's draft strategic plan and numerous other policies and activities demonstrate the value the university places on engagement. However, many stakeholders are vital to ensure that the initiative is successful.

Faculty. Before the newest policies were put into place, UB's retirement policies limited retirement payment and involvement options. The current Engaged Retirement Policy overcame these limitations and alerted faculty to potential new opportunities. The initiative is still new to most faculty and will bear fruit over time. There is anecdotal evidence of interest in engagement activities among current faculty. Many midcareer faculty, having achieved tenure, are ready to reinvigorate their professional lives. These faculty seem to value the changes in retirement policy and are receptive to the concept of the active retirement.

The Association of Retired Faculty will announce enrichment opportunities to its members. The association and the college deans are aware of the benefits that productive retirees may bring. Beyond the positive publicity resulting from faculty outreach, retirees can provide important workforce augmentation benefits. While they may not see themselves as mentors for junior faculty, they are valued by students for their experience. In addition, in tight budgetary times the university can use academically qualified retirees to help maintain college professional accreditation at lower cost. Their contribution simplifies and adds flexibility to faculty workforce planning.

Administration. The provost and deans are members of the president's Executive Committee, which meets regularly and responds to the president's strong support for work-life balance. As noted in the references, the president and provost approved and supported policies affecting retiring faculty. In-kind contributions are indicative of administration support. For example, staff members are dedicated to the implementation of this project and policies. The Office of Human Resources plays an important role in advising a specific prospective retiree about financial and health-care benefits. Provisions are provided for retired faculty to use office space, and recently, a retired faculty space has been designated for conducting research, participating in seminars, and partnering with community organizations. The president and provost approve and formally recognize faculty with the emeriti designation. Retired faculty are invited to college and university events.

USM. As part of USM, each policy developed for UB must be compliant with USM policies. Within the last 5 years, UB developed several new USM-compliant initiatives. Existing administrative relationships can be used to cooperate with other universities in the system. One of UB's important links to USM is the Council of University Faculty Senates (CUSF). CUSF is composed of two faculty representatives from each campus and shares information and collaborates on system-wide faculty governance. Many important work-life and community engagement issues have been implemented uniformly across the system as a result of CUSF activities.

USM presidents and provosts maintain frequent contact. As a winner of the Sloan Award for Faculty Career Flexibility, UB garnered attention and interest from other USM universities. The current initiative is similarly recognized. After our engaged retirement ecosystem is in place, UB can reach out to other system schools to communicate our system and collaborate.

Community partners. Given UB's location, we find that our community's needs and demands are greater than our resources. In fact, developing contacts with community partners is an ongoing activity. Each of the colleges and schools has contacts with alumni, the general public, and external business, nonprofit, and government organizations. Existing contacts have been developed to enrich student learning by recruiting experts as class speakers and providing real-world experience through an extensive series of projects and internships. For example, the Law School continually brings noteworthy speakers, judges, and practicing attorneys to campus for the benefit of both its students and the community. The Yale Gordon College of Arts and Sciences, the College of Public Affairs, and the Merrick School of Business (MSB) maintain an extensive speaker series in which local and nationally known experts share their expertise with students, faculty, and the local business community.

The faculty also manage service-learning projects and supervise internships. For example, each MSB department chair oversees an internship program in a certain area. The chair is responsible for identifying and recruiting suitable students and internship sites. To provide sufficient numbers of internship sites, chairs work with their faculty's professional contacts and university development staff. The current community buy-in and contacts will be valuable for potential faculty engagement activities.

Engagement Priorities

We contend that faculty should be engaged earlier in their careers to facilitate their success in retirement. Representatives from the Strategic Planning Committee, the provost's and deans' offices, the UFS, and UB21 committees were included in a planning group to identify UB priorities for engaging faculty. As a result of the deliberation, several critical areas were identified, including supporting current initiatives embodied in programs, workshops, and institutes distributed among the colleges. Efforts to enhance and foster innovation as well as changes in the technological environment emerged as important themes. One priority is equipping our students to live and thrive in a digital world, which will require new philosophies, teaching and interacting methods, and techniques for learning. As noted earlier, each school and college has significant and important ongoing community engagement activities that can benefit current and retired faculty.

Implementation

Implementation of the engaged retirement ecosystem relies on solid support from all elements of the university. Fortunately, UB's president, Robert Bogomolny, has designated faculty work-life and engagement as his legacy. During his tenure at UB, great strides have been made with the help of the earlier Sloan award and support from our administration. That commitment and aid raised the importance of faculty engagement in the set of competing university priorities. Several initiatives support community engagement activities of current faculty, which can provide the foundation for the engagement of retired faculty.

In many cases faculty have the aptitude to engage in the community, but they may not have refined or developed their skills or services to the degree needed. The university can step in to provide opportunities for professional development. Such development opportunities not only make a faculty member a more capable professional but also increase his or her value to the community and the marketplace. Currently, the UB Bank of America Center for Excellence in Learning, Teaching, and Technology (CELTT) provides opportunities for faculty and staff to discuss, share, and promote best practices. With regard to community engagement, the codirectors facilitated a faculty learning community on fostering experiential learning in courses. A UB21 catalyst grant funded a faculty group to survey service-learning and experiential activities on campus, as well as host experts to help faculty become more engaged through their classrooms.

Some specific activities in support of faculty involvement with targeted objectives before retirement are already supported, including the following:

- course releases to allow preparation
- service assignments to foster activity
- strategic planning for each faculty member to include targeted organizations and projects and expected outcomes
- matching of faculty to projects and organizations
- UB21 Catalyst grants designed to develop skills in strategic areas

Recently, the Office of Academic Innovation, reporting to the provost, was established within the Division of Academic Affairs. One aspect of this office is promoting and creating experiential and community engagement activities with faculty. The Office of Career Services also builds relationships with organizations. All these initiatives support current faculty, which is critical for fostering faculty commitment throughout their careers and thus increasing the likelihood that they will remain engaged after retirement.

The focus group findings informed and prompted two specific actions. One is finalizing with the Office of the President a "retirement recognition" package of services. The second is using a variety of sources to develop an engaged retirement plan that creates a sense of community and promotes the idea of UB as the faculty's intellectual legacy. For the engaged retirement ecosystem to thrive, UB needs to establish a mechanism or provide opportunities for those faculty transitioning into retirement to explore how they might continue to contribute to UB, its students, and its future, as well as direct their talents to community outreach activities.

Responsibility for Implementation

The ultimate responsibility for fostering an engaged retirement ecosystem lies with the university president, who has pledged his complete support to faculty work-life issues and engagement. However, because the specifics of each particular form of faculty engagement differ by academic unit, each dean will be responsible for implementation in his or her unit. Implementation will require department and division chairs to be involved and active in the process. In addition, the UFS approved the creation of the Association of Retired Faculty to provide a vehicle for improving the quality of life of retired faculty and opportunities for postretirement enrichment and engagement.

Conclusion

UB has benefited greatly from both of its Sloan awards. The awards have changed the expectations of faculty and the administration and created a climate of collaboration and creativity. We have come to view academic retirement as one stage in a continuum of productivity. To be effective, engaged retirement requires a foundation of shared values, preparation, support, and direction—an engaged retirement ecosystem consisting of a self-sustaining community of active faculty, cooperative external communities, and the university as a whole. It should not be an 11th-hour venture or an afterthought. Instead, it may well be the culmination of a career of learning and service that benefits all. Like saving for retirement, preparing for an engaged retirement should be done earlier rather than later.

References

Bond, R., & Paterson, L. (2005). Coming down from the ivory tower? Academics' civic and economic engagement with the community. *Oxford Review of Education, 31*(3), 331–351.

Brown, M., Aumann, K., Pitt-Catsouphes, M., Galinsky, E., & Bond, J. T. (2010, July). *Working in retirement: A 21st century phenomenon.* New York: Families and Work Institute.

Llewellyn, G., Balandin, S., Dew, A., & McConnell, D. (2004). Promoting healthy, productive ageing: Plan early, plan well. *Journal of Intellectual and Developmental Disability, 29*(4), 366–369.

Saks, A. M. (2006). Antecedents and consequences of employee engagement. *Journal of Managerial Psychology, 21*(7), 600–619.

Simpson, M., Richardson, M., & Zorn, T. E. (2012). A job, a dream or a trap? Multiple meanings for encore careers. *Work Employment and Society, 26*(3), 429–446.

Trower, C. A. (2012). *Success on the tenure track: Five keys to faculty job satisfaction.* Baltimore: Johns Hopkins University Press.

University of Baltimore. (2010a). *Faculty phased retirement.* Baltimore: Author.

University of Baltimore. (2010b). *Policy for emeritus and emerita faculty.* Baltimore: Author.

University of Baltimore. (2010c). *Policy for engaged retirement and privileges of all retired faculty.* Baltimore: Author.

University System of Maryland (USM). (2010). *Powering Maryland forward: USM's 2020 plan for more degrees, a stronger innovation economy, a higher quality of life.* Adelphi, MD: Author.

Wilson, L. B., Harlow-Rosentraub, K., Manning, T., & Carroccio, J. (2008). Preparing for the baby boomers: Lifelong learning and civic engagement in active-adult communities. *Seniors Housing and Care Journal, 16*(1), 67–82.

12

COLLABORATIONS WITH THE COMMUNITY

Katherine Haldeman, *George Mason University*

George Mason University, in Fairfax, Virginia, is recognized internationally for its innovation, diversity, and entrepreneurial spirit. Mason offers a wide variety of degree programs, dynamic faculty and staff, and a diverse student body on multiple campuses throughout Northern Virginia. For university faculty, Mason provides innovative programs that facilitate a smooth retirement transition, including a faculty retirement transitions leave program, a medical bridge program, comprehensive pre-retirement education programs with financial counseling, life-planning seminars, and the Retirement Connection program (http://hr.gmu.edu/worklife/connection), which encourages Mason retirees to stay connected to the university. Mason's interest in helping faculty and staff transition to retirement has been long-standing. This commitment is reflected in the current programs offered and in the new creative retirement transition programs that are being developed. In addition, Mason values its connection with the surrounding community and collaborates with community organizations to provide retirement transition seminars and to facilitate opportunities for fulfilling life experiences following retirement. The university has been actively involved in meaningful collaborations with Fairfax County and other community nonprofit organizations. For retiring Mason faculty, these collaborations potentially provide rewarding opportunities for involvement within the community.

George Mason University and Community Collaborations

Community outreach is highly valued at George Mason University, and both faculty and staff at various levels actively contribute to this goal. Outreach opportunities include volunteering in the community within nonprofit organizations, local school systems, and health-care institutions in the area. The resulting collaborations are fundamental to our institutional identity and figure strongly in our strategic vision. Faculty in particular can make valuable connections and build a network of contacts with the broader community (Office of Government and Community Relations, 2013).

Because George Mason University values the surrounding community, we collaborate with local organizations to provide retirement transition seminars and to facilitate opportunities for fulfilling life experiences following retirement. Past and ongoing collaborations are with Fairfax County, Leadership Fairfax (www.leadershipfairfax.org), Volunteer Fairfax (www.volunteerfairfax.org), the Positive Aging Coalition (http://positiveaging coalition.wordpress.com), and the Osher Lifelong Learning Institute (OLLI; www.olli.gmu.edu). The resulting programs from a number of these community collaborations are detailed in this chapter.

Your Next Chapter: Charting the Course to Your Retirement

In 2008 Dr. Lois Tetrick, then director of the Industrial and Organizational Psychology Program at George Mason University, collaborated with Dorothy Keenan, supervisor of senior services in the Fairfax County Department of Community and Recreation Services, and others to host a local session of the Second Annual Positive Aging Conference. The goal of the conference was to advance a national conversation about positive aging. It was simulcast from the University of Minnesota (see their website for more information: www.csh.umn.edu/index.htm).

Following the conference, Tetrick, Keenan, and others formed the Positive Aging Coalition in January 2009 to assist people who were transitioning into retirement by helping them find pathways to meaningful work and opportunities for significant community service following retirement. Positive Aging Coalition members collected feedback from the participants of the 2008 conference in the hopes of finding which topics were of interest to transitioning retirees. Four themes emerged as being important to this population in achieving a "purposeful life": "re-careering (encore careers), community involvement (civic engagement), life-long learning, and healthy aging (fitness, wellness, and social connectedness)" (Positive Aging Coalition, n.d.).

Following this analysis of important themes, Tetrick and Keenan were inspired to partner in the creation of a course focusing on retirement transitions, titled Your Next Chapter: Charting the Course to Your Retirement. Fairfax County provided funding through a contract agreement, between George Mason University and Fairfax County, to develop the course and offer it jointly to Fairfax County employees and George Mason University employees. Fairfax County wanted to collaborate with George Mason University on the development of this course because of the credibility that Mason faculty would bring to the venture. Per the contract, George Mason University was responsible for the development of the Your Next Chapter program and the specific program curriculum, with Fairfax County providing final approval of the curriculum and the process, as well as some of the staff to implement the program. The mission of the program was to provide opportunities for adults of retirement age to explore personal resources, attitudes, preferences, motivation, skills, and interest in order to create individual plans to stay healthy, active, and connected to families, friends, and communities during the transition into retirement. The specific goals were as follows:

1. Identify personal motivators of transitioning retirees as they explore their next stage of life.
2. Identify personal skill sets and other resources that may be applied in retirement.
3. Develop an awareness of self as it relates to retirement.
4. Explore opportunities for career changes, community engagement, life-long learning, fitness, wellness and leisure in Northern Virginia.
5. Develop an individual plan for retirement.

George Mason University was to implement the Your Next Chapter pilot program at various county facilities, and the county agreed to provide coordination of the project, including identifying county resources necessary to accomplish the agreed-upon project tasks, identifying participants who would be included in the pilot program, and training Mason staff on relevant county policies and procedures (D. Keenan, personal communication, 2012).

A pilot program of Your Next Chapter was offered in September 2009. The course was taught to Mason faculty and staff and to county employees by educators from George Mason University and Fairfax County who had been certified as Too Young to Retire (2Young2Retire) facilitators. The instructors' training course was based on the book *Too Young to Retire: 101 Ways to Start the Rest of Your Life* (Stone & Stone, 2002). Each of the participants received an official acknowledgment that they had been trained as 2Young2Retire facilitators (www.2young2retire.com).

During the Your Next Chapter pilot program, a variety of program formats were tried. First, four 2-hour sessions, every other week, were offered. Then, in response to feedback from participants, the program was offered as two half-day sessions. Finally the program was adapted into one all-day workshop. For Mason employees, the all-day session seemed to be the most appealing. In all versions, the course involved 8 hours of time. Fairfax County employees seemed to prefer either the two half-day or the four 2-hour sessions. Therefore, we have concluded that the desired format will vary depending on the population being served.

The Your Next Chapter course is both interactive and thought provoking, as the emphasis is shifted from the financial aspects of retirement to the social implications of this pivotal transition period. A person's career gives him or her social contact, recognition, a daily routine, a chance to use skills, and opportunities to be productive. Most of the baby boomers want a retirement that fulfills many of these same needs. The uncertainty of transitioning into what's next can be daunting for many individuals. Participants who took the class discussed topics such as changing roles within their relationships, career and part-time work, the value of community involvement, changing family commitments, and enjoying a life of leisure. They had an opportunity to reflect on their own goals, and they were provided with tools to create an individual, customized retirement plan.

Because George Mason University places such value on its continued connection to the surrounding community, and because the program had been successful since its inception in 2010, Your Next Chapter was offered to the public as a noncredit workshop through the university. The course was offered in several formats throughout the county, with each class totaling 8 hours, and class materials were provided. For example, recently the course was offered to the community as a one-session class, on a Saturday and a Thursday, from 8:30 a.m. to 5:00 p.m. A couples-only version was also offered on a Saturday from 8:30 a.m. to 5:00 p.m. (L. Tetrick & D. Keenan, personal communication, 2012). The grant from Fairfax County that funded the Your Next Chapter course ended in the fall of 2013. Tetrick is seeking additional grant funding and considering other funding options (e.g., tuition fees) to maintain this well-received program.

Lifetime Leadership Program

According to the Corporation for National and Community Service (2007),

> Over the past two decades, a growing body of research indicates that volunteering provides not just social benefits, but individual health benefits as well. The research has established a strong relationship between volunteering

and health. Those who volunteer have lower mortality rates, greater functional ability, and lower rates of depression later in life than those who do not volunteer. (p. 1)

As a result of a partnership among Leadership Fairfax, Volunteer Fairfax, George Mason University, the Positive Aging Coalition, Fairfax County Neighborhood and Community Services, and the Fairfax County Area Agency on Aging, the Lifetime Leadership Program (LLP) was created in 2012 to educate and train retirees who want to offer their skills and leadership expertise by volunteering within the community (Leadership Fairfax, 2012). The LLP is administered by Leadership Fairfax and is self-funded by course tuition fees. It addresses the themes of civic engagement, encore careers, and social connectedness. Participants enjoy new social and community connections while learning more about Fairfax County and its needs as they convert a wealth of knowledge into meaningful roles. This 2½-month program includes five biweekly sessions and provides an overview of ways for retirees to transition into their next chapter of life by informing participants of the needs within the community and training retirees to contribute their talents and skills. The leadership course is designed for retirees who want to move their lives from "success to significance" and helps program participants recognize their potential in the second half of their lives. The course provides transition training for both high-level volunteering and community engagement and is designed on the basis of the belief that retirees offer a wealth of experience, leadership, and vitality to the community. With a lifetime of accumulated skills and experiences, participants in the LLP are inspired to connect and make a difference by volunteering in the community.

Leadership Fairfax was able to contribute its expertise in running programs and currently oversees the program, providing oversight and handling logistics. George Mason University provides curriculum development and speakers to address lifelong learning, encore careers, leadership, social entrepreneurship, and legacies. Fairfax County provides information regarding county collaboration with the state, issues in the county, and county resources. Volunteer Fairfax assists in matching the skills of the program participants, who want to volunteer, with nonprofit organizations that need support. The Positive Aging Coalition assists in connecting interested people to the LLP (D. Keenan, personal communication, 2012).

Osher Lifelong Learning Institute

The Osher Lifelong Learning Institute (OLLI), an affiliate of George Mason University, with three locations in Northern Virginia, provides opportunities for mature adults to explore intellectual and cultural subjects, as well as to share their experiences and talents. Participants enjoy learning with "no homework, no exams, no required college degree, and no age threshold" (OLLI, 2013). For an annual fee of only $360, members may take as many classes as they like throughout the year; the institute also offers an introductory rate of $150 for limited offerings. Classes meet between 9:40 a.m. and 3:40 p.m. on weekdays during four seasonal terms for a total of 26 weeks per year. Members also enjoy campus privileges, such as use of the Mason libraries and bookstore and discounts at dining services, health and fitness facilities, the Center for the Arts, and more. Many ongoing activities and clubs are available throughout the year, including the Investment Forum, History Club, OLLI Players (readers' theater), Computer Club, and Photography Club. Prospective members may visit up to two class sessions of any course or activity (as space is available) at no charge.

OLLI members participate in resource groups that develop over 360 courses and activities each year. Members brainstorm ideas for courses that would be of interest and recruit qualified speakers and instructors who volunteer their time and talents. Approximately half of OLLI courses are facilitated or taught by OLLI members themselves (some of whom are Mason retirees), 25% are taught by Mason faculty, and the remainder of the instructors are recruited from the vast array of expertise available in the Washington, DC metropolitan area.

Community Collaborations

These programs, and others, are made possible because of the importance George Mason places on community involvement. As a public institution, George Mason University provides School Assistance & Volunteer Service Leave, a Commonwealth of Virginia policy, which allows Mason classified and administrative or professional faculty to receive paid leave of up to 16 hours per year or in some cases 24 hours per year. Volunteering in the community has been supported throughout the years. At Mason, if faculty want to be involved in a project that has a service component, the academic departments are generally supportive. This is in large part because of the culture at George Mason, where community collaborations are valued and supported by the upper levels of management, as mentioned earlier. Academic departments recognize what is gained by the university when their faculty and staff partner with the community and the local county. As an example, Tetrick, the Mason point person for the Your Next Chapter course, was encouraged by the center that initially housed the program, her home department, and the dean of the College of Humanities and Social Sciences to expand her local community involvement. This resulted in her helping to develop the LLP. In addition, academic departments recognize that these community connections may already exist because many outstanding members of the Fairfax County and greater Washington metropolitan area community serve as adjunct faculty at Mason, bringing their expertise and experience into the classroom, thus benefiting Mason students and Mason programs (L. Tetrick & D. Keenan, personal communication, 2012).

Challenges of Implementation

Community collaboration is not always seen as a major mission or major component of a faculty position. This can be a challenge to the development and implementation of collaborative programs. The collaborations count as a service component within a faculty position, but several of them have also served as research projects. On the issue of retirement, some program participants may think that their retirement transitions or plans to volunteer are too personal to be part of a research project, so researchers must find a way to collect the information they need without compromising the privacy of the participants. Regardless of the type of partnership that ensues, it is recommended that a contract be written and signed between the collaborating parties (e.g., the university, the county, and other community organizations) so that each partner knows what his or her responsibility is during the completion of the project and beyond.

Sustaining collaborative programs can be difficult if the academic institution or the community organizations do not decide to institutionalize the new programs. At Mason, an advisory committee has been established to explore ways to make these programs and community collaborations sustainable. Mason, for example, offered a trial pilot of the Your Next Chapter course specifically for the general public. The course offered was successful, and planners are now looking at the possibility of developing a Continuing Education course to be offered to the community as a way of nurturing the partnership. Other possibilities include development of formal public-private partnerships with Fairfax County. We continue to look for grant funding for continued research associated with these programs and yet to be developed programs (L. Tetrick, personal communication, 2012).

Dorothy Keenan, now retired as the supervisor of senior services in the Fairfax County Department of Community and Recreation Services, was a pioneer in bringing community partners together to achieve a common goal. These are her suggestions for others who want to create collaborative partnerships:

- Establish a relationship—Look for what you have in common. Look for parallel themes and common goals for partnerships. University faculty or administrators can develop relationships and network with the surrounding community by becoming members of community boards or commissions.
- Identify resources—What can each partner provide or do for the project? Look for complementary skills or resources.
- Identify the key players within each organization—Make it clear how the project benefits each of the partners involved.
- Understand your target audience—Do the research to determine what they want and need. Determine the best way to reach them when it is time to market the program.
- Set strategic goals and outcomes—Use these in program development and in creating the evaluation process.
- Develop a time line—Write a report if you fall behind on the time line. Review and readjust the time line as needed.
- Start with a pilot program.
- Evaluate on the basis of expected and realized outcomes.
- Revise the program on the basis of program evaluation results.
- Continue to update the program on the basis of new research and current relevant resources. (D. Keenan, personal communication, 2012)

Retirement Transitions Education

Because Mason is able to benefit from a robust involvement with our community, we also help faculty plan for ways to stay connected and engaged beyond the formal and structured programs listed earlier. Many of our pre-retirement programs are open to prospective retirees as well as their spouses or partners. Our life-planning seminars have the goal of preparing faculty and staff to age well, and our Retirement Connection program encourages faculty and staff to stay connected to the institution after retirement (Human Resources and Payroll Department, 2013). Both of these programs are administered by the Work/Life Team within the Human Resources and Payroll Department.

Research indicates that people plan more for a 2-week vacation than they do for their retirement, yet pre-retirees today say they want fulfillment and meaning in their later years (Freedman, 2011). To achieve these goals, they need encouragement, insight, and an action plan from a retirement transitions coach. The Human Resources and Payroll Department of George Mason University has long wanted to provide individualized, one-on-one counseling for retirement transition planning. Frequently, such counseling has not included guidance regarding the major social and psychological changes that this life transition involves. Today, with more employees bearing the responsibility for preparing for a secure retirement, a growing number of employers are offering retirement coaching as part of their benefits package. Barbara Hogg, retirement communication leader at Aon Hewitt, states that retirement looks a lot different from decades past. "We are seeing an emerging interest in providing more retirement counseling to the rank and file," she explained. The coach is someone who "can handhold the employee through the process of retirement," including the logistics of certain decisions and understanding of the steps along the way (cited in Gurchiek, 2011).

Mason is taking a holistic, full-spectrum approach to retirement preparation. The Human Resources and Payroll Department is developing a program that focuses on planning a lifestyle to support health, meaning, and purpose during the phase of life following retirement. The professional retirement coaching program will provide one-on-one retirement coaching for individuals who want this specific assistance. These topics include, but will not be limited to, managing and structuring time, keeping life orderly and in sync with the beat of the culture and world around us, and finding a sense of utility, purpose, or meaning in life. A pilot study for the new retirement coaching program is under way to provide a more personalized program. During one-on-one retirement transition coaching, program participants are working with certified retirement transition coaches to understand what effect the retirement process will have on their physical and emotional health and overall wellness, as well as how to avoid feeling a lack of purpose after retiring. Our stated objectives for the one-on-one retirement transition coaching program are to facilitate the process of establishing lifelong goals for each program participant and assist them as they make the transition to retirement. Through this program, participants will identify values, skills, and talents that they can use in retirement and they will develop a plan for making the transition into retirement, which will consist of "to do" items for retirement preparation and a time line for the completion of these items.

We have conducted three faculty focus groups on retirement transition programming. In each focus group, we asked faculty the following questions:

- What have your colleagues, friends, or relatives told you about retirement?
- What are key issues or concerns about your future retirement?

- What is the most challenging part of planning for retirement (e.g., deciding where to live, determining what to do during retirement, coordinating retirement timing with a significant other)?
- What are some ways in which Mason could make the retirement transition more manageable and smoother for faculty?

We are using the data from the faculty focus groups to improve and enhance our faculty retirement transition programs and to better assist our faculty in preparing for this major life change.

Life Planning and the Encore Stage

Life planning is investigating preferences and meaning in life beyond money. It engages an individual in systematically thinking through the possibilities for the remainder of his or her life. It is a process conducted to help people (a) focus on the true values and motivations in their lives, (b) determine the goals and objectives they have as they see their lives develop, and (c) use these values, motivations, goals, and objectives as a framework for making choices and decisions in life that have financial and nonfinancial implications or consequences.

Participants in the life-planning process make successful transitions possible by addressing needed job training, identifying in which fields jobs will be available (e.g., health care, education, the emerging green economy, and aging), and customizing their plans as necessary. At Mason we believe that the time has come to develop a new paradigm suited to the encore stage of life, blending vocational preparation, personal transformation, and intellectual stimulation. Renewal and reevaluation of one's life path occurs through a look back over one's life and then looking forward to incorporate personal values, skills, and motivations. Encore careers provide income, new meaning, and social impact, which can enhance society at large (Freedman, 2011).

The retirement transition programs at George Mason University are being designed to address the encore stage. We expect to assist our faculty in preparing for a fulfilling life after retirement by providing opportunities for them to remain healthy, active, and connected to their families, friends, and communities. We hope to help facilitate connections that lead to community service, lifelong learning, meaningful work, self-discovery, and well-being in retirement.

Conclusion

Faculty retirees have a lifetime of accumulated skills and experiences. We hope that through all the programs outlined in this chapter, retirees will be inspired to transform their wealth of knowledge and experience into meaningful new roles. For some, retirement may involve entering new paid positions, becoming volunteers in their community, using their skills, expressing their values, and finding meaning in their later years.

References

Corporation for National and Community Service. (2007, April). *The health benefits of volunteering: A review of recent research*. Retrieved from http://www.nationalservice.gov/pdf/07_0506_hbr_brief.pdf

Freedman, M. (2011). *The big shift: Navigating the new stage beyond midlife*. New York: Public Affairs.

Gurchiek, K. (2011, March 7). *Retirement coaching gives employees a handle on future: More than just handing employees a to-do list for retirement planning*. Retrieved from the Society for Human Resource Management website: http://www.shrm.org/hrdisciplines/benefits/articles/pages/retirementcoaching.aspx

Human Resources and Payroll Department, George Mason University. (2013). *Retirement connections*. Retrieved from http://hr.gmu.edu/worklife/connection

Leadership Fairfax. (2012). *Lifetime Leadership Program (LLP)*. Retrieved from http://www.leadershipfairfax.org/lifetimeleadersprogram

Office of Government and Community Relations, George Mason University. (2013). *A university engaged*. Retrieved from http://relations.gmu.edu/community-relations/information-resources/a-university-engaged/

Osher Lifelong Learning Institute (OLLI), George Mason University. (2013). Retrieved from http://www.olli.gmu.edu

Positive Aging Coalition. (n.d.). Retrieved from http://positiveagingcoalition.wordpress.com/about/

Stone, H., & Stone, M. (2002). *Too young to retire: 101 ways to start the rest of your life*. New York: Penguin Group.

PART FIVE

TAPPING INTO THE BIGGER PICTURE: MISSIONS, SYSTEMS, AND NATIONAL ASSOCIATIONS

13

WORKING WITHIN YOUR INSTITUTIONAL MISSION

Mary Kochlefl, *Xavier University*

According to Hindu tradition, life is divided into stages (Smith, 1991). Whereas the first half of life is composed of student and then householder stages, the second half of life consists of retirement and renunciation stages. According to Huston Smith, noted scholar of world religions, Hindus describe the retirement stage as traditionally beginning with the arrival of the first grandchild. It is also considered the time when an individual can withdraw from the responsibilities that characterize the householder stage, such as family, vocation, and civic social obligations, and instead focus internally. Smith describes the importance of this phase: "For many years society has exacted its dues; now relief is in order lest life end before we understand it" (p. 40). Spiritual adventurers in this phase were known as "forest dwellers" as they pursued self-discovery in solitude, which required taking leave of their families and homes. This time, explains Smith, is "for working out a philosophy, and then working that philosophy into a way of life" (p. 40). Those in the final stage of life, renunciation, become further detached, even from geographical connection, and released so from limitations that they are virtually anonymous.

When Father Leo Klein, SJ, a Jesuit priest at Xavier University, encountered this description as a faculty member teaching a course on world religions, the conceptualization of human life as stages, particularly the intentionality around later life, struck him as significant. In 2007, having served

159

as vice president for mission and ministry at Xavier and then retired himself, Klein wanted to lead others in conversation about purposeful self-discovery during, or heading into, the retirement stage. Called Second Fifty: Spirituality in Later Life Issues, Klein's program was designed by himself and several Xavier alumni initially for alumni only, and then it was expanded to include retired or retiring Xavier faculty and staff. Klein thought Second Fifty met a need he had often heard expressed by older friends and colleagues, namely, the need to make sense of one's life by reflecting on the past and seeking meaning for retirement. It required, as Hinduism had expressed, freeing oneself from the family and work obligations of earlier years and intentionally approaching later life as having its own new purpose.

For Xavier to offer a program such as Second Fifty is highly appropriate given its mission as a faith-based institution in the Jesuit and Catholic traditions. The Jesuit value of *cura personalis*, care for the whole person, calls the university to be concerned with multiple dimensions (including the intellectual, moral, and spiritual dimensions) of the lives of its students, employees, and alumni. Xavier's Center for Mission and Identity is charged with orienting faculty and staff to this mission and providing ongoing programs of education and support. This charge is increasingly important as the number of clerical Jesuit faculty decline and lay faculty and staff must play a more significant role in maintaining the university's Jesuit mission and values. The center offers as its cornerstone program Assuring the Future Mission and Identity of Xavier (AFMIX), which engages faculty and staff in a 2-year educational process on the Ignatian vision and its role in the classroom and other learning environments. The program includes readings, lectures, and reflection enhanced by weekly group discussions. Almost 200 faculty and staff have participated since 1999 in one of the seven AFMIX cohorts. The center more recently has developed a comprehensive mission orientation for members of Xavier's Board of Trustees and new senior administrative leadership.

The Ruth A. and Robert J. Conway Institute for Jesuit Education, which is part of the Center for Mission and Identity, focuses more specifically on supporting faculty in their engagement with Xavier's mission. Unique among the 28 Jesuit colleges and universities in the United States, Xavier's Conway Institute promotes and enhances the infusion of contemporary Ignatian-driven teaching methods in the classroom. A faculty member serves as the Conway Institute's director of faculty programs, receiving release from half of his or her teaching responsibilities to provide creative leadership for mission-related activities involving faculty. The faculty member holding this position rotates every 1 to 3 years. In addition, the Conway Institute annually supports a faculty fellow to undertake a pedagogical project that makes a significant mission-related impact on the curriculum, learning environment, and students' academic experience at Xavier and beyond. The Conway faculty fellow receives a summer stipend, project budget, and release from teaching responsibilities to complete the proposed project. Conway faculty fellows have engaged in a wide range of projects that have addressed issues such as sexual justice on a Jesuit campus, international service-learning in computer science, and accessibility in online courses.

Several of the Conway Institute's programs have been targeted toward particular phases of faculty life, with the acknowledgment that different needs and opportunities present themselves as faculty move through their careers. The Ignatian Mentoring Program, for example, pairs faculty—typically junior faculty—with tenured faculty in their same college to discuss the Jesuit mission and identity in relation to their own disciplines and careers. The Time to Think Program was offered in 2009–2010 to support and encourage midcareer faculty reflection on the three primary spheres of professorial activity (teaching, scholarship, and service) within an Ignatian academic context. The Xavier Mission Academy, started in 2011–2012, similarly focuses on mid- and late-career faculty, providing them with a working knowledge of Xavier's mission and the tools needed to further integrate that mission into their classes in personally and professionally appropriate ways.

Although Xavier has been offering mission-oriented programming to all faculty and staff for many years, an intentional focus on late-career faculty has been created more recently, informed by faculty development models already in place at Xavier. These new offerings include a mission-focused program through the Conway Institute specifically addressing late-career faculty issues called Taking Time to Reflect, as well as a faculty learning community (FLC) on faculty legacy projects, operated through Xavier's Center for Teaching Excellence (CTE). For the Taking Time to Reflect Program, guiding questions, readings, and images are presented in modules online, narrated by senior faculty. These readings guide small-group conversations among late-career faculty who participate in the program's monthly meetings. The FLC targeted to senior faculty, started in fall 2012, is engaged in a yearlong conversation about the issue of legacy. Led by two faculty facilitators, the FLC has nine additional members. All three of Xavier's colleges—Arts and Sciences; Social Sciences, Health, and Education; and the Williams College of Business—are represented. Xavier's CTE, which opened in fall 2010, has to date hosted 16 FLCs, which in total have engaged more than 130 faculty (out of a full-time faculty numbering approximately 350). Adopted from a successful model started at Miami University of Ohio in 1979, Xavier's FLCs have addressed faculty desires for community building tied to deeper exploration of teaching-related issues.

Second Fifty: Spirituality in Later Life Issues

The new programs targeted to late-career faculty are being designed to include consideration of Xavier's Jesuit Catholic mission, including the spiritual dimension of the retirement phase as addressed in Second Fifty. In its original configuration, Second Fifty met nine evenings, approximately once every 3 weeks, from October through April. Each 2-hour meeting started with a brief discussion with the whole group followed by smaller group conversation facilitated by committee members and included appetizers and beverages. Participants also receive materials, including books and DVDs. Participants pay a fee of $110–$150 to cover the costs of mailings, food, and materials. The sessions progressed through a range of topics using readings and films, read and viewed before the sessions, as starting points for reflection and discussion. The program concluded with a final session devoted to wrap-up conversation (See Table 13.1.).

A key text for the program is *The Gift of Years: Growing Older Gracefully* by Sister Joan Chittister, OSB (2008). In this book Chittister hopes to address what is lacking in gerontology, namely, "awareness of the spiritual dimensions of the only part of life that gives us the resources we need to make a long-term evaluation of the nature and meaning of life itself" (p. x). Echoing Hinduism, Chittister claims,

> But perhaps the most important dimension of aging well lies in the awareness that there is a purpose to aging. There is a reason for old age, whatever our state of life, whatever our social resources. There is intention built into every stage of life, no less this one than any other. (p. xi)

Her chapters on topics such as legacy, transformation, and adjustment usefully guide reflection for sessions of Second Fifty. These and other readings are supplemented by films, including *Tuesdays With Morrie* (Forte, Winfrey, & Jackson, 1999), which documents newspaper columnist Mitch Albom's conversations with his 78-year-old sociology professor who is dying from Lou Gehrig's disease, and *Away From Her* (Iron, Urdl, Weiss, & Polley, 2006), about a couple married 50 years who struggle after the wife develops Alzheimer's disease. These films serve to raise issues regarding health, legacy, and loss, which are more fully explored during discussion.

Second Fifty participants engage in activities such as creating a heritage or ethical will. With its origins in the Hebrew Bible, the ethical will (*Zevaoth* in Hebrew) is a document for passing along values to subsequent generations. As Jacob on his deathbed offered his blessing to his sons and named his desired burial place (Genesis 49:1–33), so too more recent iterations of the ethical will focus on providing direction and communicating a legacy. This

TABLE 13.1

Second Fifty Schedule

Meeting	Topic	Readings/films
1	Introduction and Orientation: Transformation	Chittister, J. (2008). "Transformation." In *The gift of years* (pp. 39–43). New York: BlueBridge. Smith, H. (1991). "The stages of life." In *The world's religions* (pp. 40–41). New York: HarperCollins.
2	Review of Your Life: Memories/Reconciliation/ Wholeness	Chittister, J. (2008). "Regret." In *The gift of years* (pp. 1–5). New York: BlueBridge. Guntzelman, L. (2008, December 31). We measure time but what's it about? *Western Hills Press*, B2. Hassel, D. (1977). "Prayer of personal reminiscence: Sharing one's memories with Christ." *Review for Religious, 36*, 213–226. Maclay, E. (1990). "Occupational therapy." In *Green winter: Celebration of later life*. New York: Henry Holt. (Original work published 1977) Tolstoy, L. (2004). *The death of Ivan Ilyich*. New York: Bantam Classics.
3	Your Image of God	Arias, J. (1973). *The god I don't believe in* (pp. 1–4). St. Meinrad, IN: Abbey Press. Chittister, J. (2009, August 29). "The god who beckons." *National Catholic Reporter*. Retrieved from http://ncronline.org/news/spirituality/god-who-beckons Fischer, K., & Hart, T. (1986). Images of God. In *Christian foundations: An introduction to faith in our time* (pp. 34–49). New York: Paulist. Himes, M. (1995). "Living conversation." *Conversations on Jesuit Higher Education, 8*, 21–27. Weintraub, J. (Producer), & Reiner, C. (Director). (1997, October 7). *Oh, God!* [Motion picture]. United States: Warner Brothers Pictures.

(Continues)

TABLE 13.1
Second Fifty Schedule (Continued)

Meeting	Topic	Readings/films
4	Growing Older: Loss, Limitation, and Possibilities	Choice of book or film: Genova, L. (2007). *Still Alice.* New York: Gallery Books. Forte, K., & Winfrey, O. (Producers), & Jackson, M. (Director). (1999, December 5). *Tuesdays with Morrie* [Motion picture]. United States: Carlton America & HARPO Productions. Iron, D., Urdl, S., & Weiss, J. (Producers), & Polley, S. (Director). (2006). *Away from her* [Motion picture]. Canada: Capri Releasing & Lionsgate Films. Also: Chittister, J. (2008). "Adjustment," "Fulfillment," and "Limitations." *The gift of years.* New York: BlueBridge.
5	Your Spirituality, Your Wisdom	Chittister, J. (2008). "Spirituality." *The gift of years* (pp. 179–183). New York: BlueBridge. Frankl, V. (2006). *Man's search for meaning.* Boston: Beacon Press. (Original work published 1946) Rohlheiser, R. (1998). "What is spirituality?" *The holy longing* (pp. 3–19). New York: Doubleday. Sirach, chapter 1. 1 Corinthians, 1:17–25.
6	The Role of Prayer	Chafets, Z. (2009, September 20). "Is there a right way to pray?" *New York Times Magazine,* 42–47.
7	Your Legacy	Chittister, J. (2008). "Legacy." *The gift of years* (pp. 215–218). New York: BlueBridge.
8	Dying as Part of Living	Bernardin, J. C. (1998). *The gift of peace.* New York: Doubleday.

document is often contrasted with or seen as supplementing the distribution of material possessions specified in a traditional last will and testament. It provides the opportunity to articulate, as Chittister (2008) calls it, our "immaterial legacy" (p. 216). Says Chittister, "Our legacy is far more than our fiscal worth. Our legacy does not end the day we die. We have added to it every moment of our lives" (p. 217). And as "the crowning moment of the aging process," legacy is also the "major task" of later years; it is a work that remains in progress and that can be intentionally shaped so as to leave behind the meaning that we intend and that can guide others. "In this period of life," Chittister concludes, "we have both the vision and the wisdom to see that the legacy is what we want it to be" (p. 217).

In Second Fifty the heritage-will activity is conducted during the session on legacy. Discussion during this meeting is prompted by the following questions:

- What "real issues" are especially important to you at this time in your life? Has there been a change in what you consider "real issues" as you've grown older?
- What specific ways, besides a written document, could you use to help your loved ones know of the legacy you want to leave them?
- What attitude toward life do you want to leave behind?
- Is there someone with whom you should make amends so that you don't leave a legacy of hurt?
- Is there a specific work or project or goal you want to accomplish before you die?

The heritage will can be thought of as a love letter addressed to a specific individual or group, such as the entire family, "loved ones," or friends. Adapted from the article "Estate Planning: How to Draft an Ethical Will" by Vanessa Cross (2009), the following prompts are used for drafting the document:

- The world I grew up in was . . .
- I am grateful to you for . . .
- Here are some important lessons I've learned in my life . . .
- My definition of happiness (or success or satisfaction) is . . .
- The books that are dearest to my heart are . . .
- There are many things I changed my mind about as life went on. Here are some of them . . .

Participants in Second Fifty have valued the program and its emphasis on preparing them to live more conscious, spiritually integrated lives.

Responding to a survey at the end of the year, participants cite the variety of materials and the small-group discussion as important aspects of the program. They find it beneficial to stay in the same small groups through the program so that trust can be built among members. Some participants describe Second Fifty as filling a gap in addressing the spiritual aspect of later years. One wrote on the survey, "It's very valuable to be able to discuss such important issues with fellow travelers and to hear their stories and feedback. There is so much out there about aging, retirement planning, etc. but most lack a spiritual perspective." Others value stepping outside their daily responsibilities to reflect intentionally on their retirement, as Hinduism promotes. One participant said the program "helped me realize I have much to gain and to give in the later years of life. It helped me in making the decision to retire and to embrace a less 'scheduled' daily life."

Although the program has had as many as 46 participants in the nine-evening format, attendance has varied, and alumni have shown more interest than retired faculty. For spring 2013 Second Fifty was offered in a three-Saturday format to see if this schedule is more convenient. Retiring faculty, who have been invited to participate in the last two sessions, seem less interested in addressing their later years immediately when their careers shift to retirement. Their hesitance may confirm what one Second Fifty participant considered a drawback to the program, what she called an emphasis on the last quarter rather than second half of life. Faculty may be less willing, at least immediately, to let go of a career identity that can be so interwoven with their personal lives and less eager to examine retirement as a new and distinct phase.

Taking Time to Reflect

To assist faculty before they retire, and while they are possibly contemplating that transition, Xavier has enhanced existing faculty development efforts with opportunities directly addressing the late-career perspective. The Taking Time to Reflect Program, developed by Debra Mooney Corcoran, PhD, assistant to the president and chief mission officer at Xavier, was offered by the Conway Institute for Jesuit Education for the first time in fall 2013. The program includes seven Web-based sessions with videos, readings, activities, and reflection questions, coupled with monthly group meetings facilitated by the Conway Institute director of faculty programs. The sessions ask faculty to revisit topics, such as Jesuit history and values, addressed in other mission-related programming. These topics are considered, primarily through the activities, reflection questions, and group meetings, from the late-career faculty perspective. For example, in the session on Ignatian spirituality, the activity invites participants to engage in a daily reflection such as St. Ignatius Loyola's *Examen*, a series of introspective prompts focused on expressing gratitude, petitioning for knowledge of God and self, reviewing the day, responding to the review, and looking forward. This is expanded to an Ignatian Annual Examen, a reflective review of the past year guided by similar prompts. The session on Xavier's history includes reflection questions similar to the heritage-will exercise in Second Fifty. Inviting participants to consider their individual connections to the development of the institution, the questions include the following: (a) In what ways have I influenced the history of Xavier? and (b) How do I want to be remembered by my fellow colleagues?

The Taking Time to Reflect Program fits well within an existing scope of mission-related programming that faculty will likely have participated in earlier in their careers at Xavier. By connecting faculty's individual paths to the institutional mission and history, the program will engage faculty in reflection on their personal journeys in ways that are both familiar and non-threatening. Although the program is not overtly focused on retirement or spirituality, it may help faculty examine their life's work at Xavier in meaningful ways that will help them transition to the retirement phase when they are ready.

Faculty Learning Community and Fellowship on Legacy Projects

Xavier's CTE started an FLC on faculty legacy projects in fall 2012 as a means of enhancing existing faculty development efforts with a new opportunity targeted to late-career faculty. FLCs have been popular at Xavier for connecting faculty across departments and colleges and providing opportunities to engage in conversations related to teaching. An important aspect of FLCs is their focus on the individual projects of participants. Although community building is critical to the model, FLCs are encouraged to move beyond discussion to some type of implementation, ideally experimentation by faculty in their classes. However, unlike committees or task forces, which are familiar models for faculty, FLCs do not operate under a charge; they are not tasked with fixing a problem or putting forward a recommendation. Their direction and use of time and budget are determined by the members themselves, led by one or two facilitators. For its yearlong exploration, the group is given a $10,000 budget that can be spent on up to $500 in professional development funds per member, as well as expenses related to meetings (including food), retreats, dissemination, and projects.

The Faculty Legacy Project FLC has not been entirely typical of FLCs supported by Xavier over the last 3 years. Because of the grant funding supporting it, through the Alfred P. Sloan Award for Best Practices in Faculty Retirement Transitions, the topic was initiated by the CTE and then facilitators were recruited to lead the community. The FLC also began in late fall 2012, instead of August, so it did not quite run the full academic year as other FLCs have. The call for applications was successful, even though it went out midsemester, and attracted interested participants from all three of Xavier's colleges.

Given the creative space to consider legacy projects, the members have generated a range of ideas they are now pursuing. Several participants are interested in capturing the history of faculty and academic projects at Xavier in repositories that will continue to build over time. For example, a sociologist is developing a faculty oral history project to capture the stories of faculty nearing retirement or recently retired. An education faculty member is videotaping and interviewing one of the founders of Xavier's Montessori education program, an internationally known program that was one of the first university-based programs in the United States to prepare Montessori teachers. This project will help document Xavier's Montessori history and also provide a resource for Montessori education courses. In addition to these individual projects, the group has wanted to provide input to the administration about policies related to faculty retirement and strategies for continued involvement of retired faculty in university life. To that end, several members have collaborated on a survey for senior faculty whose results will be shared broadly on campus during the 2013–2014 academic year.

The CTE is designating another FLC for 2013–2014 for a topic related to late-career faculty. Faculty interested in facilitating this FLC have been asked to propose specific topics, from which one will be selected. All faculty will then be invited to apply to participate as one of the 8–12 members of the community. In the future, senior faculty can continue to propose FLC topics related to the late-career stage in the annual open call for applications. FLCs, which are designed to be a comfortable place for faculty-led conversations, will be an appropriate means of fostering ongoing dialogue about late-career issues.

In addition to supporting a second FLC on a topic particular to late-career faculty, the CTE has offered a fellowship for 2013–2014 on the topic of legacy. This will provide an extended opportunity for a faculty member to implement a legacy project. Each year the CTE has supported three faculty fellowships, one funded through the Conway Institute for Jesuit Education, on timely topics related to teaching. While one fellowship annually focuses on Jesuit education, the other two fellowships have addressed current issues, such as sustainability, international education, community engagement, and high-impact learning practices. The faculty fellow on implementing a faculty legacy project will also participate with two other fellows in 2013–2014 to conduct significant projects with impact on the university and, potentially, other institutions of higher education. Each faculty fellow receives a summer stipend, project budget, and one-semester release from all teaching responsibilities.

The faculty legacy fellow may be chosen from the membership of the Faculty Legacy Projects FLC—one who would like to implement a larger-scale version of his or her individual FLC project—or may be another faculty member who has not participated in this FLC. In the call for fellowship proposals, the following examples were given to suggest possible fellowship topics:

- preserving the history of faculty or faculty work such as academic programs or lectures
- providing for the transitioning or sustaining of an existing program after faculty retirement
- designing and implementing opportunities for retired faculty to remain engaged at Xavier

The CTE expects that the Faculty Legacy Fellowship will result in a project of importance and also demonstrate how support for legacy projects can affect faculty individually and collectively. Future faculty fellowships may have a similar focus, as one ongoing faculty fellowship topic that has emerged is expanding an FLC topic. Faculty who have participated in FLCs related to faculty legacy or other late-career issues will be eligible to propose a fellowship project under this broad category.

Conclusion

Xavier's culture of *cura personalis* makes possible a consistent and ongoing engagement of faculty in the university's Jesuit Catholic mission. Xavier's efforts to support faculty through the stages of their careers, including their transition to retirement, draw on this charism. Second Fifty's emphasis on the spiritual dimension of later life, while overlooked in most retirement-related programming and foreign within university culture at many institutions, has context and history at Xavier and, indeed, is helping inspire and enrich faculty development efforts related to late-career stages. As Hindu tradition asserts, the later stages of life deserve dedicated time and space and warrant rich reflection. Programs focused on the transition to retirement can help faculty contemplate the meaning of their careers, which are often a life's work, comprising many years in a single profession (and sometimes a single institution) and interwoven deeply with their personal lives.

In implementing enhanced programming specific to late-career faculty, Xavier has intentionally built on existing faculty development structures, including those related to mission and teaching. Xavier's active Center for Mission and Identity now includes Taking Time to Reflect among its multiple programs addressing the spectrum of the faculty career from pre-tenure through pre-retirement. The CTE similarly is including late-career topics, such as faculty legacy, among its FLC and faculty fellowship focus areas. Adding programs specific to late-career issues within familiar faculty development structures will increase participation and interest in these efforts and help ensure their long-term sustainability. Ideally, conversation about late-career issues and retirement will become as commonplace among faculty development topics as efforts to support new and midcareer faculty. Like most higher education institutions, Xavier has a significant number of faculty in the late stage of their career or approaching retirement. Many have been shaping the university culture and the lives of Xavier students for decades. Support for these faculty recognizes the importance of their past and ongoing role in the institution.

References

Chittister, J. (2008). *The gift of years: Growing older gracefully*. New York: BlueBridge.

Cross, V. (2009, November 26). Estate planning: How to draft an ethical will. *Suite101*. Retrieved from http://suite101.com/a/how-to-draft-an-ethical-will-a173954

Forte, K., & Winfrey, O. (Producers), & Jackson, M. (Director). (1999, December 5). *Tuesdays with Morrie* [Motion picture]. United States: Carlton America & HARPO Productions.

Iron, D., Urdl, S., & Weiss, J. (Producers), & Polley, S. (Director). (2006). *Away from her* [Motion picture]. Canada: Capri Releasing & Lionsgate Films.

Smith, H. (1991). *The world's religions*. New York: HarperCollins.

RETIREMENT AT THE FRONTIER

Challenges and Benefits of Being in State Systems

Binnie Singh and Maureen L. Stanton, *University of California–Davis*

As one of 10 universities that collectively make up the University of California (UC) system, UC Davis is faced with a growing population of faculty approaching retirement age. Most of these faculty have been deeply committed to their academic lives for decades, and their dedication will potentially make it difficult for them to envision a fulfilling retirement. To address this burgeoning need, our Academic Affairs unit is seeking ways to help those faculty who either are contemplating retirement or have recently retired develop a broader and more positive vision of their postacademic lives. In this chapter we aim to share the current institutional context in which our emeriti (or soon-to-be emeriti) find themselves. We discuss opportunities for continued engagement and the challenges that face those retiring from UC Davis. In addition, we describe new developments in our unique approach to this expected postinstitutional demographic transformation and discuss how some of our efforts can offer opportunities to emeriti faculty that will facilitate system-wide efforts to build excellence in an era of unprecedented institutional change. We provide data on faculty retirements over recent years to demonstrate why creating clear pathways toward a fulfilling retirement is important to our campus and to the UC system as a whole. We also describe some of the benefits and challenges of being one campus that is developing its own retirement-focused programs within a larger institutional framework.

Last, we discuss the enhanced opportunities that UC Davis has to engage our emeriti faculty as our campus grows over the next decade.

Commitments to Guide Our Way

UC Davis is a land-grant institution built to advance the human condition through improving the quality of life for all people of California, all citizens of our nation, and the rest of the world. From our health to the economy, from the air we breathe and the food we eat to how we experience, perceive, and interpret life, UC Davis has impact through teaching, research, and public service. UC Davis is regarded, both domestically and globally, as a leader of higher education, dedicated to providing a socially relevant, world-class education. Our "Vision of Excellence" (UC Davis, 2010) is built around a series of major goals, and here we emphasize how retired faculty can contribute to the achievement of those goals. Retired faculty can be engaged in realizing the UC Davis "Vision of Excellence" in the following ways:

Foster a vibrant community of learning and scholarship. Through transformative and diverse opportunities for learning, UC Davis will inspire and prepare its students, faculty, staff, and alumni to lead and excel in solving the dynamic challenges of tomorrow's world. Emeriti faculty are invaluable as both teachers and mentors at all levels. As experienced instructors, they can devote more time and effort to the kinds of teaching that are most effective in fostering critical thinking. As successful scholars and academics, they can help to guide early career faculty on successful trajectories.

Drive innovation at the frontiers of knowledge. Building on the interdisciplinary strengths of its faculty, UC Davis will promote a collaborative environment that spurs innovations in learning and research by discovering ideas that take shape at the frontiers and intersections of academic disciplines. Many emeriti faculty continue to engage in extramurally funded research, and in so doing, they create new knowledge. As research leaders who are focused on just this aspect of academic pursuit, they can be particularly effective mentors to undergraduate researchers, graduate students, and postdoctoral scholars.

Embrace global issues. UC Davis will be the university of choice for international students, postdoctoral scholars, faculty, prestigious international and governmental exchange programs, and research enterprises that have transnational and global applications. Our emeriti population is highly international and globally engaged. Accordingly, through travel, Education Abroad, and other forms of international outreach, they elevate the global literacy of our U.S. students as well as global awareness of UC Davis as a destination for international students and scholars.

Nurture a sustainable future and propel economic vitality. UC Davis will be the preeminent university partner in advancing the economic prosperity of our region, fostering the burgeoning life-science, agricultural, and clean-energy industries of California, and investigating and sharing socially, politically, economically, and environmentally relevant solutions to global problems. Sustainability continues to be an area of interest and expertise for our emeriti and soon-to-be emeriti, many of whom have developed lifelong contacts in industry, government, and public constituencies that can be of tremendous value to faculty at earlier career stages.

Champion health, education, access, and opportunity. Guided by its commitments to social responsibility and community engagement, UC Davis will support and sustain healthy, equitable communities in which all will have access to the benefits of education and discovery. Many of our emeriti faculty remain in the area after they retire and then serve as critical liaisons between the campus and our local community. As advisers, consultants, and advocates, they help to reinforce the campus commitment to doing local good, while also building awareness and appreciation for UC Davis throughout our region.

Cultivate a culture of organizational excellence, effectiveness, and stewardship. UC Davis will provide an efficient, professional administrative organization that is committed to serving and advancing the university's academic mission. Achievement in the advancement of the university's academic mission requires knowledge and proven success. Many of our emeriti served in key campus leadership roles before retiring. In consultation with the chancellor and the Academic Senate, emeriti provide insights and experiences that aid our efforts to improve administrative processes. In addition, some emeriti are recalled to serve in interim leadership roles, whereas others may lead or join teams focused on special new projects.

The Demographics of Faculty Retirement Across the University of California System

As a system, UC is aware of the aging faculty population. Figure 14.1 shows that when UC faculty leave the system altogether, they are generally entering into retirement, as recognized by the system's eligibility rules. As a result they begin to draw down on the retirement investments that the system provides, either through our defined benefits program or our defined contributions plan.

Over a 10-year period, from 2002–2003 to 2011–2012, the average percentage of separations owing to retirements was approximately 51.4%, with retirements being the primary reason for separation since 2003–2004. Figure 14.2 highlights the trend over the same 10-year period of the separation of faculty by category, such as resignation or retirement.

Last, Table 14.1 outlines the percentages of separations that were retirements by campus, the headcount by campus, and the retirement rates by

Figure 14.1. University of California ladder and equivalent rank faculty separation type by year

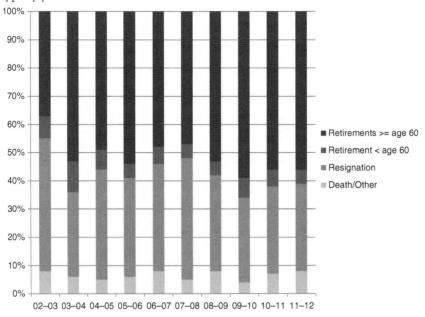

Note: Created April 24, 2013; UCOP: Office of Academic Personnel.

Figure 14.2. University of California ladder and equivalent rank faculty average age by separation type by year

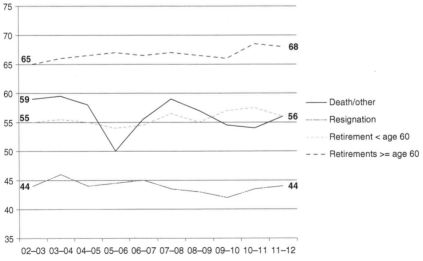

Note: Created April 26, 2013; UCOP: Office of Academic Personnel.

TABLE 14.1

UC-Wide Ladder and Equivalent Rank Faculty
Retirement Separations by Years by Campus
Total Faculty Headcounts by Year by Campus
Retirement Rates by Year by Campus
General Campus and Health Science, 2002–03 to 2011–12

	02–03	03–04	04–05	05–06	06–07	07–08	08–09	09–10	10–11	11–12	10 Year Average
Berkeley	28	57	28	55	31	28	41	47	42	35	39
Davis	34	34	33	30	30	48	31	40	49	38	37
Irvine	8	15	24	24	31	25	16	22	26	14	21
Los Angeles	11	22	28	31	29	22	26	31	63	40	30
Merced	—	—	—	1	1	—	—	3	1	—	2
Riverside	6	14	15	13	8	14	13	15	13	19	13
Santa Barbara	10	15	18	20	13	20	21	30	18	22	18
Santa Cruz	5	7	11	6	15	7	13	22	6	19	12
San Diego	13	17	15	21	16	19	15	30	30	30	19
San Francisco	1	5	11	10	6	16	12	15	15	14	32
10 Year Total	**116**	**186**	**183**	**211**	**180**	**199**	**188**	**255**	**263**	**231**	**223**
% retirements to all separations	**45%**	**63%**	**54%**	**59%**	**55%**	**54%**	**59%**	**68%**	**62%**	**61%**	

(Continues)

TABLE 14.1 (Continued)

	02–03	03–04	04–05	05–06	06–07	07–08	08–09	09–10	10–11	11–12	10 Year Average
Faculty Headcounts											
U-Wide	**8,348**	**8,644**	**8,838**	**8,910**	**8,992**	**9,142**	**9,342**	**9,389**	**9,282**	**9,180**	**9,007**
Berkeley	1,339	1,350	1,363	1,371	1,367	1,380	1,383	1,391	1,385	1,385	1,369
Davis	1,351	1,413	1,461	1,472	1,465	1,453	1,458	1,490	1,462	1,417	1,444
Irvine	863	919	959	989	1,007	1,040	1,079	1,068	1,044	1,078	1,005
Los Angeles	1,706	1,749	1,764	1,726	1,753	1,784	1,825	1,835	1,813	1,769	1,772
Merced	—	—	—	47	71	83	107	118	125	132	98
Riverside	547	574	593	586	592	626	662	653	632	628	609
Santa Barbara	766	805	816	810	807	817	813	812	796	783	803
Santa Cruz	454	482	494	500	512	511	528	530	516	514	504
San Diego	974	1,004	1,038	1,060	1,067	1,088	1,130	1,137	1,150	1,153	1,080
San Francisco	348	348	350	349	351	367	357	355	359	348	353
Retirement Rates											
U-Wide	**1.4%**	**2.2%**	**2.1%**	**2.4%**	**2.0%**	**2.2%**	**2.0%**	**2.7%**	**2.8%**	**2.5%**	**2.2%**
Berkeley	2.1%	4.2%	2.1%	4.0%	2.3%	2.0%	3.0%	3.4%	3.0%	2.6%	2.9%
Davis	2.5%	2.4%	2.3%	2.0%	2.0%	3.3%	2.1%	2.7%	3.4%	2.7%	2.5%
Irvine	0.9%	1.6%	2.5%	2.4%	3.1%	2.4%	1.5%	2.1%	2.5%	1.3%	2.0%

Los Angeles	0.6%	1.3%	1.6%	1.8%	1.7%	1.2%	1.4%	1.7%	3.5%	2.3%	1.7%
Merced	—	—	—	2.1%	1.4%	—	—	2.5%	8.0%	—	1.7%
Riverside	1.1%	2.2%	2.5%	2.2%	1.4%	2.2%	2.0%	2.3%	2.1%	3.5%	2.2%
Santa Barbara	1.3%	2.2%	2.2%	2.5%	1.6%	2.4%	2.6%	3.7%	2.3%	2.4%	2.3%
Santa Cruz	1.1%	2.2%	2.2%	1.2%	2.9%	1.4%	2.5%	4.2%	1.2%	5.8%	2.4%
San Diego	1.3%	2.2%	1.4%	2.0%	1.5%	1.7%	1.3%	2.6%	2.6%	1.2%	1.7%
San Francisco	0.3%	2.2%	3.1%	2.9%	1.7%	4.4%	3.4%	4.2%	4.2%	4.0%	3.0%

Notes: Merced shows 7 year average

CTOs include 010, 011, 030, 031, 040, 041, 210, 211, 221, 520, 521, 530, 531

Created April 19, 2013; UCOP: Office of Academic Personnel

year over a 10-year period. According to these figures, the trends in average retirement rate appear to be consistent among the campuses over the 10-year period. For example, the percentages of retirements at Berkeley and Davis, campuses that have similar headcounts, were fairly consistent, except for a couple of increased percentages at Berkeley. (UC Merced has fewer retirements because it is a new campus with a younger faculty. It also has a relatively small faculty, and so average retirements across the system are driven mostly by the older, larger campuses.)

These data confirm that separations by retirement will probably accelerate at the more established UC campuses over the next decade. The need to focus on transitioning to retirement is especially strong at UC Davis and UCLA, both of which have significant numbers of faculty 70 years of age or older.

What Does Retirement Mean to Academic Faculty Members?

The university's faculty is aging just like the rest of today's workforce. An academic, however, will likely have a different outlook on what it means to retire than a nonacademic. Most faculty have devoted their lives to scholarly activities—making discoveries and creative advances (and speaking and writing to disseminate their achievements), providing instruction and guidance to students, and participating in shared university governance. In all these activities a faculty member exercises a strong creative voice. This consuming dedication to one's work does not suddenly evaporate upon retirement, and so many faculty find it difficult to envision alternative passions that will fully engage them as emeriti.

The challenge of building a rewarding retirement is also shaped by changing demographics over time. As noted by Freedman and Moen (2005), "Health and longevity have been stretched, creating the possibility of a new decades-long stage of life between the career- and family building phase and the onset of true old age." Given the reality of longer and healthier lives, there is an urgent need to help the aging faculty population engage with the university in ways that will be rewarding for both the individual and the institution.

Productive Transition for Retirees at University of California–Davis and Beyond

The Role of Bridge Employment

Anecdotal conversations confirm that retirement is an adjustment. However, the transition to retirement can be smoothed by providing those individuals considering retirement with resources, information, and opportunities.

Bridge employment is defined as "employment that takes place after a person's retirement from a full-time position but before the person's permanent withdrawal from the workforce" (Kim & Feldman, 2000, p. 1195). Kim and Feldman (2000) studied the impacts of this type of employment on the adjustment to retirement, as well as on the quality of life in retirement. In 1999 they surveyed UC faculty retirees who took advantage of retirement incentive programs in the early 1990s. The study sample consisted of faculty who accepted an early retirement incentive available to faculty whose age and years of service totaled at least 73. The sample included 924 professors who accepted the incentive and who were also eligible for bridge employment. Surveys were deliverable to 879 faculty, of whom 371 returned surveys, yielding a 42% response rate (Kim & Feldman, 2000). Data analysis revealed several patterns that characterize the habits and preferences of postretirement faculty.

- Older workers need to maintain daily routines, especially after participating in an emotionally involved or fast-paced occupation, as they find it difficult to adjust to no structure at all.
- Older workers try to sustain structure in their daily lives by participating in the activities they value most highly.
- Individuals who have high career identification are likely to seek continuity through some form of postretirement work involvement. Among older workers whose sense of self-worth is highly tied to their professional accomplishments, participation in bridge employment, part-time work, temporary work, consulting, or professional associations will be more avidly sought and more rewarding when achieved. (Kim & Feldman, 2000, pp. 1195–1196)

Results of the survey highlight that bridge employment is useful in sustaining the well-being of middle-aged and older workers. The researchers offer two key implications: (a) there may be uncertainty and misunderstanding about the nature of bridge employment opportunities available to retirees, especially when they lose office space or administrative support; and (b) bridge employment may be an excellent way for organizations to resolve staffing problems.

Development of a New Program for University of California–Davis Faculty Considering Retirement

With the findings of the Kim and Feldman (2000) study in mind, and aware of our aging faculty, we planned a pre-retiree workshop series to further assist in retirement planning for faculty employees. In the planning phase of the program, Academic Affairs partnered with campus colleagues in Benefits and the Retiree Center,[1] and we also consulted with other campuses that had begun similar work. In particular, UC Berkeley graciously provided us with essential information included in its pre-retiree workshop series, which is designed for both academics and staff employees, as well as information about how the program was created, how it has been working, and what challenges it has faced. Berkeley also shared training materials and speaker information.

Reviewing UC Berkeley's materials, we decided to create two concurrent series, one for staff employees and one for faculty and academics. We wanted to provide faculty participants with the opportunity to be in session with their peers, allowing for more relevant dialogue, exchange of ideas, and perhaps more openness toward discussing the issues and concerns that are of particular concern to faculty. Additionally, all employees were invited to bring their spouses and partners to the series. Encouraging couples to attend together—so that the partner receives information concurrently with the faculty member—is an important aspect of the program. This helps them to navigate the pre- and postretirement years as a team. As noted by Freedman and Moen (2005),

> Twenty-first century retirements often come in pairs, as husbands and wives have to negotiate two retirements: "his" and "hers." Research shows this can be stressful for marriages, especially when one spouse wants to retire, and the other doesn't. Wives often feel they have to time their retirements to coordinate with their husbands' wishes. One woman we interviewed complained that her career had "just gotten started" and she was reluctant to leave it. (para. 21)

In addition to the usual financial sessions about money management and estate planning, we included sessions that focused on the emotional implications of the transition to retirement. One such session was on "work/life transitions," and another was on "personal fulfillment." Freedman and Moen (2005) describe the emphasis most aging individuals give to the financial aspects of retirement and the lack of attention paid to emotionally planning for what's next:

> Older workers tend not to talk about retirement. Particularly surprising is the finding that couples tend not to talk with each other about life in retirement much past thinking about ages and dates. That reminds us of people who plan their weddings down to the last detail, but not their lives as a married couple. The fact is, many people will live together retired longer than they lived together when both were in their career jobs. Whether single or married, people rarely talk to friends, and even more rarely to

colleagues, about retirement, worrying it may signal an absence of commitment and a readiness to throw in the towel, when what they really want is a well-planned second act. (para. 22)

Refinement of the Retirement Planning Sessions for University of California–Davis Faculty

The pilot of the workshop series began in 2011–2012. On the basis of the evaluations, we considered what needed to be changed and what needed to be put in place for the long-term administration of the program. As a result the series was offered again in 2012–2013 and is now an ongoing, annual workshop offered through the continued collaboration of Academic Affairs and the Retiree Center. We are especially fortunate that the current director of the Retiree Center is also the current president of the Association of Retirement Organizations in Higher Education (AROHE). (UC Davis is also an institutional member of AROHE.) The connection to AROHE is important because the association provides access to the good work being done at other institutions and allows us to consider additional programs and tools for our campus.

At the time the pilot series began, we established a webpage devoted to "Retirements and Recalls" (http://academicpersonnel.ucdavis.edu). This page is designed to be a key resource for faculty considering retirement, as well as for those who have already retired and have questions about these issues. The page contains links to policies, a fact sheet on "returning to employment after retirement," information on our pre-retiree workshop series, a link to the online "retirement calculator" on the Benefits webpage,[2] and much more.

Additional planning efforts at UC Davis include creating a toolkit for deans and academic department chairs on faculty retirements, modeled after UC Berkeley's toolkit. This collaboration is another example of how the campuses of a single system can benefit through independent creativity and subsequent collaboration. Our toolkit includes the following items:

- a checklist of restrictions and policies for faculty who are considering recall to part-time campus service[3]
- a list of frequently asked questions about faculty retirement for chairs and deans
- talking points for deans and chairs to use in conversations with faculty who may be planning for retirement, including some dos and don'ts of what to say
- resources and information for academics considering retirement

This online toolkit was recently finalized and shared with our deans, chairs, and sister UC campuses in late spring 2013.

Last, we have also initiated regular meetings with the UC Davis Emeriti Board. With this collaboration we hope to gain feedback and exchange ideas for utilizing our emeriti in ways that both benefit UC Davis and assist emeriti in remaining engaged, productive, and interested.

The Benefits of Being a University of California

The UC system provides a unique opportunity for the sharing of information and resources. What is working at one campus can be transported to another, allowing for adjustments to suit the needs of each. This model is demonstrated with system-wide policy. For example, the UC *Academic Personnel Manual (APM)* applies to all UCs, but most of the policies have a notation at the end indicating that each chancellor can establish his or her own additional policies. Each campus, then, can create implementation tools to administer the system-wide policy in a way that works for it.

As a large university system, UC has the bargaining power of 10 campuses to negotiate large-scale benefits and opportunities. An example of this is the recently added benefit of Sittercity care services for all eligible UC employees. Sittercity is a referral service that helps an employee find and select prescreened emergency backup care and other service providers, such as in-home nannies, child-care providers, elder-care providers, transportation providers, dog walkers, pet sitters, tutors, and housekeepers. All current UC employees are provided with free membership and access to the online database of nearly 2 million prescreened caregivers and services. This is a tremendous benefit for employees. Emeriti and other retirees can pay for membership to use the referral services.

Being part of a larger system provides an excellent opportunity to generate useful data that can inform policy changes. In recent years UC has established several technological systems that enable the campuses to better monitor their activities and to increase efficiencies. In the last 2 years, UC has also created an online application tool for all academic job vacancies. This tool, UC Recruit, is structured so that each campus contributes funding to maintain and enhance the features of the system. Over time the system will be able to track hiring patterns, including data on race and gender, information about advertising, and search committee composition and practices. These examples demonstrate best practices in both information sharing and in achieving cost efficiencies, as comprehensive technology is much less expensive when shared among campuses.

Another example of a benefit from membership in a large system is the recent Campus Climate Survey, which was conducted on all 10 campuses. A system-wide committee made up of representatives from all campuses and an external consultant developed the survey, and each campus was provided with the opportunity to add questions. The results of the survey will soon be released, and this information will help us consider how our campus rates on these important issues as compared to other campuses in the system. Campuses that are doing particularly well in a given area can share their best practices with those campuses that may need to improve. The Climate Survey will then be reissued several years from now to determine what impacts any changes have made since the initial offering. Further, other universities and systems outside UC will be able to learn from this information and consider changes or additions to their campuses. There are likely to be contributions to the literature based on these findings, which will have an even broader impact.

With regard to facilitating the transition to retirement, most UC campuses have similar organizational structures that address faculty issues. We can therefore learn from one another. The following example is particularly helpful because it highlights what was done at our sister campus, UC San Francisco:

> In San Mateo, Calif., the Samaritan House Free Medical Clinic was created by retired members of the clinical faculty of the University of California at San Francisco. Along with seeing more than 8,000 patients a year in two locations free of charge, the Samaritan House Free Medical Clinic has become a favorite rotation for the university's medical students and residents—a place where they come to learn medicine under the guidance of experienced physicians. (Freedman & Moen, 2005, para. 33)

This example illustrates how another UC campus provides opportunities for retired faculty to play a role in community service, while also training medical students and residents. This is the type of example that is valuable for our system to share so that each campus can tweak the model to suit individual regional needs. Not having to "reinvent the wheel" is an enormous advantage.

Overall, UC emeriti are encouraged to continue their involvement with their campuses after they retire. Nine of the 10 UC campuses have emeriti associations, which are dues-supported membership organizations that have received official recognition as campus affiliates by the UC regents (the newest UC campus, UC Merced, does not yet have enough emeriti to form an association). Five of the 10 campuses have campus-funded retiree centers with full-time staff (UC Berkeley, UC Davis, UCLA, UC Irvine, and UC San Diego), and one campus has a center with a part-time staff member (UC Santa Barbara). The emeriti associations and retired staff associations on all the remaining campuses except for UC Merced are advocating for the establishment of campus-funded retiree centers.

All UC emeriti associations and retiree centers offer robust programming and services for UC emeriti. Programs and services vary by campus, but include the following:

- Continuation of university e-mail service
- Library privileges
- Discounts at campus eateries, retail outlets, sporting events, and performing arts venues
- Reduced-fee or complimentary parking passes (on some campuses)
- Free notary service (on some campuses)
- Educational programs
- Social events
- Day trips and world travel
- Emeriti service awards and research grants
- Representation on Academic Senate, campus committees, task forces, and other volunteer groups

On the UC Davis campus, the UC Davis Emeriti Association (UCDEA) coordinates the Video Records Project, which creates an oral history of the campus by filming interviews with emeriti. The videos—nearly 400 to date—are shown several times each week on the local public access television station and are archived in the university library.

The UC emeriti associations have organized on a system-wide level to form the Council of University of California Emeriti Associations (CUCEA), which advocates on behalf of emeriti with the UC Office of the President. Each campus sends one or two representatives to biennial CUCEA meetings, during which representatives from the Office of the President provide updates on any issues that might affect emeriti and listen to concerns from the campus representatives. This system-wide model has been very effective, as it has created an ongoing two-way dialog with the UC Office of the President and provides a strong unified voice for emeriti concerns.

Every three years CUCEA conducts a bio-bibliographical survey of emeriti at each of the UC campuses. This survey clearly demonstrates the valuable contributions of UC emeriti and has been used to successfully advocate for emeriti rights and privileges. The results of the most recent survey, which covered the years 2009–2012, showed the following:

- 51% of the survey respondents are still teaching (36% on their home campus and 15% elsewhere)
- 43% received extramural funding
- Collectively, respondents had written 600 books, 6,000 articles, 1,000 book chapters, and a myriad of abstracts and reports
- A high number of respondents serve on campus committees (advisory groups, departmental committees, doctoral committees, etc.)

Additionally, a large percentage of emeriti contribute financially to the university. This percentage varies by campus, but a survey at UC Irvine revealed that more than 50% of their emeriti contribute money to campus initiatives. UC emeriti are an extremely valuable resource who contribute significantly to the teaching, research, and service missions of the UC system. As observed by John Vohs, president of the UC Davis Emeriti Association, "UC emeriti contributions are almost the equivalent of an eleventh UC campus." Learn more about CUCEA and see the results of the most recent bio-bibliographical survey at http://cucea.ucsd.edu.

Challenges at the Frontier

Being part of a large university system certainly also has challenges. Because the UC system is so large, the speed at which change can occur is limited. As an example, changing a policy in the system-wide *APM* requires a series of reviews that can take several years. Any opportunity for input is useful, but there needs to be recognition of the additional time and effort needed to put new programs in place. Although UC ladder-rank faculty are not unionized, a number of academic employees are represented and part of a bargaining agreement across the UC system. The need to confer on policy changes and bargain new contracts on a regular basis can also limit the speed at which change can occur.

At UC Davis, and across the UC system, faculty retirements are expected to accelerate over at least the next decade. This represents both an opportunity and a challenge, and our approach at UC Davis has been to seek solutions that mutually benefit our aging faculty and our institution. The interests of these two groups are not mutually exclusive, as senior and soon-to-be retiring faculty have much they can contribute to the university, if they remain engaged. Our retirement transition workshops will continue to provide potential retirees with information about opportunities for engagement that will provide a bridge from full-time faculty employment to a less engaged time of life. Through our pre-retirement series workshops and collaborations with our sister campuses, we aim to make UC Davis known as an institution that provides its faculty with respect and support throughout their careers and beyond.

UC Davis has a unique opportunity to improve retirement and the transition to retirement through our 2020 Initiative, "an ambitious plan to build on the institution's excellence, create a more diverse community of scholars, and achieve financial stability" (Katehi, 2011). The initiative commits our campus to add up to 5,000 new students by 2020, along with corresponding increases in graduate students, faculty, staff, and facilities.

We believe that increased engagement of emeriti faculty will be essential for the success of the 2020 Initiative. The demographic profile of our faculty guarantees that retirements will continue to increase over the next few years as the student population increases. Without the concerted efforts of recalled faculty, our campus will face a broadening gap in addressing student needs in teaching, advising, and mentoring. While new faculty will also be hired to meet the demands of 2020, they may not be hired as quickly as necessary to meet students' needs. Emeriti faculty can both fill these gaps and also help us plan for these exciting changes. UC Davis is in position and ready to continue efforts to be a premier research institution that meets the demands of all employees, including retiring faculty.

Author Note

All data and figures were provided by the UC Office of the President, Office of the Vice Provost–Academic Personnel. We want to thank Kellie Jean Hogue, formerly of UC Davis Academic Affairs, who assisted in research and data gathering for this work. We also want to thank Sue Barnes, director of the UC Davis Retiree Center, for additional information provided on the UC Emeriti and Retirement Association system-wide.

Notes

1. The UC Davis Retiree Center was established in 2006 as a collaboration among the UC Davis Retiree Association, the UC Davis Emeriti Association, and the UC Davis administration.

2. The "retirement calculator" provides estimates of income in retirement. The tool is managed by UC and available to all employees.

3. Recalled faculty have been hired back to work following a brief period of no employment after retirement. These employees are limited to working no more than 43% of a full-time position per month, inclusive of all recall appointments. On the Academic Affairs website, recall activity examples include using extramural funds for research, teaching (including teaching in summer sessions and leading a summer abroad program), volunteering to teach freshman seminars, advising students, serving on committees, and serving in an administrative position.

References

Freedman, M., & Moen, P. (2005). Academic pioneer "the third age." *Chronicle of Higher Education, 51*(34), B1.

Katehi, L. P. B. (2011). *2020 initiative*. Retrieved from the UC Davis website: http://chancellor.ucdavis.edu/initiatives/2020_Initiative/index.html

Kim, S., & Feldman, D. C. (2000). Working in retirement: The antecedents of bridge employment and its consequences for quality of life in retirement. *Academy of Management Journal, 43*(6), 1195–1210.

University of California (UC)–Davis. (2010). *Vision of excellence*. Retrieved from http://vision.ucdavis.edu/plan.html

15

ASSOCIATION OF RETIREMENT ORGANIZATIONS IN HIGHER EDUCATION

Sue Barnes and Janette C. Brown,
Association of Retirement Organizations in Higher Education

M any faculty, consciously or subconsciously, fear loss after retirement—loss of identity and relationships with colleagues and students—as well as diminished intellectual stimulation and connection to their colleges and universities. Some struggle to envision a productive and meaningful life after retirement, whereas others never consider leaving academe. Retired faculty have sometimes expressed feelings of "falling off a cliff" or "suddenly becoming invisible."

Through the creation of retiree organizations, retiree centers, and emeriti colleges,[1] an increasing number of colleges and universities are providing programs to help faculty with bridging the transition to retirement. These programs are also vehicles for connecting retired faculty with their institutions and engaging their expertise for the common good. Across the nation cultures are changing at academic institutions as campus leaders recognize the value of their retired faculty's wisdom, knowledge, and experience. These retirees can provide great value to important interdisciplinary and intergenerational initiatives that contribute to the institution, the local community, and the larger world.

Beginning in the early 1990s, campus and retiree leaders across North America began to network as the movement to establish retiree organizations started to grow. Informal conversations ultimately resulted in the formation of the Association of Retirement Organizations in Higher Education (AROHE), incorporated as a nonprofit association in 2002. With the motto "Advocate, Educate, Serve," the association provides educational outreach and networking opportunities to assist institutions of higher education with the creation, development, and maintenance of organizations that serve retired faculty and staff.

Today AROHE is a small but growing association of nearly 100 member organizations representing over 100,000 retired faculty and staff at institutions of higher education in the United States and Canada. Leadership draws from visionaries among the retiree population and the campus leaders who serve them. It includes researchers with analytical expertise, administrators with organization and management experience, and academics with intellectual and social acumen. AROHE has conducted several research surveys to gather information on national trends and has developed a start-up kit for campuses that wish to establish retiree organizations.

Three common types of retiree organizations have formed on university campuses: retired faculty or staff associations, campus-funded retiree centers, and emeriti colleges. Each of the three types of organizations specializes in slightly different functions, and several campuses have more than one type of organization.

Retiree Associations

Retired faculty and retired staff associations typically operate as alumni associations do. These associations are usually affiliated with their universities but operate as separate entities. Often begun as advocacy groups or social clubs, associations have grown to provide valuable services, programs, and benefits and have become important partners in furthering their institutions' educational missions. On some campuses emeriti/retired faculty have formed associations separately from retired staff, whereas on other campuses faculty and staff have joined together in a single entity. These organizations are usually primarily funded by member dues; however, many receive additional funding, staff support, or space from their academic institutions, and a large percentage engage in fund-raising drives for scholarships or other philanthropic projects.

Campus-Funded Retiree Centers

In recent years more retiree associations have advocated for the establishment of campus-funded retiree centers to serve the ongoing needs of retired faculty and staff and to maintain mutually beneficial campus connections. As confirmed by AROHE research, academic institutions that support and engage their retirees reap the rewards of higher levels of volunteerism and engagement in campus initiatives, such as mentoring programs and philanthropic projects.

Campus-funded retiree centers typically serve as the office of record for retirees. They provide information and referrals, organize retiree programs, connect retirees with volunteer opportunities, and provide a place where retirees can interact with each other and their institutions. Some centers also provide pre-retirement planning programs to optimize the retirement preparation and transition phase. Centers are typically housed within academic affairs, human resources, or development/advancement offices. Many centers receive funding from more than one institutional entity and augment their budgets with fund-raising drives and fee-based programming.

Emeriti Colleges

Emeriti colleges are campus-funded retiree organizations that focus primarily on academic and research endeavors. Emeriti colleges often offer enrichment courses for mature adults, organize speakers' bureaus to offer lectures for their surrounding communities, award research grants, and publish scholarly journals. Most emeriti colleges receive the majority of their funding from their universities and augment their budgets with fee-based programming and member dues.

Retiree Organization Structure and Funding

Retiree organizations vary tremendously in structure and funding. No single path to success fits all faculty groups or institutions. Some were created from the bottom up by a group of interested retirees who set out to create an organization to serve themselves and their host institutions. Others were formed from the top down by senior officials at institutions. A few organizations focus primarily upon activities of benefit to retirees, but most pursue a mix of service initiatives along with retiree benefits and activities.

The strength of a retiree group is often directly proportional to the financial assistance provided by the institution and to the interest shown by senior academic officials. Some groups have acquired a considerable measure

TABLE 15.1
Sources of Funding for Retiree Organizations

Source	Percentage of survey respondents
Dues (mandatory)	44%
Provost's or chancellor's office	43%
Dues (voluntary)	25%
Foundation/development office	22%
Fund-raising	16%
Human resources	11%
Endowment	9%
Academic unit budget	6%
Academic affairs/academic senate	6%
Alumni office	6%
Institutional grant funding	4%
Outside grant funding	1%

of stability with institutional funding for staff and operating expenses as well as assigned office and activity space, whereas others are "operating on a shoestring," figuratively hanging on by their fingertips. The most successful retiree organizations are recognized as an important part of the institutional mission. The majority of campus-based retiree organizations have not evolved to this stage, but most receive some level of resources from their institutions.

AROHE surveys have documented the funding sources of retiree organizations. The results of the most recent survey (Brown & Pearson, 2012) are given in Table 15.1.

Retiree Organization Programs and Activities

Retiree organizations offer a wide variety of programs and services to enrich the lives of academic retirees and help them to continue their connections with their academic institutions. Typically, they include the following:

- *Volunteer/service programs*: Retired faculty volunteer in many capacities, including serving on graduate student committees, judging symposia, and acting as jurors for mock law school trials. Retiree organizations often play a role in these volunteer efforts. Some retiree organizations have developed formal volunteer corps to assist with campus initiatives when called upon, others act as intermediaries to connect retirees with volunteer opportunities, and still others create partnerships with community volunteer organizations.

- *University advocacy programs*: University employees may not necessarily initiate direct contact with legislators on behalf of the university, but retirees, as an independent group, can prepare position papers, write letters to the editor, and otherwise provide information to state legislators to highlight critical needs at the university.
- *Fund-raising*: Retirees are often critical philanthropic partners. They participate in annual fund-raising efforts, legacy project funding, and capital campaign drives.
- *Retirement-planning programs*: Frequently, organizations partner with human resources or academic affairs departments to offer retirement-planning programs. Retirees who are several years into retirement can provide valuable perspectives for individuals who are in the planning stages.
- *Educational workshops*: Regularly scheduled breakfast or lunch programs with speakers are a mainstay for the majority of retiree organizations. Several also offer conferences, colloquiums, or symposia. Speakers may be current faculty, emeriti, alumni, or local or regional experts.
- *Social programs*: Monthly or quarterly social programs, such as barbecues, wine tastings, and other formal and informal gatherings, are another popular offering.
- *Student mentoring programs*: Many different types of mentoring programs match undergraduate or graduate students with retired faculty. Some institutions assign retired faculty to dormitories, where they eat with the students and are available to consult on programs, study habits, and career choices.
- *Consultant/adviser programs*: Retired faculty often serve on committees or task forces to provide input on such projects as long-term plans or assessments of space needs. They also can provide institutional history that is often a critical component of campus decisions.
- *Living history projects*: These projects create audio or video interviews with retired professors to preserve institutional history and document faculty contributions. DVDs are often catalogued at the library and are available for public viewing online or through local television programming.
- *Scholarship programs*: Student or staff scholarships or awards are funded through dues, special events, or fund-raising drives.

- *Speakers' bureaus*: Speakers' bureaus provide presentations to community groups, sharing the expertise and experience of participating retirees.
- *Interest groups*: Investment clubs, book clubs, bridge clubs, and other interest groups provide retirees with opportunities to share common interests.
- *Campus tours*: Organizations keep retired faculty engaged in the campus by offering tours of new buildings, research laboratories, and arts facilities.
- *Travel programs*: Day trips to local points of interest and multiday tours to more distant destinations offer convenience and security for retirees. World travel is often scheduled in conjunction with the alumni association or established tour operators.
- *Newsletters/e-mail updates*: Most groups annually publish two to four newsletters, and many provide more frequent e-mail communications that feature activities of the retiree organization, legislative actions affecting retirees, vignettes by retirees who are pursuing interesting hobbies or careers, and campus service opportunities.
- *Teaching/recall-to-service programs*: In most instances retired faculty teaching or continuation of research is arranged through their former academic departments and is usually the result of a personal knowledge of the retired faculty's abilities. Retiree organizations can play a role in connecting retired faculty with these opportunities.

The 2012 AROHE survey illustrates the programs and activities offered by responding organizations (Brown & Pearson, 2012). See Table 15.2.

TABLE 15.2
Retiree Organizations' Programs and Activities

Programs and activities	Percentage of survey respondents
Host social events (e.g., breakfasts, luncheons, or other)	81%
Maintain a retiree e-mail list	77%
Maintain retiree contact records	64%
Maintain contacts with retiree groups at other institutions	53%
Provide requested assistance for the administration	49%
Provide guidance to newly retired employees	44%

(Continues)

TABLE 15.2
Retiree Organizations' Programs and Activities (Continued)

Programs and activities	Percentage of survey respondents
Host a retiree recognition day, reception, or similar event	42%
Present community lectures, discussions, or performances	36%
Promote cultural or artistic endeavors	33%
Preserve or write university or retiree organizational histories	31%
Host clubs or educational groups (e.g., bridge club, book club, or investment group)	30%
Offer pre-retiree retirement education workshops	29%
Offer wellness, health, and aging programs	29%
Provide scholarships for students	27%
Present retiree awards	26%
Offer programs involving volunteerism, civic engagement, service-learning, or community outreach	25%
Raise funds for student scholarships	23%
Offer retiree exhibits of creative efforts (e.g., art, photography, or poems)	22%
Develop memorials for recently deceased members	21%
Provide volunteers for community educational programs	18%
Offer computer classes for retirees	17%
Teach retiree courses or workshops	17%
Advise, mentor, and honor specific students	15%
Raise funds for retiree lectures, programs, and awards	15%
Publish or write profiles of distinguished professors and administrators	12%
Raise funds for the institution	11%
Offer retiree reemployment opportunities	9%
Teach graduate classes	7%
Teach undergraduate seminars or orientations	7%
Mentor new faculty	4%
Meet with prospective students, parents, or other campus visitors	4%

Retired Faculty Benefits

Retiree organizations actively advocate for enhanced retiree benefits. These benefits are often important to retired faculty and can be a valuable incentive when considering whether and when to retire. Many of these benefits encourage retired faculty to stay connected with their institution and ease their transition from active faculty to retired status. They commonly include the following:

- continuation of campus e-mail
- use of campus libraries
- use of campus computer services
- access to office space (either in their home department or school or in an emeriti center)
- continuation of health care
- free or reduced-fee campus parking
- discounts at campus venues and events (e.g., athletics, recreational facilities and programs, performing arts, retail outlets, dining establishments)

Starting a Retiree Organization

There are likely as many approaches to starting a retiree organization as there are active groups at academic institutions. However, as mentioned briefly earlier in this chapter, there are two general organizational structures. The first is the top-down approach. In this case, a senior administrator at an institution is persuaded, often in concert with a group of interested retired faculty, that starting an active retiree organization is in the institution's best interests.

This decision is typically followed by an allocation of office space; development of a budget for operating costs, programs and activities, and staffing; and agreement on a specific mission. A liaison between the retiree group and the administration is typically appointed, and the chair of the retiree group has a reporting relationship to a senior official—often the provost, the director of advancement/development, or the director of human resources. This approach usually has greater success because it includes an institutional commitment to the fledgling retiree group, plus a clear indication that the retirees are regarded as important to the host institution.

The alternative is the bottom-up approach, in which interested retired faculty decide to create a retiree organization and approach the administration for both encouragement and financial assistance. This approach can succeed with a supportive administration, but it can also be problematic if the administration doesn't accord a high priority to the viability of the group. On many campuses retirees have successfully advocated for space, funding, and other support to create robust retiree organizations, but it often can take many years to establish an adequately funded organization.

While there are many models for and many approaches to starting a retiree organization, key steps can ease the process and shorten the time from start-up to a fully established and engaged organization:

- *Join AROHE*: This organization is a vital source of information and contacts with people and schools that can provide advice and useful models to fit any college or university considering a retiree organization.
- *Survey retirees*: Conduct research to determine the retirees' interests and their willingness to serve in various capacities to organize and maintain a retiree organization.
- *Provide campus service*: Before asking for campus support, organize retiree initiatives to provide valuable service to the campus through teaching, researching, or mentoring. Start creating partnerships with key campus departments.
- *Seek support*: Meet with top administrative leaders and other campus constituents (faculty and staff) early in the process of starting an organization. In this connection, be aware of the campus political culture. Keep everyone informed and, ideally, involved with the initial exploration and later development of the retiree organization.
- *Identify a champion*: Things happen on campus when there are well-respected individuals and groups who identify with and help promote a new idea. Every new idea needs advocates.
- *Create a task force*: If the campus shows support for a retiree organization, ask for the creation of a task force that includes high-level campus administrators and retirees. This step can be important for legitimizing the project and garnering important support from the campus.
- *Submit a written proposal*: A written proposal formalizes the request. The proposal should outline the benefits to the campus for providing support for a retiree organization, anticipated functions of the organization, administrative reporting lines, budget needs, and space requirements.
- *Continue efforts as necessary*: On many campuses, it takes several years of continued effort to establish a retiree organization and gain support from the academic institution.

Conclusion

Retiree organizations, including retired faculty associations, emeriti colleges, and campus-funded retiree centers, can become the home department for many different collaborative campus projects—places where retired faculty can complete their capstone projects and connect with other retired and active faculty to create innovative, multidisciplinary, and multigenerational programs.

Especially in difficult economic times, the resources that colleges or universities invest in retiree organizations are repaid many times over as retired faculty continue to contribute to their institutions through teaching, research, service, and financial support. Retiree organizations that are recognized and supported as part of the institutional framework become essential and effective partners that contribute to the overall success of the institution.

Note

1. AROHE research shows that institutions vary in their practices of conferring emeritus and emerita status upon retired faculty (and sometimes administrators); therefore, in this chapter, the plural term *emeriti* is interpreted loosely and generously as honor for academic service.

Reference

Brown, J. C., & Pearson, L. (2012). *2010–2012 AROHE survey of college and university retiree organizations*. Los Angeles: Association of Retirement Organizations in Higher Education.

PART SIX

CHALLENGES OF AND OPPORTUNITIES FOR IMPLEMENTATION

16

UNIVERSITY OF WASHINGTON RETIREMENT TRANSITION OPTIONS FOR TENURED FACULTY

Cheryl A. Cameron and Rhonda Forman,
University of Washington

The University of Washington has a long history of supporting its faculty in their retirement transitions. In the face of the most drastic economic downturn in decades, faculty at the traditional retirement age struggled with the realities of an uncertain financial future. During this period the university, not surprisingly, observed a decline in the annual number of faculty retirements. In response, the University of Washington administration and faculty began discussing how to incentivize faculty retirement, with the goal of addressing the needs of both the faculty and the institution. Faculty asked for a program that would address their need for enhanced fiscal certainty during retirement in the face of unstable retirement portfolios and escalating health-care costs. The administration wanted a program that would help address the realities of the budget crisis—both budget cuts and succession planning—while it minimized the risk of losing faculty who were mission critical. This chapter describes the three retirement transition options offered by the University of Washington to support tenured faculty in the process of preparing for retirement, deciding to retire, or phasing into retirement.

Faculty Retirements in the First Decade of the 2000s

During the academic years of 1999–2000 through 2011–2012, an average of 43 tenured faculty retired from the university each year. Table 16.1 shows the pattern of retirement over this 13-year period, which includes fluctuation in the number of retirements per year and a gradual increase in the average age at retirement. The number of retirements is noticeably lower in academic years associated with the current economic crisis (i.e., 2008–2009 and 2009–2010).

During this time faculty who wanted a smoother transition to retirement used the Partial Reemployment Policy, which allowed the institution to employ them according to state regulations on the reemployment of retirees. Additionally, for years the university, on a case-by-case basis, had allowed faculty to voluntarily agree to forgo their right to partial reemployment in exchange for an individually arranged retirement transition agreement more suited to their needs. Using the existing Partial Reemployment Policy as part of the framework for a new retirement incentive option became the foundation for the university's planning. This framework had the potential to permit the implementation of a program that added new benefits for faculty while it minimized the need for additional resource investments by the institution.

TABLE 16.1
Retirement of Tenured Faculty by Academic Year

Academic year	Number of retirements	Average age at retirement
1999–2000	49	65.8 (7 < 62)
2000–2001	62	65.0 (7 < 62)
2001–2002	46	65.6 (7 < 62)
2002–2003	26	67.4 (2 < 62)
2003–2004	32	66.0 (4 < 62)
2004–2005	41	67.8 (2 < 62)
2005–2006	49	65.3 (5 < 62)
2006–2007	44	66.8 (2 < 62)
2007–2008	41	67.6 (4 < 62)
2008–2009	34	66.8 (3 < 62)
2009–2010	37	67.4 (6 < 62)
2010–2011	59	67.7 (4 < 62)
2011–2012	44	69.5 (0 < 62)

TABLE 16.2

Transition to Retirement Options for Tenured Faculty

Option	Description
Partial Reemployment Policy	Policy by which the institution vests a right to 5 years of partial reemployment (up to a maximum of 40% time) with tenured faculty who are at least 62 years of age
Individualized retirement transition agreements	Individualized arrangements whereby a tenured faculty member with a vested right to partial reemployment voluntarily agrees to forgo that right and to set a definitive and irrevocable time line for retirement in exchange for adjusted workloads and responsibilities before retirement that facilitate the fulfillment of career-culminating activities
Voluntary Retirement Incentive Program	Periodically available option that permits tenured faculty to elect to forgo their vested right to partial reemployment in exchange for a lump-sum contribution to a tax-free medical expense account if they sign up during the open election period and agree to retire in the specified retirement period

The result was the implementation, in 2010, of the Voluntary Retirement Incentive (VRI) Program in which tenured faculty could agree to forgo their right to reemployment after retirement in exchange for a university contribution to a medical expense account. The university now offers three ways for faculty to transition into retirement, listed in Table 16.2.

Partial Reemployment Policy

Policy Description

Washington State law permits a faculty member who retires from a state institution of higher education to be reemployed after retirement up to 40% time (RCW 28B.10.420 [2][d]). Consistent with this provision, the University of Washington vests with tenured faculty the right, beginning at age 62, to be reemployed up to a maximum of 40% time for instructional or research purposes for 5 years after the date of retirement. This policy is intended to support individual faculty members with their retirement transition, while it also supports the institution by retaining a core of committed senior faculty who can assist academic units as they adjust to changing personnel profiles.

When a retiree's reemployment is funded from state or tuition funds, the assigned duties must be classroom teaching unless the reemploying unit agrees to other instructional assignments. Arrangements for instructional, research, or other designated duties of reemployed retired faculty are made by agreement between the department chair—or dean in the case of an undepartmentalized school or college—and the retired faculty member. Decisions about teaching load and equivalent percentages of support are made at the local level, taking into account traditional teaching loads within the reemploying unit. There is no guarantee that the reemployment assignments specifically requested by the retiree will be available and offered. Efforts are made to accommodate a retiree's desires for class scheduling, but the needs of the unit's programs and curricula take precedence over individual requests. A retiree does not need to elect reemployment in each year of the vested 5-year reemployment period, but skipping a year does not extend the 5-year period. Retirees are required to notify their department chair or dean by December 1 of the preceding year of their election to be reemployed to ensure that they are planned into the curriculum. The university extends the 5-year reemployment option to professorial faculty retiring from its "without tenure by reason of funding" and "research" appointment tracks if funding is available; however, they are not considered to have a vested right to reemployment.

Significance of Vesting

As a state agency the University of Washington is obligated to comply with the Ethics in Public Service Act (Chapter 42.52 RCW). One of its provisions is a restriction on the receipt by state employees of gifts or things of economic value that could be expected to influence or be considered a reward for their action or inaction (RCW 42.52.140).

The University of Washington's Partial Reemployment Policy creates a vested right available to tenured faculty who remain employed until the age of 62, which may not be unilaterally revoked. Therefore, when faculty members elect to enter into a retirement transition agreement in which they receive a benefit in exchange for forgoing this vested right, they have entered into a transaction in which there is "consideration," that is, the giving of something in exchange for something else. This precludes the transaction from being interpreted as a receipt of a gift. For this reason the framework for individual retirement transition agreements and the VRI Program involves a faculty member's decision to voluntarily forgo a vested right under the Partial Reemployment Policy.

The University of Washington considers the Partial Reemployment Policy to be a significant benefit to its tenured faculty. Of the University of Washington's participant responses to the American Council on Education (ACE)/Sloan survey on best practices in faculty retirement transitions, over 47% indicated they were satisfied with their ability to work part-time in retirement. In addition, the Partial Reemployment Policy was identified as one of the "best things" the University of Washington does to make the retirement transition smoother for faculty.

Pattern of Use

To understand the pattern of use of the Partial Reemployment Policy, the records of the tenured faculty who retired in the 8 academic years from 1999–2000 through 2006–2007 were reviewed. This time frame for review was selected because these retirees had the potential to use the full 5 years of their vested right to reemployment. More recent retirees are still in the period of their vested right to reemployment.

1999–2000

Forty-nine tenured faculty retired in 1999–2000. Seven of the retirees did not have a vested right to reemployment because of their age; another four of the retirees had entered into an individualized retirement agreement in which they agreed to forgo their vested right to reemployment. Of the 38 retirees with a vested right to 5 years of reemployment, 12 (31.6%) were not reemployed at any time during the 5-year period following retirement. The pattern of reemployment of the remaining 26 retirees is reported in Table 16.3.

2000–2001

Sixty-two tenured faculty retired in 2000–2001. Seven of the retirees did not have a vested right to reemployment because of their age. Another 15 of the retirees had entered into an individualized retirement agreement in which they agreed to forgo their vested right to reemployment. Of the 40 retirees

TABLE 16.3
Pattern of Reemployment by 1999–2000 Retirees

Years of reemployment	*Cumulative level of reemployment*				
	Full 40%	*Partial 33%–39%*	*Partial 20%–32%*	*Partial 1%–19%*	*Total*
5	0	4 (15.4%)	0	0	4 (15.4%)
4	3 (11.5%)	3 (11.5%)	1 (3.8%)	2 (7.7%)	9 (34.6%)
3	0	2 (7.7%)	0	2 (7.7%)	4 (15.4%)
2	0	2 (7.7%)	0	1 (3.8%)	3 (11.5%)
1	2 (7.7%)	1 (3.8%)	1 (3.8%)	2 (7.7%)	6 (23.1%)
Total	5 (19.2%)	12 (46.2%)	2 (7.7%)	7 (26.9%)	26

TABLE 16.4
Pattern of Reemployment by 2000–2001 Retirees

Years of reemployment	*Cumulative level of reemployment*				
	Full 40%	*Partial 33%–39%*	*Partial 20%–32%*	*Partial 1%–19%*	*Total*
5	1 (3.8%)	3 (11.5%)	3 (11.5%)	0	7 (26.9%)
4	1 (3.8%)	3 (11.5%)	4 (15.4%)	0	8 (30.8%)
3	1 (3.8%)	1 (3.8%)	2 (7.7%)	1 (3.8%)	5 (19.2%)
2	1 (3.8%)	1 (3.8%)	2 (7.7%)	0	4 (15.4%)
1	0	0	1 (3.8%)	1 (3.8%)	2 (7.7%)
Total	4 (15.4%)	8 (30.8%)	12 (46.2%)	2 (7.7%)	26

with a vested right to 5 years of reemployment, 14 (35.0%) were not reemployed at any time during the 5-year period following retirement. The pattern of reemployment of the remaining 26 retirees is reported in Table 16.4.

2001–2002
Forty-six tenured faculty retired in 2001–2002. Seven of the retirees did not have a vested right to reemployment because of their age. Another eight of the retirees had entered into an individualized retirement agreement in which they agreed to forgo their vested right to reemployment. Of the 31 retirees with a vested right to 5 years of reemployment, seven (22.6%) were not reemployed at any time during the 5-year period following retirement. The pattern of reemployment of the remaining 24 retirees is reported in Table 16.5.

TABLE 16.5
Pattern of Reemployment by 2001–2002 Retirees

Years of reemployment	*Cumulative level of reemployment*				
	Full 40%	*Partial 33%–39%*	*Partial 20%–32%*	*Partial 1%–19%*	*Total*
5	3 (12.5%)	4 (16.7%)	2 (8.3%)	1 (4.2%)	10 (41.7%)
4	1 (4.2%)	1 (4.2%)	1 (4.2%)	1 (4.2%)	4 (16.7%)
3	0	3 (12.5%)	0	2 (8.3%)	5 (20.8%)
2	1 (4.2%)	1 (4.2%)	1 (4.2%)	0	3 (12.5%)
1	0	0	0	2 (8.3%)	2 (8.3%)
Total	5 (20.8%)	9 (37.5%)	4 (16.7%)	6 (25.0%)	24

TABLE 16.6
Pattern of Reemployment by 2002–2003 Retirees

Years of reemployment	Cumulative level of reemployment				
	Full 40%	Partial 33%–39%	Partial 20%–32%	Partial 1%–19%	Total
5	0	5 (29.4%)	1 (5.9%)	2 (11.8%)	8 (47.1%)
4	2 (11.8%)	1 (5.9%)	1 (5.9%)	1 (5.9%)	5 (29.4%)
3	0	2 (11.8%)	0	0	2 (11.8%)
2	1 (5.9%)	0	1 (5.9%)	0	2 (11.8%)
1	0	0	0	0	0
Total	3 (17.6%)	8 (47.1%)	3 (17.6%)	3 (17.6%)	17

2002–2003

Twenty-six tenured faculty retired in 2002–2003. Two of the retirees did not have a vested right to reemployment because of their age. Another four of the retirees had entered into an individualized retirement agreement in which they agreed to forgo their vested right to reemployment. Of the 20 retirees with a vested right to 5 years of reemployment, three (15.0%) were not reemployed at any time during the 5-year period following retirement. The pattern of reemployment of the remaining 17 retirees is reported in Table 16.6.

2003–2004

Thirty-two tenured faculty retired in 2003–2004. Four of the retirees did not have a vested right to reemployment because of their age. Another five of the retirees had entered into an individualized retirement agreement in which they agreed to forgo their vested right to reemployment. Of the 23 retirees with a vested right to 5 years of reemployment, eight (34.8%) were not reemployed at any time during the 5-year period following retirement. The pattern of reemployment of the remaining 15 retirees is reported in Table 16.7.

2004–2005

Forty-one tenured faculty retired in 2004–2005. Two of the retirees did not have a vested right to reemployment because of their age. Another five of the retirees had entered into an individualized retirement agreement in which they agreed to forgo their vested right to reemployment. Of the 34 retirees with a vested right to 5 years of reemployment, 10 (29.4%) were

TABLE 16.7
Pattern of Reemployment by 2003–2004 Retirees

Years of reemployment	*Cumulative level of reemployment*				
	Full 40%	*Partial 33%–39%*	*Partial 20%–32%*	*Partial 1%–19%*	*Total*
5	2 (13.3%)	2 (13.3%)	1 (6.7%)	1 (6.7%)	6 (40.0%)
4	0	0	0	2 (13.3%)	2 (13.3%)
3	1 (6.7%)	1 (6.7%)	1 (6.7%)	0	3 (20.0%)
2	0	0	1 (6.7%)	0	1 (6.7%)
1	0	1 (6.7%)	0	2 (13.3%)	3 (20.0%)
Total	3 (20.0%)	4 (26.7%)	3 (20.0%)	5 (33.3%)	15

not reemployed at any time during the 5-year period following retirement. The pattern of reemployment of the remaining 24 retirees is reported in Table 16.8.

2005–2006
Forty-nine tenured faculty retired in 2005–2006. Five of the retirees did not have a vested right to reemployment because of their age. Another 11 of the retirees had entered into an individualized retirement agreement in which they agreed to forgo their vested right to reemployment. Of the 33 retirees with a vested right to 5 years of reemployment, 18 (54.5%) were not reemployed

TABLE 16.8
Pattern of Reemployment by 2004–2005 Retirees

Years of reemployment	*Cumulative level of reemployment*				
	Full 40%	*Partial 33%–39%*	*Partial 20%–32%*	*Partial 1%–19%*	*Total*
5	4 (16.7%)	3 (12.5%)	3 (12.5%)	3 (12.5%)	13 (54.2%)
4	3 (12.5%)	1 (4.2%)	2 (8.3%)	0	6 (25.0%)
3	0	2 (8.3%)	1 (4.2%)	0	3 (12.5%)
2	0	0	2 (8.3%)	0	2 (8.3%)
1	0	0	0	0	0
Total	7 (29.2%)	6 (25.0%)	8 (33.3%)	3 (12.5%)	24

TABLE 16.9
Pattern of Reemployment by 2005–2006 Retirees

Years of reemployment	*Cumulative level of reemployment*				
	Full 40%	*Partial 33%–39%*	*Partial 20%–32%*	*Partial 1%–19%*	*Total*
5	1 (6.7%)	4 (26.7%)	1 (6.7%)	0	6 (40.0%)
4	1 (6.7%)	0	0	0	1 (6.7%)
3	1 (6.7%)	0	0	0	1 (6.7%)
2	0	1 (6.7%)	1 (6.7%)	2 (13.3%)	4 (26.7%)
1	1 (6.7%)	1 (6.7%)	0	1 (6.7%)	3 (20.0%)
Total	4 (26.7%)	6 (40.0%)	2 (13.3%)	3 (20.0%)	15

at any time during the 5-year period following retirement. The pattern of reemployment of the remaining 15 retirees is reported in Table 16.9.

2006–2007
Forty-four tenured faculty retired in 2006–2007. Two of the retirees did not have a vested right to reemployment because of their age. Eleven of the retirees had entered into an individualized retirement agreement in which they agreed to forgo their vested right to reemployment. Of the 31 retirees with a vested right to 5 years of reemployment, 12 (38.7%) were not reemployed at any time during the 5-year period following retirement. The pattern of reemployment of the remaining 19 retirees is reported in Table 16.10.

TABLE 16.10
Pattern of Reemployment by 2006–2007 Retirees

Years of reemployment	*Cumulative level of reemployment*				
	Full 40%	*Partial 33%–39%*	*Partial 20%–32%*	*Partial 1%–19%*	*Total*
5	2 (10.5%)	6 (31.6%)	3 (15.8%)	0	11 (57.9%)
4	0	1 (5.3%)	0	2 (10.5%)	3 (15.8%)
3	0	0	0	0	0
2	0	0	3 (15.8%)	2 (10.5%)	5 (26.3%)
1	0	0	0	0	0
Total	2 (10.5%)	7 (36.8%)	6 (31.6%)	4 (21.1%)	19

Summary of Pattern of Use

There is substantial variation year to year among the retirees as to their status and use of the vested right to reemployment. Of the 349 retirees over the 8-year period from 1999–2000 to 2006–2007, only 250 had a vested right to 5 years of reemployment at the time of retirement. The percentage of retirees with a vested right to 5 years of reemployment varied across the years from 64.5% to 82.9% (see Table 16.11).

Of the retirees who did not have a vested right to reemployment, 36 were less than 62 years of age at the time of retirement. The percentage of retirees less than 62 years of age at the time of retirement ranged from 4.5% to 15.2% across the years. While individuals who retire before the age of 62 do not have a vested right to reemployment, reemploying these retirees is not prohibited and may be possible on an as-needed basis. In addition, these retirees may continue their medical, dental, and life insurance policies indefinitely if they apply for them at the time they retire. They can choose from the plans that are available to employees or elect a Medicare Supplement Plan at the time they become eligible for Medicare.

Sixty-three of the retirees had entered into an individualized retirement transition agreement before retirement. The percentage of individualized agreements ranged from 8.2% to 25.0% across the years. The arrangements for 46 of the retirees with an individual retirement transition agreement included relinquishing the full 5-year vested right to reemployment, whereas for 17 of the retirees the agreement included forgoing only a fraction of the 5-year vested right. Determinations with regard to the number of vested years that would be relinquished were based on the type and extent of responsibilities that were being exchanged (e.g., number and type of course reductions).

As seen in Table 16.12, of the 250 retirees with a vested right to reemployment, 84 (33.6%) did not elect to be reemployed at any time during the 5-year period following retirement. Over the reported years there was substantial variation with the percentage electing not to be reemployed ranging from 15.0% to 54.5%, with the lowest percentage in the year with the lowest number of retirees with a vested right to reemployment.

Of the 166 retirees who elected to be reemployed, 65 (39.2%) were reemployed in each of the 5 years following retirement and 103 (62.0%) were reemployed in 4 or 5 of the years following retirement (see Table 16.13). The number of retirees who limited their reemployment to only 1 or 2 years was 39 (23.5%). In general, the retirees who have a vested right to 5 years of reemployment and elect to be reemployed do so over the majority of the years available to them.

Of the 166 retirees who elected to be reemployed, 33 (19.9%) were reemployed to the maximum extent permissible (i.e., 40% time) during the

TABLE 16.11
Retiree Status at Time of Retirement

	1999–2000	2000–2001	2001–2002	2002–2003	2003–2004	2004–2005	2005–2006	2006–2007	Total
Total retirees	49	62	46	26	32	41	49	44	349
Retirees less than 62 years of age	7 (14.3%)	7 (11.3%)	7 (15.2%)	2 (7.7%)	4 (12.5%)	2 (4.9%)	5 (10.2%)	2 (4.5%)	36 (10.3%)
Retirees with an individualized retirement agreement	4 (8.2%)	15 (24.2%)	8 (17.4%)	4 (15.4%)	5 (15.6%)	5 (12.2%)	11 (22.4%)	11 (25.0%)	63 (18.1%)
Retirees with vested right to 5 years of reemployment	38 (77.6%)	40 (64.5%)	31 (67.4%)	20 (76.9%)	23 (71.9%)	34 (82.9%)	33 (67.3%)	31 (70.5%)	250 (71.6%)

211

TABLE 16.12

Retiree Use of Right to Reemployment

	1999–2000	2000–2001	2001–2002	2002–2003	2003–2004	2004–2005	2005–2006	2006–2007	Total
Retirees with vested right to 5 years of reemployment	38	40	31	20	23	34	33	31	250
Retirees who did not elect to be reemployed	12 (31.6%)	14 (35.0%)	7 (22.6%)	3 (15.0%)	8 (34.8%)	10 (29.4%)	18 (54.5%)	12 (38.7%)	84 (33.6%)
Retirees who elected to be reemployed	26 (68.4%)	26 (65.0%)	24 (77.4%)	17 (85.0%)	15 (65.2%)	24 (70.6%)	15 (45.5%)	19 (61.3%)	166 (66.4%)

TABLE 16.13
Reemployment Patterns of Retirees With Vested Right to 5 Years of Reemployment

	1999–2000	2000–2001	2001–2002	2002–2003	2003–2004	2004–2005	2005–2006	2006–2007	Total
Retirees who elected to be reemployed	26	26	24	17	15	24	15	19	166
Retirees reemployed for 5 years	4 (15.4%)	7 (26.9%)	10 (41.7%)	8 (47.1%)	6 (40.0%)	13 (54.2%)	6 (40.0%)	11 (57.9%)	65 (39.2%)
Retirees reemployed for 4 or 5 years	13 (50.0%)	15 (57.7%)	14 (58.3%)	13 (76.5%)	8 (53.3%)	19 (79.2%)	7 (46.7%)	14 (73.7%)	103 (62.0%)
Retirees reemployed for 1 or 2 years	9 (34.6%)	6 (23.1%)	5 (20.8%)	2 (11.8%)	4 (26.7%)	2 (8.3%)	7 (46.7%)	5 (26.3%)	40 (24.1%)
Retirees reemployed at the 40% time maximum level	5 (19.2%)	4 (15.4%)	5 (20.8%)	3 (17.6%)	3 (20.0%)	7 (29.2%)	4 (26.7%)	2 (10.5%)	33 (19.9%)
Retirees re-employed at the 33%–40% time level	17 (65.4%)	12 (46.2%)	14 (58.3%)	11 (64.7%)	7 (46.7%)	13 (54.2%)	10 (66.7%)	9 (47.4%)	93 (56.0%)

years that they were reemployed, and 93 (56.0%) were reemployed in the range of 33%–40% time during the years that they were reemployed. It is interesting to note that the most common level of reemployment over the years (5 out of the 8 years) is the 33%–39% time level. This pattern may be partially accounted for by the fact that a retiree who elects to be reemployed in only one quarter of the 9-month academic year has a maximum reemployment option of 33% (i.e., 100% for one quarter). The Partial Reemployment Policy requires that the retiree receive full payment in the quarter in which the reemployment services (e.g., teaching) are delivered.

Voluntary Retirement Incentive Program

Program Description

The VRI Program is an alternative retirement benefit available to eligible tenured faculty whereby retirees elect to forgo their vested right to partial reemployment in exchange for a tax-free medical expense account. The faculty retiree and eligible dependents can use the fund to pay medical expenses after retirement. The medical expense account receives a onetime, lump-sum contribution from the state-funded position in the academic unit that the tenured faculty member is vacating on retirement. The contribution is based on the faculty member's 9- or 12-month state-funded (tenure-backed) position. The contribution amounts to 25% of the 5-year value of the state-funded 40% reemployment. For example, a faculty member with a $100,000 annual salary if reemployed at 40% over 5 years would earn a taxable income over that period of $200,000. This same faculty member could receive $50,000 as a onetime, lump-sum, tax-free deposit in a medical expense account at the time of retirement.

The contribution limits for 100% tenured faculty are a minimum of $25,000 and a maximum of $100,000. Proportional contribution limits apply to faculty with partial tenure. For example, a faculty member with a $100,000 annual salary and only 50% tenure would receive $25,000 as a contribution to a medical expense account.

The VRI was first offered in 2010 with an open election period from May 1, 2010, to December 31, 2010. The retirement window was May 1, 2010, to June 30, 2011. The open election period for the second offering of the VRI was October 1, 2011, to March 31, 2012. The retirement window was October 1, 2011, to December 31, 2012.

Eligible participants were informed of the VRI option through two personalized mailings that included a program brochure and instructions on the process for electing to participate. For each program offering, the first mailing went out during the month preceding the open election period. The second mailing went out 3 months before the end of the open election period. In the month before the end of the open election period, an e-mail was sent to all eligible participants reminding them of the closing date of the open election period. The deans and chancellors of all academic units with eligible participants were provided with the names of the eligible faculty and brochures for distribution.

Pattern of Use

The pattern of retirement reported in Table 16.13 indicates that 17 (45.9%) of the 37 retirees in 2009–2010 elected the VRI, 41 (69.5%) of the 59 retirees in 2010–2011 elected the VRI, and 24 (54.5%) of the 44 retirees in 2011–2012 elected the VRI. There are 16 additional retirees who elected the VRI who will be included in the 2012–2013 report when it is available.

In 2010 there were 590 tenured faculty who were eligible to elect to retire under the first offering of the VRI option. Of those eligible 58 (9.8%) elected to retire under the VRI. The profile of the faculty electing to retire under the VRI is summarized in Table 16.14.

In the period since retirement, 16 (27.6%) of the VRI retirees have been reemployed even though they did not have a vested right to reemployment. The reemployment of nine of these was limited to the year immediately following retirement. Two were reemployed at the maximum level of 40%, one at a partial level of 33%–39%, one at a partial level of 20%–32%, and five at a partial level of 1%–19%. Another retiree has been reemployed in 1 year since retirement at a partial level of 1%–19%, but it was not the year immediately following retirement. Six of the VRI retirees have been reemployed every year since retirement. One was reemployed at the maximum level of 40%, two at a partial level of 33%–39%, two at a partial level of 20%–32%,

TABLE 16.14
Profile of 2010–2011 Voluntary Retirement Incentive Retirees:
First Voluntary Retirement Incentive Offering

Academic rank	*Average age*	*Average payment to medical expense account*
Professor (49, or 84.5%)	68.5 (range of 62–82)	$55,686
Associate professor (8, or 13.8%)	65.6 (range of 62–69)	$39,809
Assistant professor (1, or 1.7%)	73	$42,804
58 total	68.2 (median of 67.5)	$53,274

and one at a partial level of 1%–19%. The average age of those who have been reemployed is 68.6, whereas the average age of those who have not been reemployed is 68.0.

During the same retirement period, an additional 24 tenured faculty retired. The average age of the non-VRI retirees was 66.6, with a median of 67. Eight of the non-VRI retirees did not have a vested right to reemployment because they were less than 62 years of age and were therefore not eligible to elect to participate in the VRI. Of the other 16 non-VRI retirees, three (18.8%) have not yet elected to be reemployed, while the remaining 13 (81.3%) have been reemployed. Of the reemployed group, eight have been reemployed in each year following retirement. Five were reemployed at the maximum level of 40%, one at the partial level of 33%–39%, one at the partial level of 20%–32%, and one at the partial level of 1%–19%. Of the remaining five reemployed non-VRI retirees, two have been reemployed in 2 years at the maximum level of 40%, one has been reemployed in 1 year at the maximum level of 40%, one has been reemployed in 2 years at the partial level of 1%–19%, and one has been reemployed in 1 year at the partial level of 1%–19%. The average age of those who were reemployed is 70.2, whereas the average age of those who have not been reemployed is 71.7.

As seen in the comparison of the reemployment patterns of VRI retirees and non-VRI retirees in Table 16.15, the non-VRI retirees are generally reemployed for a greater number of years after retirement and at a higher percentage of time.

In 2011 there were 608 tenured faculty who were eligible to elect to retire under the second offering of the VRI. Of those eligible 40 (6.6%) elected to retire under the VRI. The profile of the faculty electing to retire under the VRI is summarized in Table 16.16.

In the year since retirement, only seven (17.5%) have been reemployed: two at the maximum level of 40%, one at a partial level of 33%–39%, two at a partial level of 20%–32%, and two at a partial level of 1%–19%. The average age of those who were reemployed was 67.0, whereas the average age of those who have not been reemployed was 69.6.

During the same retirement period, an additional 22 tenured faculty retired. The average age of the non-VRI retirees was 70.1, with a median of 71. Two of the non-VRI retirees had entered into individual retirement agreements in which they had agreed to forgo their vested right to reemployment and were therefore not eligible to elect to participate in the VRI. Of the other 20 non-VRI retirees, four (20%) have not yet elected to be reemployed, whereas the remaining 16 (80.0%) have been reemployed. Of the reemployed group, seven have been reemployed at the maximum level of 40%, two were partially reemployed at the level of 33%–39%, five were partially reemployed

TABLE 16.15
Reemployment Comparison of 2010–2011 Voluntary Retirement Incentive and Non–Voluntary Retirement Incentive Retirees

Level of reemployment	VRI retiree					Non-VRI retiree				
	40%	33%–39%	20%–32%	1%–19%		40%	33%–39%	20%–32%	1%–19%	
Number of retirees employed for 1 year	2	1	1	6	10 (62.5%)	1	0	0	1	2 (15.4%)
Number of retirees employed for 2 years	0	0	0	0	0	2	0	0	1	3 (23.1%)
Number of retirees employed all years since retirement	1	2	2	1	6 (37.5%)	5	1	1	1	8 (61.5%)
Total	3	3	3	7	16	8	1	1	3	13

TABLE 16.16

**Profile of 2011–2012 Voluntary Retirement Incentive Retirees:
Second Voluntary Retirement Incentive Offering**

Academic rank	Average age	Average payment
Professor (33, or 82.5%)	70.2 (range of 63–86)	$54,387
Associate professor (7, or 17.5%)	64.4 (range of 62–68)	$36,636
40 total	69.2 (median of 68)	$51,281

at the level of 20%–32%, and two were partially reemployed at the level of 1%–19%. The average age of those who were reemployed was 71.4, whereas the average age of those who have not been reemployed was 66.5.

Like the 2010–2011 non-VRI retirees, the 2011–2012 non-VRI retirees are generally reemployed at a higher percentage of time (see Table 16.17).

Of particular note is the pattern of non-reemployment by non-VRI retirees. Three (18.8%) of the 2010–2011 non-VRI retirees and four (20.0%) of the 2011–2012 non-VRI retirees have not elected reemployment to date. This is a lower nonuse rate than was observed in the general review of the use of the reemployment policy, which had an average nonuse rate of 33.6%. Although specific information regarding the reasons for nonuse is not available, an explanation may be unanticipated health issues or personal obligations that have restricted the retirees' availability. Other explanations may include the retirees' need for additional information when making the decision to elect the VRI option or lack of familiarity with the reemployment policy. Some faculty had a difficult time deciding whether to give up their vested right to reemployment. For those who did not have plans to reemploy, electing the VRI may have been an easy investment decision. On the other hand, for those whose identity is closely tied to their relationship with the

TABLE 16.17

**Reemployment Comparison of 2011–2012 Voluntary Retirement
Incentive and Non–Voluntary Retirement Incentive Retirees**

	VRI retiree				Non-VRI retiree			
Level of reemployment		40%	33%–39%	20%–32%	1%–19%		40%	33%–39%	20%–32%	1%–19%
Number of retirees reemployed since retirement	7	2	1	2	2	16	7	2	5	2

university and who thus may want to continue to work part-time, the decision may have been more difficult from both a personal identity and financial perspective.

Conclusion

At the University of Washington, the Alfred P. Sloan Award for Best Practices in Faculty Retirement Transitions has provided an opportunity to reflect on the faculty's use of the retirement transition options that are available. Reviewing the use patterns of the Partial Reemployment Policy was a manual effort that the institution had not previously undertaken. Before the review many believed institutional myths regarding the use of the policy, such as most retirees are reemployed for no more than 1 to 2 years. But that myth was in fact not confirmed by the review. Instead, it was found that approximately one-third of retirees with a vested right to reemployment do not elect to be reemployed. Of those who do elect reemployment, however, almost two-thirds are reemployed for at least 4 years. We also learned from the ACE/Sloan faculty survey that faculty consider the Partial Reemployment Policy to be a valuable retirement transition tool.

As the university developed the VRI program, a concern that the university would expend resources to fund medical expense accounts for retirees who had no intention of being reemployed was expressed. The use data provided in this chapter show that about one-third of retirees with a vested right to reemployment do not elect to be reemployed. Therefore, it is likely that some of the VRI retirees would not have pursued reemployment if they had elected to retire without the VRI program. However, would they have retired at the time of the VRI offering if the incentive had not been available? This question remains a subject of future investigation.

The reemployment history of VRI retirees suggests that the program captured some faculty who intended to reemploy after retirement. In fact, 23 (23.5%) of the 98 VRI retirees have been reemployed since retirement. How many intended to reemploy after retirement but have not because of the VRI election is unknown. In addition, how many would have elected to retire in the same time frame if the VRI Program had not been offered is unknown. Did VRI serve as an incentive to retire? An assessment of the VRI Program from an institutional and faculty perspective will be enhanced by the deeper understanding of the retirees' eligibility for and use of retirement transition options as reported in this chapter. The next phase of the assessment requires studies of faculty eligible to retire, retirees, and academic units of employment. The university plans to conduct these assessments in 2013–2014, and we hope to report on those outcomes as well.

References

Revised Code of Washington, RCW 28B.10.420, Annuities and retirement income plans—Retirement at age seventy—Reemployment, conditions when. (2013). Retrieved from http://apps.leg.wa.gov/rcw/default.aspx?cite=28B.10.420

Revised Code of Washington, Chapter 42.52.140 RCW, Ethics in Public Service. (2013). Retrieved from http://apps.leg.wa.gov/rcw/default.aspx?cite=42.52&full =true

Revised Code of Washington, RCW 42.52.140, Gifts. (2013). Retrieved from http://apps.leg.wa.gov/rcw/default.aspx?cite=42.52.140

17

DEVELOPMENT OF A NEW RETIREMENT PROGRAM AT PRINCETON

Joan Girgus and Sandra Johnson, *Princeton University*

In the fall of 2008, the faculty and administration at Princeton University sought to develop a fair and transparent retirement program that would encourage faculty to retire. In February 2010 Princeton announced the institution of this new faculty retirement program, which joined three existing retirement programs and was designed to be the program of choice for Princeton faculty as they approach retirement. This chapter describes the evolution of the new program and the process that was used to institute it, the relationship of the new program to the three existing programs, and the initial results of its institution. The chapter also describes how Princeton supports the continuing scholarly work of its faculty after retirement, and Princeton's plans for the continuing enhancement of a smooth transition into retirement for faculty.

Background and Rationale

Before 1994 mandatory retirement ages were legal in many states, and most colleges and universities were able to set a mandatory retirement age for their faculty. Princeton's mandatory retirement age varied from 68 years of age between the end of World War II and 1970, to 65 years of age between 1970 and 1985, to 70 years of age from 1985 until 1994, when new federal legislation made it illegal to have a mandatory retirement age. The university's institution of a mandatory retirement age through this period meant that there was steady and regular turnover of faculty as senior faculty retired and junior faculty were hired to replace them. This meant that Princeton—and indeed universities generally—could plan for a constant flow of new ideas, new approaches, and even new fields and disciplines. In other words, between the end of World War II and 1994, intellectual renewal in the academy depended profoundly on the presence of a mandatory retirement age.

After a 1994 federal law prohibited colleges and universities from having a fixed retirement age for tenured faculty, Princeton instituted three programs that we hoped would permit (and encourage) faculty to choose the path to retirement that suited them best in the absence of a mandatory retirement age. Although we thought the average age of retirement would increase somewhat in the absence of a mandatory retirement age, we imagined there would be a brief period of years during which there would be relatively few retirements, followed by a steady stream of retirements once a new average age of retirement was established. We thought faculty would continue to retire because of a combination of factors: readiness to do something different than they had been doing as faculty members, an interest in reorganizing and rebalancing the time they spent on teaching and scholarship, the incentives that were built into each of the three new retirement programs we were instituting, and a desire to contribute to the opportunities for renewal of their departments and disciplines that are inherent in the hiring of young faculty who have only recently received their PhDs and who will provide the best of the new intellectual ideas and approaches in their teaching and scholarship.

The following are brief descriptions of the three programs that were instituted at that time (and that continue to exist to this day):

- *General Retirement Plan and Retirement Bonus*: Under this plan, tenured faculty members who commit before July 1 of any year to retire from the university on July 1 of the following year receive from the university on the date of their retirement a cash grant equal to the amount that the university contributed to the faculty member's TIAA-CREF or Vanguard retirement accounts during the final year of service before retirement.
- *Basic Phased Retirement Plan*: This plan permits half-time duty for a period of up to 4 years, with the formal agreement of the participating faculty member to retire from the university at the end of that period. During that 4-year period, participating faculty members receive half of their full-time-equivalent (FTE) salaries, which is either set

through the usual process of annual review or is the average salary of all professors of the same rank in the university, whichever is larger. Faculty members may teach full-time one term per year and be absent from campus the other term, and they are permitted to teach at other institutions during those terms that they have no duties at Princeton.

- *Enhanced Phased Retirement Plan*: This plan provides half-time service for a period of up to 2 years, with the formal agreement of the participating faculty member to retire from the university at the end of that period. During this 2-year period, participating faculty members receive two-thirds of their FTE salaries. Again, the FTE salary either is set through the usual process of annual review or is the average salary of all professors of the same rank in the university, whichever is larger.

If these programs had indeed led Princeton faculty to retire at the rate they were retiring when Princeton had a mandatory retirement age (although at a slightly older average age), departments and the university would have experienced a brief hiatus in retirements but, after that, would have been able to continue to plan for the constant renewal that is so crucial to the evolution of intellectual life and scientific discovery. But this is not what happened. After 1994 some faculty at Princeton retired at or before age 70, but the vast majority did not. Indeed, many faculty seemed not to know how to decide when to retire. In the 15 years following the lifting of a mandatory retirement age, the Princeton tenure-track and tenured faculty grew by 51 overall, but the number of assistant professors decreased by 27 and the number of tenured faculty (associate and full professors) grew by 78, largely because Princeton continued to grant tenure to deserving assistant professors while tenured faculty were choosing to continue their lives as tenured faculty members well past the age at which faculty had previously been required to retire. By 2008–2009 the percentage of faculty at Princeton who were tenured had grown to 77% from 72% in 1993–1994; 15.4% of the faculty were older than age 65 as compared to 5.3% in 1993–1994, and 6.5% of the faculty were aged 71 or higher as compared to 0% in 1993–1994.

In the face of these numbers, Princeton decided that it needed to look for a new approach to faculty retirement for several reasons. First, the decline in the number of positions for new PhDs limited the opportunities for the profession to renew itself and threatened the loss of a generation of scholars and the new ideas and intellectual approaches they would bring with them. Second, the smaller number of opportunities to hire assistant professors hindered Princeton's efforts to diversify its faculty. The senior faculty now reaching retirement age is largely a White male group that went to graduate school

40–50 years ago. The young people who are in graduate school and completing their PhDs now may not be as diverse in gender and race as we would like, but they are a much more diverse group than the senior faculty nearing retirement age. Finally, we were concerned that increasingly the details of each faculty member's retirement plan were worked out individually between the faculty member and the dean of the faculty. This led faculty considering retirement to believe that a better deal could always be negotiated and that others were getting a better deal than they were. It also led the university to want to develop a retirement plan that would be the same for everyone and that would be seen as fair—even generous—by everyone.

Thus, in the fall of 2008, David Dobkin, Princeton's dean of the faculty, instituted a process designed to see whether a new retirement plan could be developed that would encourage faculty to begin thinking about retirement earlier than they had been and that would then ultimately return the "normal" retirement age for faculty to between age 65 and 70. The process began with a series of four focus groups led by Dobkin that took place over the course of 5 weeks. A total of 19 tenured faculty representing a range of disciplines participated in these focus groups with four to six faculty members in each group. The participants were chosen for several reasons: they were thought leaders, they were probably nearing retirement, they were people who might have helpful ideas on the subject, or they were particularly effective department chairs. Dobkin laid out the two following issues: (a) the secrecy of our current process doesn't serve us well because everyone thinks everyone else is getting a better deal and (b) the current plans are not providing us with the faculty renewal opportunities that we need to maintain ourselves as a major research university. He then opened the floor for discussion. The comments from the faculty in these focus groups were remarkably consistent.

First, people clearly believed that "70 is the new 60." People are more vital than before; they both want to and can work longer than they could even 20 years ago. At the same time there was agreement that it is important to encourage retirement in order to create the "churn" of new ideas and foci in departments and to create career paths for young scholars, including our own graduate students. For this to happen, senior faculty must be encouraged to retire, and departments must be given permission to appoint assistant professors to replace them.

Second, there was complete agreement about the centrality of several aspects of any new retirement plan that have nothing to do with providing resources: there should be no special deals; transparency and openness are crucial; retiring faculty must feel that they have the full respect of the university and their colleagues; and this is not about the money, it is about ego and dignity. Participants in the focus groups emphasized the importance of recognizing that when a faculty member decides to retire, he or she is contributing to the overall good of the university and the academy more generally. Along these same lines, focus group participants urged the dean to find things that retirees can do to help the university.

The resource question that received the most attention in all four focus groups was office (and lab) space after retirement. Many—indeed, most—Princeton faculty want to continue their research and scholarship after they retire, and so space and the proximity of colleagues and intellectual interlocutors are important to them. Office space was not only seen as important by everyone; it was also seen as a problem because some departments have space for retirees and others don't. For some faculty this can be solved by providing central space that is designated for retired faculty, but other faculty will see having space near their departmental and scholarly colleagues as crucial to their well-being and thus to their willingness to retire. Additionally, some focus group participants thought that teaching opportunities after retirement could be an issue for some faculty, although that concern came up less frequently than one might have expected.

Before convening the first focus group, Dobkin had developed an outline for the new retirement plan. In the course of the focus group discussions, this draft plan was changed in various ways, such as increasing the size of the retirement bonuses. In October 2008 this new iteration of the plan was brought to one of the quarterly meetings of department chairs and program directors for discussion; this group reiterated most of the points raised in the focus groups. The president and the dean of the faculty used this opportunity to describe the important role department chairs must play in discussions with faculty about retirement. Since department chairs work with faculty on the trajectories of their research and teaching, they are the ones who will have to be responsible for raising questions about retirement with faculty. Although department chairs are not expected to discuss retirement plans with faculty in any detail, the president and dean of the faculty made it clear that the university does expect them to encourage appropriate faculty to talk with the dean of the faculty or the associate dean who has been designated as the person who will work out plans for individual faculty.

By October 2008 another factor intervened: the country in general and thus all universities were in the grip of extreme economic uncertainty. As the stock market slid dramatically lower, and faculty watched their retirement accounts shrink before their eyes, it became clear that faculty were going to be reluctant to consider retirement until things stabilized, no matter how attractive the new plan was. Thus, Princeton put the planning process on hold. By the fall of 2009, the overall financial situation at Princeton had stabilized sufficiently to return to the question of a new retirement plan. Faculty were feeling more secure about considering retirement as the stock market, and thus their retirement accounts, recovered much of the ground they had lost in the fall of 2008. Therefore, Dobkin convened an ad hoc committee of eight tenured faculty members to review the plan that had been under discussion the year before. This group represented a mix of faculty with special expertise on the economy and on issues concerning retirement along with several long-standing department chairs. Dobkin reviewed the plan developed in 2008 with them, asked their advice about any revisions that should be made, and asked whether the recession was sufficiently in the past to roll out a new plan at this point. The dean specified a series of goals for the new retirement plan:

- to incentivize the tenured faculty to embrace 65–70 as an appropriate retirement age if they so choose
- to be transparent and clear about the options that are available and ensure that everyone has access to the same options
- to allow individual faculty members to determine the path toward emeritus status that works best for them
- to allow faculty to continue to be productive members of the university community after retirement at the level that seems right for them

The ad hoc committee met several times and added an additional retirement option (described later in the chapter) to those that had previously been specified. In January 2010 the new plan was presented to a meeting of department chairs and program directors. During the time the ad hoc committee was meeting and considering the new retirement plan, the proposed plan was also being reviewed by Princeton's legal counsel, who advised several changes. For example, the original version of the plan considered by the ad hoc committee spread a bonus payment out over several years in order to ease the tax burden on retiring faculty. Princeton's legal counsel made it clear that any bonus would have to be paid to the faculty member in its entirety at the time the retirement agreement was signed, and so the plan was changed to reflect this requirement.

In February 2010 Dobkin sent all faculty a letter highlighting the goals of the new plan and detailing how the new plan would work. At the monthly university faculty meeting in March 2010, Dobkin reviewed the details of the new plan and answered questions from the faculty. In that same month he and Associate Dean Sandra Johnson met with small groups of faculty who were interested in considering retirement and walked them through the details of the new plan.

TABLE 17.1
Bonus Rates

Faculty member's age	65	66	67	68	69
Premium as a multiple of salary	1.50	1.25	1.00	0.75	0.50

The New Retirement Plan

The new plan is an age-based retirement-incentive plan that offers a bonus at the time of signing an agreement to retire as well as an opportunity to enter phased retirement for some number of years after signing. It works in the following way: To be retirement eligible, a faculty member must be at least 55 years old and have at least 10 years of half-time or greater service at Princeton. Faculty who are eligible for retirement can sign a retirement agreement under the new plan when they are between the ages of 65 and 69. At the end of the month in which the agreement is signed, the faculty member is paid a bonus that is a multiplier of the faculty member's salary or the average salary of all faculty at that rank, whichever is greater. The bonus begins at 1.5 times salary at age 65 and declines by .25 times salary each year after that through age 69 (see Table 17.1).

A faculty member who signs a retirement agreement between the ages of 65 and 69 is also eligible to continue teaching half-time for up to 3 years, with the number of years of half-time teaching dependent on the age of signing (see Table 17.2).

Faculty members who wish to teach full-time up to retirement may instead choose a bonus equal to 1 year of their final salary at retirement by signing a retirement agreement before turning 67 that commits the faculty member to transfer to emeritus status not later than the end of the academic year in which he or she turns 70. This option was added to the plan in the fall of 2009 at the suggestion of the ad hoc faculty committee.

We believe the new retirement plan both provides a fair benefit to those who choose to retire and enables us to open up positions for scholars at the beginning of their academic careers who will form the future of Princeton. The new plan has proved to be popular with Princeton faculty. At the time it was instituted, there were 72 faculty members who were at least age 65

TABLE 17.2
Teaching Options

Faculty member's age	65	66	67	68	69
Possible number of years of phased teaching	3	3	2	2	1

but had not yet turned 70. Because nine of these faculty had already signed retirement agreements, there were 63 faculty eligible to participate in the initial offering of the new retirement plan, and 18 (29%) of the faculty in this group elected to do so. There was a separate initial offering of a bonus of 1.5 times salary with opportunities for up to 3 years of phased teaching for those faculty who had already turned 70 when the new retirement plan was instituted, and 49% of those eligible in this group elected to participate. (This separate offering for faculty over the age of 70 was available for only 4 months, after which the new retirement plan has been available only to faculty between the ages of 65 and 69.) Altogether, 35 faculty members signed retirement agreements under the new retirement plan during the first 6 months after it was instituted.

It is important to note that the three retirement plans that were already in existence when the new plan was instituted continue to be available to faculty. Since the institution of the new retirement plan, those plans are particularly used by those who do not wish to retire by the age of 70.

In implementing the new retirement plan, we have realized the importance of continuing to provide individual conversations with an associate dean of the faculty to those faculty who are considering retirement. Although the options are clearly described on the Dean of the Faculty website, each faculty member understandably sees his or her situation as unique, and although the broad parameters of the retirement arrangements are the same for all faculty, there are always details that are best worked out on an individual basis with a human touch.

Supports for Continuing Research and Scholarship After Retirement

The majority of Princeton faculty wish to continue their research and scholarship after retirement, and some would like occasional opportunities to teach. Thus, in addition to the standard supports that most colleges and universities provide for retirees (e.g., health benefits and access to the programs of the institution's employee assistance provider), Princeton provides a number of supports designed to enable retired faculty to continue to pursue their research and scholarship.

- Tenured faculty in good standing are appointed to the ranks of professor or associate professor emeritus when they retire, and faculty who hold endowed chairs may keep the names of their chair in the emeritus title.

- Whenever possible, emeriti faculty are assigned office space as available and needed. It is sometimes possible to do this in the faculty member's home department. Alternatively, there is some shared central office space for retired faculty. This is one of our larger challenges as the majority of retiring faculty want to have offices, and like many universities, Princeton is short of office space, even shared office space.
- Some departments are able to continue to provide some secretarial and computing support for emeriti faculty.
- Faculty retain their university computing privileges when they are granted emeritus status. In particular, there is no change to their existing Princeton e-mail address upon becoming an emeritus faculty member.
- Emeriti faculty continue to have use of the library on the same basis as active faculty.
- Emeriti faculty are assigned on-campus parking permits on the same basis as active faculty.
- Emeriti faculty may be appointed as senior scholars if they serve as principal investigators on sponsored research projects or maintain active research programs at the university. Appointments and re-appointments to the rank of senior scholar are normally for renewable 1-year terms on the recommendation of the sponsoring department. Senior scholars have no specific responsibilities in teaching or research but are encouraged to participate in department, center, and institute programs and to interact with faculty, researchers, and students in informal settings.
- Faculty who can support 50% of their annual salary through grants and contracts can request that they be appointed to the research staff as benefits-eligible senior research scholars after they retire from the faculty. Their initial FTE salary at this rank is a 12-month salary equivalent to their academic year salary plus 2.5/9ths of summer salary (i.e., 1.278 times the academic year salary).
- Emeriti faculty in the humanities and social sciences are eligible to request grants from the University Committee on Research in the Humanities and Social Sciences (UCRH&SS) in support of their scholarly research. Grants are made for a great variety of purposes. Among the most frequent are travel and living expenses necessary for research away from home, research assistance, research materials, and subvention of publication.
- Senior research scholars who are retired faculty are eligible to apply for learned society travel funds. These funds provide reimbursement of transportation and hotel expenses for conferences or learned society

meetings (held within or outside the United States), provided that the retired faculty member is delivering a paper, chairing a session, participating as an invited discussant, or serving with the learned society as an officer.

- Emeriti faculty continue to have access to the remaining funds in their research accounts. Retiring faculty also receive an additional $5,000 in their research accounts in order to help ease the transition in their scholarship and research. These funds may be used to pay for research-related expenses, such as the purchase of books and other research materials, including databases and software; the employment of research assistants; payment of subventions; payment of translation expenses for research materials; research-related travel; and other research-related expenditures. (These funds may not be used by faculty to pay themselves a salary or summer salary.)
- Laboratory space, when available, is provided for retired faculty as long as their research continues to be supported by outside grants.
- Emeriti faculty may carry to completion the supervision of those doctoral students whom they were advising before retirement (but may not accept new graduate students after retirement).
- Emeriti faculty may accept postdoctoral fellows and other researchers to work with them.
- There are opportunities for postretirement teaching. These are determined by the department chair in consultation with the dean of the faculty based on departmental needs and constraints. Post-retirement teaching is limited to one course a year up to a maximum over the entire retirement of three courses. When retired faculty members engage in postretirement teaching, they are paid at the rate of a lecturer with the rank of professor, and during the semester they teach, they hold the title of lecturer with the rank of professor in addition to their emeritus professorial title.

Princeton Faculty Views of the Current Practices

As part of the application process for the Alfred P. Sloan Award for Best Practices in Faculty Retirement Transitions, the American Council on Education (ACE) surveyed both the currently active Princeton faculty and the retired faculty. All the questions asked how satisfied faculty were regarding a set of retirement-related issues, using the following scale: very dissatisfied, dissatisfied, neutral, satisfied, very satisfied, don't know, and not applicable (N/A). We were pleased that the Princeton faculty had the highest satisfaction scores of all the colleges and universities that applied for the award in the following categories: posttenure review and other options, phasing and transitioning supports, financial planning and medical insurance, and ongoing supports and opportunities in retirement. In addition, Princeton faculty were the second-most satisfied group in the category of campus culture regarding senior faculty.

We were particularly pleased with the percentage of faculty who declared themselves "very satisfied" with specific aspects of what is provided for the retirement transition at Princeton. On questions about the following provisions, the "very satisfied" responses of Princeton faculty were at least 10 percentage points higher than the responses of all research universities and all participating institutions:

- ability to phase to retirement
- amount of time given to colleagues to phase into retirement
- senior colleagues being valued by their junior colleagues
- senior colleagues being valued by the students
- employee assistance program
- ability to participate in continued health insurance
- ability for partners and dependents to participate in health insurance
- office space on campus
- research opportunities
- library privileges
- e-mail privileges
- social/fitness (e.g., gym access, faculty facilities, commencement activities)
- participation in lectures, performing arts, and international opportunities

Plans for the Future

As we contemplate the current set of retirement options and support services for retired faculty, we believe our next steps should be to help faculty begin thinking about and planning for retirement at much earlier stages in their careers. We are primarily concerned with helping faculty plan for a financially secure retirement by initiating their engagement at the beginning of their careers. We also would like to develop programs for faculty in the latter stages of their careers who might be concerned that they haven't yet planned adequately for retirement. To these ends we are working on instituting financial counseling for incoming assistant professors designed to introduce them to the benefits of supplemental retirement annuity accounts. We also are working on instituting more elaborate financial planning counseling for faculty as they are promoted to full professor or come to Princeton as full professors. Finally, we are exploring programs to help those faculty who are not planning to continue their scholarly and research activities after retirement think about how they might structure their postretirement lives so that they are more fulfilling. We believe (and the faculty survey responses support the idea) that our current postretirement supports work well for those faculty who wish to continue their research and scholarship but provide fewer supports for those faculty who would like to undertake new ventures after they retire from their faculty positions.

18

RETIREMENT PROGRAMS AND PLANS AT GEORGIA TECH

Spotlight on a Technological University

Rosario A. Gerhardt, *Georgia Institute of Technology*

The Georgia Institute of Technology (Georgia Tech) is part of the University System of Georgia (USG), which comprises more than 35 higher education institutions that must share limited resources while advocating for their unique needs and advancing their distinctive missions. Georgia Tech currently boasts a student body of approximately 21,000 and a faculty of nearly 1,000 (Office of Institutional Research and Planning, 2013), mostly focused on training engineers, with smaller programs in the sciences, computing, architecture, business, and liberal arts. When G. P. "Bud" Peterson joined Georgia Tech as president in April 2009, he was faced with a number of issues resulting from the economic downturn: state-mandated furloughs, a difficult outlook regarding new faculty hiring, and a professoriate whose original plans to retire were thwarted because of low investment returns or the inability to sell their homes. Now, nearly 4 years later, the economy has begun to turn around, and faculty who are eligible to retire or have postponed retirement are finding it easier to take the plunge. This chapter discusses the retirement benefits and programs that Georgia Tech provides to make retirement a viable and attractive option for faculty in the absence of a mandatory retirement policy, as well as to ensure that the institute continues to benefit from the contributions retirees make to our ongoing pursuit of institutional excellence and effectiveness. The chapter concludes with some anecdotal information obtained from the Georgia Tech news archives and interviews with more than 20 retirees, as well as some tentative next steps for further enhancing the retiree experience at Georgia Tech.

Georgia Tech Faculty

We have made strides in diversifying the professoriate. Active Georgia Tech faculty during spring 2012 were 71% White, 22% Asian, 4% Black or African American, and 3% Hispanic or Latino/a. We had a total of 179 female professors out of a total of 897 active faculty (20%). In addition, as indicated in Figure 18.1, 59% of female faculty and 44% of male faculty are under 44 years old.

While more than 100 faculty are of retirement age, we have recently increased our faculty ranks so that the number of assistant and associate professors now exceeds the number of full professors. Most full professors are between the ages of 45 and 54, and the average age at retirement is 64. These trends are shown in Figure 18.2, in which the faculty are presented by rank and age. As of March 2012 there were 243 retirees, of which 146 held emeritus status.

Assessing Awareness of Retiree Benefits

As part of the competition for the Sloan Award for Best Practices in Faculty Retirement Transitions, tenured, tenure-track, and retired faculty were asked to respond to an American Council on Education (ACE) questionnaire

Figure 18.1. Comparison of the active faculty during spring 2012 as function of gender and age.

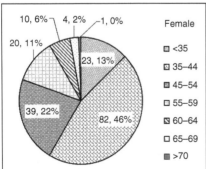
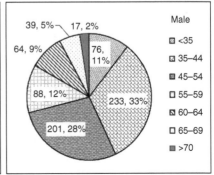

Figure 18.2. Number of active faculty during spring 2012 as function of rank and age.

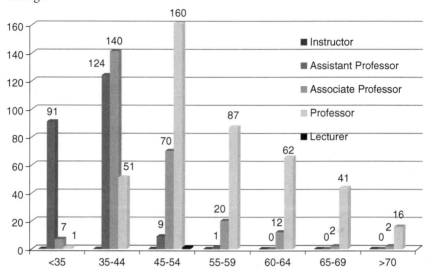

about the retirement transition programs available to them. Of those who responded, 15.1% were emeritus faculty, 55.6% were full professors, 17.5% were associate professors, and 11.9% were assistant professors. The majority of those who responded had been at Georgia Tech for more than 20 years. In view of this workforce stability, it was surprising to learn that a fairly large percentage of those who responded were not familiar with many of the retirement options and benefits available to them. However, this is apparently fairly common, as faculty at most institutions that participated in the survey indicated a similar lack of awareness. On the other hand, most Georgia Tech respondents felt that the campus culture valued senior colleagues, and a great number expressed satisfaction with the financial planning and insurance options available. (See chapter 2 for more details about the aggregated responses to the various questions.)

The following sections describe the retirement options available to tenured and tenure-track faculty at the Georgia Institute of Technology and some of the changes implemented over the years that have helped secure a brighter future for our retirees.

Faculty Retirement Benefits

Georgia Tech offers a comprehensive benefits package designed to meet the diverse needs of our faculty and staff. Our benefits are competitive and are an important component of the total compensation package. Georgia Tech offers a robust choice of health and welfare plans including medical, dental, vision, flexible spending, disability, and life insurance plans.

Teachers Retirement System of Georgia Versus Optional Retirement Plan

All regular faculty and staff are required to participate in either the Teachers Retirement System (TRS) or the Optional Retirement Plan (ORP). Supplemental retirement plans allow for additional savings opportunities. The TRS program is a defined benefit plan with a 6% employee contribution and an 11.41% employer contribution. TRS has a 10-year vesting period, 2% per year income replacement, and disability retirement at 10 years of service at any age. The ORP is a defined contribution plan offered to salaried, exempt employees only. The plan requires a 6% employee contribution and has a 9.24% employer contribution. Vesting is immediate, and service providers include VALIC, Fidelity, and TIAA-CREF. Supplemental retirement plans include 403(b) tax-sheltered annuity plans and a 457(b) deferred compensation plan. Employees can contribute up to $17,000 pretax for 2012 (and an additional $5,500 for employees age 50 and over) and may enroll and make changes to their election at any time. A Roth 403(b) is available for after-tax contributions.

Health Insurance Options

Georgia Tech faculty have two comprehensive medical plans to choose from: the Open Access Point of Service (POS) and the Health Savings Account (HSA) Open Access POS. The HSA Open Access POS is a qualified high-deductible health plan (HDHP) that offers lower premiums in exchange for a higher deductible and allows employees to contribute up to $3,100 for individual coverage and up to $6,250 for family coverage on a pretax basis. This money can be used to satisfy the deductible or other qualified medical expenses. Employees age 55 or older may contribute an additional $1,000 per year. Contributions to this account roll over every year and can also be used as an additional source of disposable income after age 65 without penalty. Both plans are administered by Blue Cross Blue Shield (BCBS) of Georgia.

To continue health benefits from Georgia Tech after retirement, faculty must meet retirement eligibility requirements defined in the USG (2009) *Board of Regents Policy Manual* as follows:

- Have been employed by the USG for the last ten (10) years in a regular, benefitted position and have attained age 60; or,

- Have at least twenty-five (25) total years of benefitted service established with a State of Georgia sponsored retirement plan, of which the last five (5) years of employment must have been continuous and with the USG. An early pension benefit penalty will apply to an individual who elects to participate in the Teachers Retirement System of Georgia, or in the Employees Retirement System, if he/she decides to retire with between twenty-five (25) and thirty (30) years of benefitted service prior to attaining age 60; or,
- Have at least thirty (30) total years of benefitted service established with a State of Georgia sponsored retirement plan, of which the last five (5) years must have been continuous and with the USG.

Reemployment After Retirement

When a faculty member retires from Georgia Tech and is receiving benefits from the TRS, the Employees Retirement System, or the Regent's Retirement Plan, he or she may be reemployed by the institute only with approval from the USG Board of Regents and under the following conditions:

- The reemployment must be approved by the institute's president.
- The retiree must have a minimum break of 30 days between the effective date of retirement and the effective date of reemployment.
- The work commitment of a rehired retiree must be less than half-time.
- The salary paid to a rehired retiree must be less than 50% of the annual benefit-base compensation earned at the time of retirement.
- The salary paid to a rehired retiree must be consistent with his or her work commitment.

Over the past few years, the Faculty Benefits Committee has discussed the need for an additional retirement incentive, especially for tenured faculty who are eligible to retire but who have not, in part because there is no longer a mandatory retirement age. As an example, the committee has offered faculty on the TRS plan full summer employment for, say, 2 years in a row right before retirement—which can boost their retirement earnings—in exchange for a firm retirement date. This option is taken advantage of primarily by faculty whose fields of expertise do not rely on external funding and who often teach over the summer months. But many faculty in the science, technology, engineering, and mathematics fields, such as those in the College of Engineering, the College of Computing, or the College of Sciences, have their summer paid for via external grants and do not need this incentive.

Maintaining Access to E-Mail, Office Space, and Labs

Tenured faculty at a technology-focused university such as Georgia Tech establish an extensive network of interaction beyond the classroom. Because of the complexity and variety of their research and rapidly changing technology, physical and online access to libraries, laboratory facilities, electronic communications, and other resources are vital. Georgia Tech faculty who wish to maintain their access to these resources may apply for emeritus status. A policy established by the USG Board of Regents states that an institution's president may, at his or her discretion, confer the title of emeritus or emerita on any retired faculty member who at the time of retirement had 10 or more years of honorable and distinguished service in the USG. In addition to the system requirements, Georgia Tech has institute-specific requirements that faculty must satisfy to be awarded emeritus status.

The following procedure is normally used to develop recommendations:

- Faculty seeking the emeritus title must submit a written request to the head of their department or unit before their planned retirement date. They may also give consent to be nominated for emeritus status by a colleague within the same unit.
- If the unit has a designated Faculty Advisory Committee, the unit head will forward the request, along with a detailed vita of the faculty member, to that committee. The unit's Faculty Advisory Committee will then submit a written recommendation (either positive or negative) to the unit head.
- The unit head will then prepare and forward a written recommendation (either positive or negative), along with the Faculty Advisory Committee's recommendation (if applicable) and the faculty member's vita, to the president for final action.
- The unit recommendation should be conveyed to the president and the candidate no later than 3 months after the request date.

Retirement Track Options for Rehired Faculty

There are many ways retired tenured faculty can contribute to the betterment of Georgia Tech, its students, and its junior faculty. We offer three tracks that retired faculty can take to continue to be engaged in the institution.

Research Track

Faculty may continue to apply for research grants, support graduate students and postdocs, and maintain their research activity as long as the guidelines for reemployment are followed. Many faculty who have chosen this route continue to supervise the research of PhD students and postdocs for years. Other faculty choose to collaborate with junior faculty and help them get their research off the ground. Others take on more visible leadership research positions. A few choose to accept employment at other institutions of higher learning, and others go back into the extensive data they collected over the years and publish long-overdue research articles.

Teaching Track

Faculty may continue to teach courses on an ad hoc basis as long as there is a need. For example, a number of retired faculty have recently chosen to teach required courses around the world at Georgia Tech's various international programs. Retired faculty often have the time and flexibility to teach abroad and use this opportunity to engage with our students. Faculty may also teach on the Georgia Tech campus if needed. Most often they teach courses that are required for a large number of students, specialized courses that were developed by the retired faculty themselves, and courses for which Georgia Tech has not yet found a replacement professor.

Service Track

This is the track most often followed by senior faculty who served as administrators right before retiring. They may choose to come back to work on various committees or special assignments on a part-time basis. Retired faculty can serve on specialty committees, help review promotion and tenure packages, or serve in a variety of interim leadership positions while a replacement is being found.

Other Retiree Engagement

Regardless of whether retirees plan to fully retire or continue their association with Georgia Tech through teaching, part-time employment, or emeritus status, Georgia Tech offers several other programs and organizations that show them they are valued and keep them connected to the institute.

Retirement Dinner Banquet

All Georgia Tech administrative staff and faculty are invited to a grand fete honoring retiring faculty, which features personalized tributes to each retiree. Retiring faculty must apply to be included. An e-mail is sent to all retiring employees, but the application information can also be downloaded from the Human Resources website.

Silver Jackets

Silver Jackets is a Georgia Tech retiree organization that was spearheaded by Maureen Glass, a retiring administrative manager, in 2007 (Pavlik, 2011). This organization holds monthly meetings in the spring and fall semesters, during which presentations of interest to retirees are given. For example, in November Silver Jackets presents benefits options so retirees can decide whether they should change their benefits during the open enrollment period. In addition to the monthly meetings, Silver Jackets members also volunteer to assist at blood drives and participate in volunteer activities around the state.

Alumni Association

Some retirees also take advantage of the many activities provided by the Georgia Tech Alumni Association and remarked in interviews that the trips offered by the association are getting better all the time.

Words From the Wise

Interviews with approximately 20 retired faculty in the spring of 2013 revealed that their activities are as diversified during their retirement years as they were when they were part of the professoriate at Georgia Tech. Several said they are now more physically active, taking time to bike, run, or swim regularly, while others have become more involved with the arts, volunteering with Atlanta Symphony Hall, the Center of Puppetry Arts, and other venues in the city of Atlanta. Yet others have taken up painting or gardening as a full-time avocation.

During the individual interviews, several major themes were repeated:

- Have a plan beyond wanting to use the time for travel or relaxation.
- Prepare for having an unstructured life and the emotional changes that may result.
- Work out the details of how to get the most from Medicare and health-care benefits.

- Consider talking to a financial planner about managing retirement income, especially if you are part of the ORP, which has a fixed amount of savings (unlike the TRS program, which has an automatic cost of living increase of 1.5% every 6 months), or if you have more than one retirement account.
- Be aware that what works for someone else may not be the best option for you, and do your homework.
- If you are on the TRS system and have obtained 40 years of credit, do not keep working; your retirement salary is already at a maximum.
- Take advantage of online access to the library.
- Enjoy life.
- Volunteer; it will do you good.

Next Steps

In Georgia Tech's ongoing efforts to provide support and engagement opportunities for retirees, we are exploring several new initiatives, including the following:

- *Benefits survey*: We currently do not survey the faculty about their knowledge of or satisfaction with the retirement transition supports, but we are considering adding questions on this subject in future faculty surveys that will follow up our initial climate assessment study.
- *Competition for postretirement legacy projects*: We plan to hold an internal competition to encourage Georgia Tech retirees to serve as mentors to young faculty, complete intellectual projects (e.g., books or software), participate in international activities, and participate in research related to age and disabilities.

We also intend to solicit additional funds from different sources to contribute to new programs at Georgia Tech so that these programs become sustainable.

References

Office of Institutional Research and Planning, Georgia Institute of Technology. (2013). Retrieved from http://www.irp.gatech.edu/

Pavlik, A. (2011). Silver Jackets keep retirees connected. *The Whistle, 36*(24), 3. Retrieved from http://www.whistle.gatech.edu/archives/11/nov/28/112811.pdf

University System of Georgia (USG). (2009). *Board of Regents policy manual.* Retrieved from www.usg.edu/policymanual/

PART SEVEN

CONCLUSION

19

WHAT LEADERS MUST DO

Ensuring Smooth Faculty Retirement Transitions

Claire A. Van Ummersen, *American Council on Education*

Much attention has been focused on early faculty career stages—recruiting, retention, and advancement—but because of the concern for age discrimination, institutions have not been as aggressive in developing opportunities and support structures for senior faculty in the culminating years of their careers, when they begin to think about retirement. The result has been that senior faculty often feel marginalized and hunger for respect from colleagues, recognition of their achievements, and support appropriate to their career stage. Only recently have institutions come to understand what faculty need at this latter stage and how they might provide for them without seeming unfair to others or, worse, incurring penalties under the age discrimination statutes. When we began studying the culminating stages of faculty careers, as detailed in the first two chapters, we recognized that common elements helped administrators to create building blocks for success. Most important, we've found that campuses with a culture that was already strained or under pressure had a difficult time addressing sensitive and personal issues, such as the culminating stages of faculty careers and retirement issues. If the culture was already fractured, efforts to move faculty into retirement were often met with suspicion and disregard. If the problems of culture were not addressed, or even acknowledged, while reforms were being carried out, then change was likely to be slowed or halted. The authors of the chapters in this book have shared best practices and models for support that will work in many different types of institutions—large and small, from research universities to liberal arts colleges, both public and private. They also have revealed the creativity of the recipients of the Sloan Award for Best Practices in Faculty Retirement Transitions in providing services that satisfy faculty and accomplish institutional goals at a reasonable cost.

This final chapter reviews the key themes presented in this book, discusses the role of culture change in the planning and implementation stages of retirement transition programs, and provides tips on implementation for campuses seeking to create win-win environments for their institutions and their faculty.

Review of Key Themes

When we asked the award-winning campuses to provide examples of best practices that might be replicated in other settings, we noticed similar topics and themes. We have thus divided the book into parts addressing these six major themes: (a) Setting the Context; (b) The Psychosocial Aspects of the Culminating Stages of Faculty Careers; (c) Institutional Structures That Support the Culminating Stages of Faculty Careers; (d) Senior and Emeriti Faculty Contributions to Local Communities; (e) Tapping Into the Bigger Picture: Missions, Systems, and National Associations; and (f) Challenges of and Opportunities for Implementation.

The chapters in Part One discuss how higher education arrived at its current state of affairs regarding faculty retirement and the culminating stages of faculty careers. As the baby boomers age, campuses are beginning to see how much of a priority retirement should be for strategic human resource planning. Sustaining and replenishing human capital is critical to the proper functioning and renewal of the academy. Chapters 1 and 2 also provide the context for this book, describing how the campuses were selected, what was learned during the competition administered by the American Council on Education (ACE), and what were the common trends in the data from our surveys.

The chapters in Part Two discuss the psychosocial aspect of faculty life, which is especially pronounced in liberal arts colleges and institutions that have strong ties to their local community. Albright College provides us with an alternate view of community and engagement, through the Japanese concept of *fureai*, and encourages administrators to reflect on the current faculty community as an instrument of support for phasing and retiring faculty. Mount Holyoke College considers the relevancy of developmental theory in addressing retirement, specifically the push-pull influences in a faculty member's life in the culminating years of his or her career. Carleton College addresses how faculty are both supported by and support the local community, especially through ongoing local governance and civic engagements.

The chapters in Part Three look at the formalized structures that campuses can put in place to facilitate and smooth the retirement transition for senior faculty. These chapters address time-honored policies and programs that many institutions have but also offer institutional variations on these traditions. San José State University (SJSU), for example, has reinvented its midcareer faculty retreats, originally intended for associate professors, to help senior faculty plan for retirement. Housed in the Emeriti Center and funded by an endowment, the University of Southern California's Living History Project creates and stores archival-quality video interviews of retired faculty (and staff). Among other offerings for retired faculty, these videos signal the institution's commitment to helping faculty develop a legacy of their academic careers. Bentley University revitalized its phased retirement program by offering more flexible, 1-, 2-, or 3-year commitments. This change increased faculty satisfaction and usage. Finally, Skidmore College seized an opportunity to work with a retiring and long-serving faculty member and developed the Retiree Initiative Planning Group, which serves as an association for retired employees.

The chapters in Part Four highlight the community partnerships that senior and retired faculty have created. Wellesley College uses its Emeriti Faculty Steering Committee to develop and coordinate local seminars and activities to strengthen its connections with the town of Wellesley and its surrounding neighbors. The University of Baltimore has constructed an engaged ecosystem for its senior and retired faculty and has created a formal Engaged Retirement Policy. George Mason University, through a contract with Fairfax County, VA, offers local residents and university employees a variety of encore career engagement activities and courses designed by university faculty, such as Your Next Chapter: Charting the Course to Your Retirement, and the Lifetime Leadership Program.

Part Five steps back from the discussion of programs and offerings for senior and retired faculty and reframes discussions about retiring and retired faculty in a variety of ways. First, Xavier University builds upon the Jesuit mission of *cura personalis* in its Second Fifty programming, which helps participants evaluate the presence of spirituality in their lives. Next, the University of California–Davis explains how being in a university system, especially one as large as the University of California (UC) system, can benefit faculty. Davis can collect data on retirement trends from other UC institutions, offer its faculty a competitive retirement plan negotiated on a larger scale, and study the effectiveness of slight adjustments to retirement incentives in a controlled environment. Last, because many of the chapters discussed retiree organizations, we asked the Association of Retirement Organizations in Higher Education to briefly describe the advantages they offer their member institutions.

Part Six provides portraits of three campuses whose leadership successfully turned known challenges for senior faculty into opportunities for positive change. The University of Washington worked with faculty to address their concerns over retirement and developed a new Voluntary Retirement Incentive Program that complies with state laws on retirement benefits and provides individual medical expense accounts. Princeton University built on its retirement programs by conducting focus groups to learn what faculty needed to make the transition to retirement smoother. An ad hoc committee developed a new plan that is age based; provides financial incentives; and, most important, is consistently and fairly applied to eligible faculty. Finally, the Georgia Institute of Technology, while upholding a state-enforced restriction on phased retirement, offers retired faculty seeking reemployment three options: a research track, a teaching track, and a service track.

Change and Culture in Higher Education

The rate of change in the world today is much faster than in past decades. Higher education is faced with constrained resources, changing demographics, increasing faculty longevity resulting from better health, and the uncapping of the mandatory retirement age. Likewise, its environment is volatile, uncertain, complex, and ambiguous. Higher education leaders must adapt their institutions to these changes more quickly. Although the current situation is confounding, it also provides unparalleled opportunities to balance the composition of faculty to meet institutional goals of diversity and to ensure institutional capacity to maintain program excellence and competitive positioning for recruiting students, faculty, and research funding. Leaders must understand the dynamics of these changes and the necessity of developing win-win solutions for both the faculty's and the institution's long-term success.

As previously mentioned, understanding campus culture is essential in making any type of faculty-related change. We found in our research that faculty have long memories. The administration's previous attempts at reform, even from decades ago, are often resurrected during new discussions about reform. As described in Part Two, faculty are often deeply connected and committed to the preservation of institutional culture and want to ensure their institution's success for generations to come.

Therefore, we encourage administrators to address changes in culture by signaling full support for the new programs and policies their institution is implementing. The first signal is funding. The University of Washington discussed funding a medical expense account to help faculty in planning for retirement. Several campuses funded emeriti centers, retirement associations, or retired faculty development grants. Another signal is training. We found that faculty often rely more on their peers than on department chairs, websites, or faculty handbooks for information. Some campuses use their retired faculty as a reliable source of information, asking them to conduct sessions for faculty thinking about retirement. A few schools acknowledged that their department chairs or deans need training to become more comfortable in discussing retirement plans with faculty. All of these behind-the-scenes efforts provide administrators more credibility in interactions with faculty. Campuses can also signal their support for faculty in their latter career stages. SJSU offers Staying Alive retreats to help revitalize faculty. The University of Southern California posts Living History videos of current (and retired) faculty on YouTube and has dedicated space for viewing them in the Gerontology Library. The University of Baltimore has an official engaged retirement policy on its books. Several campuses provide office and library space to their emeriti and retired faculty. These public signals and policies go a long way to ensuring faculty that their institution will support them in retirement.

Campuses can also signal their support by helping faculty prepare for the retirement transition. Several schools encourage faculty to engage with their communities well before their retirement. These collaborations are often part of the service expectation for seasoned faculty, but they are also useful mechanisms during the transition to retirement. For example, at George Mason University staff and faculty take part in much of the community retirement-related programming. With the baby boomers beginning to retire in large numbers, there will be an increasing need for encore careers, such as those described in chapter 12.

All the campuses we worked with had a variety of financial planning options. In assisting faculty with financial planning, it is safer to use independent third parties (e.g., TIAA-CREF, Fidelity, or the state retirement office) to provide these services. Our interviews with faculty also indicated that they would like to have an evaluation of their financial status from an independent financial planner in addition to the private or state retirement plan personnel. SJSU has created a retirement calculator that can be used by qualifying faculty throughout the California State University system.

Aside from providing various supports and programs for pre-retirement faculty, institutions have begun to focus on ways to make emeritus status more substantive and attractive to senior faculty. They are expanding the services of existing emeriti organizations or developing new ones to assist retiring faculty with lifestyle and self-esteem issues that often delay retirement. These organizations working with their institutions create a natural bridge from a full-time commitment through a phasing opportunity to a new experience. From numerous studies we know that much health and well-being comes from volunteering and altruism as well as living a productive life rich in social interactions.

As budgets tighten and the numbers of emeriti and retirees grow, institutions will likely assist and depend on emeriti organizations more and more to support retirees and to undertake responsibility for providing courses and intellectual engagement. These organizations are also becoming an important link to their communities—working with nonprofits, providing volunteers to assist with courses and activities in senior centers and schools. Emeriti organizations, with some creative thinking, could utilize the "workforce" of emeriti faculty to create programming and thus develop a new revenue stream for colleges and universities. This win-win solution would bring alumni and their former professors together to the benefit of both groups and the institution. Further attention needs to be given to the relationships among institutions, emeriti organizations, the internal community, the external community, and alumni groups. As resources become more restricted and demographics continue to change, all of these relationships will bring value to institutions and allow for the achievement of the mission and the enhancement of core values. These positive relationships, and positive signals of change, will help create an environment in which senior faculty are valued by their students, their colleagues, and the administration.

Words to the Wise on Implementation

Navigating between an institution's needs and the needs of loyal, long-serving faculty is a tricky balancing act. Campuses must be aware of several potential pitfalls as they discuss the topic of retirement with faculty. Good practice involves the following:

- *Formal written policies*: If there are no formal written policies, then the first step will be to decide how to involve faculty in the process of developing these new policies. To begin the process, the provost and faculty senate can jointly appoint a special committee with membership selected from senior faculty ranks or provide the faculty as a whole with draft policies for comment. Each institution, depending on its governance structure, will likely choose a different route.
- *Clear and transparent policies*: Before policies are implemented, they should be reviewed by legal counsel, and those involving payouts should also be reviewed by tax experts to protect both the faculty member and the institution.

- *A strong communications campaign*: Once policies are in place, campuses will need a well-developed, multipronged communication plan, taking advantage of websites, e-mail, social media, and old-fashioned face-to-face programming. Each institution will need to tailor its message to reflect its current circumstances and its program's benefits for senior and emeriti faculty and the institution. The goal is to provide information to faculty explaining what supports are available, how to access them, and where to get additional answers to questions.

In addition to providing these services, institutions will need to educate both their human resource and academic administrators—beginning with department chairs, deans, and chief academic officers—to be certain they know how to properly engage faculty in discussions about retirement. Always remember that retirement decisions are voluntary and cannot in any way be influenced by coercion. However, administrators can ask about someone's retirement plans if they follow the key rules. Institutions can, as they develop yearly planning goals or longer-range plans, approach faculty to learn their intentions by doing the following:

1. asking a broad range of faculty at the same time
2. clearly stating that the information is requested for institutional planning purposes only and that people will not be held to their responses
3. asking for the information in writing so that faculty have time to respond at their convenience or to choose not to respond at all

Finally, institutions need to prepare to make the "business case" for why it is important to strengthen senior faculty in their culminating career stage, in their bridge to emeriti or retiree status, and in their adjustment to a new relationship with their institutions. Senior and emeriti or retired faculty have much to contribute—they have accrued intangible assets, contacts, knowledge, and experience—and can use their talents to mentor students and younger faculty, assist with grant writing, make connections among researchers, engage in positive promotion of the institution, teach, conduct research, and provide volunteer service.

Higher education institutions must become more agile and cost-effective in how they operate. Investing in support for senior faculty to transition smoothly to retirement provides resources for the institution to reallocate for new programs. Many emeriti faculty are willing to teach and advise freshmen, assist with internships, and take responsibility for international student programs. This allows active faculty to concentrate on teaching and research without worrying about these time-consuming but necessary activities that enrich student learning. Satisfied retired faculty are also great ambassadors in their work with alumni and other friends of the institution, and ultimately these faculty become donors to special projects.

Senior faculty in their culminating career stage have given a major part of their lives to higher education institutions; now is the time for us to give back by assisting them with an active, satisfying, intellectually stimulating next chapter of their lives.

Lotte Bailyn is the *T. Wilson (1953) Professor of Management* and emerita at the MIT Sloan School of Management. Lotte was chair of the MIT faculty from 1997 to 1999, and was the Matina S. Horner Distinguished Visiting Professor at Radcliffe's Public Policy Institute from 1995 to 1997. She studies the relationship between managerial practice and employees' lives, with special emphasis on the dynamics of gender and diversity in business organizations and academia. Bailyn holds a BA in mathematics from Swarthmore College, an MA and a PhD in social psychology from Harvard/Radcliffe, and two honorary degrees. She is a fellow of the American Psychological Association and the Association for Psychological Science.

Sue Barnes is the director of the Retiree Center at the University of California–Davis, which provides a wide variety of programs and services to connect 8,000-plus retired faculty and staff to the Davis campus. She holds a BS degree in visual communication from Western Washington University. She is the president of the Association of Retirement Organizations in Higher Education, with her term ending in December 2014.

Janette C. Brown, EdD, is executive director of both the University of Southern California's Emeriti Center and the Association of Retirement Organizations in Higher Education and is adjunct faculty at the USC Davis School of Gerontology. Brown manages the USC Emeriti Center's programs, services, and resources for pre-retirees and retirees, conducts retiree-related research, and consults with institutions to help develop campus retiree organizations.

Laura Koppes Bryan is dean of the Yale Gordon College of Arts and Sciences and professor of psychology at the University of Baltimore. She is a U.S. Fulbright scholar and a fellow of the American Psychological Association, the Association for Psychological Science, and the Society for Industrial and Organizational Psychology.

Cheryl A. Cameron is vice provost for academic personnel at the University of Washington. She is a professor in the Department of Oral Health Sciences in the School of Dentistry and an adjunct professor in the College of Education. She holds the Virginia and Prentice Bloedel Endowed Professorship.

Margarita M. Cardona is the director of sponsored research and faculty development at the University of Baltimore. She is a certified research administrator, a National Aeronautics and Space Administration (NASA)/National Association for Equal Opportunity in Higher Education (NAFEO) Research Administration Fellow, a NASA Space Grant Fellow, and a graduate of the National Council of University Research Administrators (NCURA) Leadership Development Institute. She is currently pursuing a doctorate in public policy.

Andrea Chapdelaine is provost and vice president for academic affairs at Albright College. Dr. Chapdelaine has created several policies to support work-life balance and career success. She earned her PhD and MA in social psychology from the University of Connecticut and her BA in psychology and legal studies from the University of New Hampshire.

Kathleen Christensen is the program director of the Alfred P. Sloan Foundation's *Working Longer*, which is a program designed to deepening scholarly and public understanding of aging Americans' work patterns. Recognized for her expertise on work-family issues and workplace flexibility, Dr. Christensen planned and participated in the 2010 White House Forum on Workplace Flexibility, as well as participated in the 2005 White House Conference on Aging. In 2010, Dr. Christensen was named by *Working Mother* magazine as one of the "Seven Wonders of the Work-Life Field," which identified her as the "foremost strategic supporter of work-life research and practices." Christensen earned her PhD from Pennsylvania State University.

Caroline S. Clauss-Ehlers, PhD, is an internationally known psychologist specializing in work with bilingual families. During her 2012 sabbatical she served as visiting special assistant to the president of Mount Holyoke College. At Rutgers University, she is associate professor and program/clinical coordinator for programs in school counseling and counseling psychology.

Terence E. Diggory, professor emeritus of English at Skidmore College, serves as convener of the college's Retiree Initiative Planning Group. During his 33 years of teaching at Skidmore, he served two separate terms as chair of the English Department. He retired in 2010.

Lauren J. Duranleau is a research analyst at the American Dental Education Association. Previously, she worked at the American Council on Education, conducting research and data analysis. She earned her MPA from George Mason University and her BA in journalism and sociology from the University of Maine.

Rhonda Forman is assistant vice provost for academic personnel at the University of Washington. She has over 30 years of experience in higher education administration.

Patricia Foster is a grant and budget administrator in the Academic Affairs division at Bentley University. In partnership with colleagues in Academic Affairs, the Office of Human Resources, and other areas of the university, she serves as a liaison to the Bentley community on matters related to faculty retirement and is responsible for retirement-related research, programming, and communications. She holds a BS in business administration from the University of Delaware.

Rosario A. Gerhardt has been an engineering faculty member at the Georgia Institute of Technology since January 1991. She joined the Office of Institute Diversity at Georgia Tech on a part-time basis in November 2011. Her responsibilities include helping the vice president for institute diversity to identify key funding programs and initiatives that will increase the institute's diversity excellence and inclusion. The American Council on Education (ACE)/Sloan award is one such program.

Joan Girgus is a professor of psychology and special assistant to the dean of the faculty at Princeton University. Her teaching and research focus on personality and social psychology, and her administrative work focuses on women faculty and making Princeton a more family-friendly university.

Nathan D. Grawe is associate professor of economics (1999–present) and former associate dean of the college at Carleton College (2009–2012). As an economist he has studied financial constraints on educational attainment and the effect of recent demographic and birthrate changes for future higher education demand.

Katherine Haldeman is a retirement transitions researcher who develops and implements programs to assist faculty in their retirement transitions. Haldeman received a BA in psychology from George Washington University, a master's in health education from George Mason University, and a coach certification through the Retirement Options Coach Certification Program.

Sandra Johnson is an associate dean of the faculty at Princeton University. She has been an administrator at Princeton for the last 18 years. Her responsibilities include overseeing the faculty retirement program as well as the budget and finances for the Office of the Dean of the Faculty.

Mary Kochlefl is executive director for academic organizational development and online learning at Xavier University. Since joining Xavier in 1995, she has held several roles, including overseeing the grants office, Center for Teaching Excellence, and academic assessment efforts. Kochlefl earned her PhD in English, with a minor in religious studies, from Indiana University.

Susan A. Kress retired in 2012 from her position as vice president of academic affairs (VPAA) and professor of English at Skidmore College after 37 years of service. As VPAA, Kress focused much attention on retirement transitions at the college. She currently serves on the board of the Association of Retirement Organizations in Higher Education.

Vicki LaFarge is associate dean for academic affairs and associate professor of management at Bentley University. Dr. LaFarge earned a master's in forest science from the Yale School of Forestry and Environmental Management and a PhD in organizational behavior from Yale University. Dr. LaFarge was the recipient of Bentley's Adamian Award for Teaching Excellence, the Advisor of the Year Award, and the Martin Luther King Diversity Award.

Mary Lefkowitz taught classical studies at Wellesley from 1960 to 2005. Author or coeditor of some 10 books and numerous articles and reviews, she has been awarded several honorary degrees, a Mellon Emeritus grant, and a 2006 National Humanities Medal "for outstanding excellence in scholarship and teaching."

Kathryn L. Lynch is dean of faculty affairs and Katharine Lee Bates and Sophie Chantal Hart Professor of English at Wellesley College, where she has taught since 1983. A specialist on medieval English literature, she has edited or written four books and numerous articles and book reviews.

Jean M. McLaughlin is an associate director at the American Council on Education (ACE), where she has worked since 2006. During her time there ACE has received an additional $2.58 million in funding, out of a total of $4.1 million, from the Alfred P. Sloan Foundation to advance career flexibility for faculty through national awards programs and to disseminate best practices throughout higher education.

Joan Merdinger is former associate vice president for faculty affairs and professor emerita of social work at San José State University (SJSU). During her career at SJSU, she oversaw faculty appointment, retention, tenure, promotion, and early retirement planning. She is currently a member of the board of the SJSU Emeritus and Retired Faculty Association.

Lynn Pasquerella, president of Mount Holyoke College, is a philosopher whose career combines teaching and scholarship with local and global engagement. Her term has been marked by robust strategic planning, outreach, and commitment to a vibrant campus community. Pasquerella is a Phi Beta Kappa senator and host of *The Academic Minute*, a public radio program.

Dennis Pitta is the J. William Middendorf Distinguished Professor at the Merrick School of Business at the University of Baltimore (UB). He is also the chair of the Faculty Work Life Committee at UB. He earned his PhD from the University of Maryland–College Park's Smith School of Business.

Samantha Roy is the Sloan grant administrator at Albright College. She provides support and project management for grants awarded by the Sloan Foundation for faculty work-life balance and retirement transitions. She earned her MA in English from Binghamton University and her BA in English from Albright College.

Beverly Schneller is associate provost for academic affairs at Belmont University. She was the associate provost at the University of Baltimore from 2011 to 2013. Dr. Schneller is a Teagle Assessment scholar and the author of three books and numerous articles in the fields of British literature and women's studies.

Binnie Singh is an assistant vice provost of academic affairs at the University of California–Davis. Before that appointment, she was the director of faculty development for nearly 11 years. Singh holds a BS in psychology from UC Davis and a master's in organizational psychology from California School of Professional Psychology.

Maureen L. Stanton is the vice provost of academic affairs at the University of California–Davis and professor of evolution and ecology. An accomplished biologist and researcher, Dr. Stanton is a co–principal investigator on UC Davis's Advance initiative to increase the number of Latinas in science, which has established the Center for Advancing Multicultural Perspectives on Science.

Amy Strage is interim director of the Center for Faculty Development and professor of Child and Adolescent Development at San José State University. For the past decade she has developed and implemented a variety of programs to support faculty in all aspects of their professional endeavors and at all stages of their careers.

Claire A. Van Ummersen is currently senior adviser at the American Council on Education (ACE), where she served for 5 years as vice president of the Center for Effective Leadership and for 4 years as vice president and director of the Office of Women in Higher Education. Van Ummersen is president emerita of Cleveland State University, having served as president from 1993 to 2001. Prior to that, Van Ummersen was chancellor of the University System of New Hampshire, and she has also served with the Massachusetts Board of Regents of Higher Education.

INDEX

refute these claims. In the process, I learned a great deal about the route I should have taken to retirement from the time I accepted my first academic appointment to the time I submitted my intention to retire. Join me as I relive my long journey so that you may avoid my wrong turns and succeed in reaching your ultimate destination, a worry-free retirement, despite the risks and uncertainties you will surely face when you retire."

Sty/us

22883 Quicksilver Drive
Sterling, VA 20166-2102   Subscribe to our e-mail alerts: www.Styluspub.com

Also available from Stylus

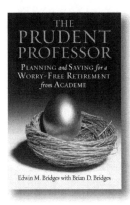

The Prudent Professor

Planning and Saving for a Worry-Free Retirement from Academe

Edwin M. Bridges and Brian D. Bridges

"In *The Prudent Professor*, Edwin Bridges, professor emeritus of Stanford, has provided an incredibly helpful guide to investment success. Targeted to members of the academic community, the book draws on his own careful research and long personal experience in building—and protecting—his retirement funds. He describes with candor where he went right—avoiding potholes—and where he went wrong—falling into them. His blunt appraisals of working with TIAA-CREF and with Vanguard (I should know!) are invaluable, indeed priceless."

—John C. Bogle,
Founder, The Vanguard Group

"Strengths of this book include its readability and accessibility to further information. Retirement is approached from the 'what you put in is what you will get out' philosophy, encouraging the reader to learn what options are best suited for themselves. As a young professional, *The Prudent Professor* is an excellent resource. A crash course in financial planning and what to expect (based on today's economic situation) when approaching retirement is explained very well."

—NACADA Journal
National Academic Advising Association

"*The Prudent Professor* is a welcome gift to every academic and professional who wants to prepare for retirement, and not just let it happen. It should be required reading for all of us who seek to invent our futures rather than simply try to predict them. The authors provide their readers with the analytic and judgmental tools to navigate through the dangerous reefs of retirement. By alternating valuable principles of investment and disbursement with Ed Bridges' own personal experiences of problem solving and critical reflection on his decisions, we come to understand our present and future choices with clarity, empathy and confidence."

—Lee S. Shulman,
President Emeritus, The Carnegie Foundation for the Advancement of Teaching

What makes this book unique is that Ed Bridges—Professor Emeritus, Stanford University—shares with you his self-education about the business of investing and retirement planning. He writes, "In schooling myself, I adopted the mind-set that I had used as a social scientist for the past forty-six years. I distinguished between fact and opinion and scrutinized the evidence behind every author's claims; moreover, I searched for research that might corroborate or